Understanding
& Designing
MARKETING
RESEARCH

Understanding
& Designing
MARKETING
RESEARCH

John R. Webb
Department of Marketing,
Strathclyde Business School,
University of Strathclyde, Glasgow, UK

INTERNATIONAL THOMSON BUSINESS PRESS
I T P ® An International Thomson Publishing Company

London • Bonn • Johannesburg • Madrid • Melbourne • Mexico City • New York • Paris
Singapore • Tokyo • Toronto • Albany, NY • Belmont, CA • Cincinnati, OH • Detroit, MI

Understanding & Designing Marketing Research

I(T)P® A division of International Thomson Publishing Inc.
The ITP logo is a trademark under licence

British Library Cataloguing-in-Publication Data
A catalogue record for this book is available from the British Library

First published 1992 by Academic Press Ltd
Reprinted 1994, 1995 by The Dryden Press
Reprinted 1999 by International Thomson Business Press

Typeset by Mathematical Composition Setters Ltd, Salisbury, UK
Printed in the UK by TJ International , Cornwall

ISBN 1-86152-464-1

658. 83/WEB

International Thomson Business Press
Berkshire House
168–173 High Holborn
London WC1V 7AA
UK

http://www.itbp.com

Contents

Preface   vii
1. Research for Marketing   1
2. The Process of Research   10
3. Secondary Data—Uses and Limitations   31
4. The Process of Sampling   45
5. Survey and Panel/Syndicated Research   68
6. Questionnaire Design   91
7. Qualitative Research   112
8. Measurement and Scales   134
9. Attitudes and their Measurement   151
10. Experimentation   173
11. Writing and Reading Research Reports   193
12. Commissioning Marketing Research   207
Appendix: Statistics and Sampling   215
Author Index   225
Subject Index   227

For Elizabeth, James, Charlotte and Thomas

Preface

Marketing research has in recent years, come to be seen as an increasingly important process in the management of organisations—especially those concerned with the production, distribution and marketing of goods and services. High levels of competition, technological innovations (both in the products themselves and in their modes of manufacture) and the demanding and increasingly discriminating nature of a widening range of consumers have all combined to increase the levels of "danger" in the environment in which organisations have to operate. There is also a growing perception that the "psychic" distance between those who consume goods and services and the organisations that seek to satisfy their demands is increasing; for multinational bodies, there is also the additional complication that there might be a considerable physical distance between the two parties. Marketing research is the process which is almost universally acknowledged to be the way in which to bridge the gulf between the various key members of the exchange process.

This book has been written as an introduction to that varied, and sometimes complicated, array of techniques which are known collectively as marketing research. It has been written with two main target markets in mind: those studying marketing research as an elective or option when working for a business qualification—degree, diploma etc., and those who commission marketing research from specialist agencies and are not as clear as they would like to be about what, exactly, is meant by certain terms or techniques.

Marketing research may be divided into two main portions: the research process itself and the analysis of the results. This text concentrates, almost exclusively, on the former, the process of marketing research. For those who seek further enlightenment as to the analysis of the results, there are many excellent specialist texts on statistics and related techniques. As an introductory text, the book will explain, in clear, easy to comprehend language, those various methods and processes which are most commonly used.

Because of the fact that books are constructed on a fixed, "linear" principle, a decision has had to be made as to the order in which the topics are presented. However, the linearity of the marketing research process is something which, to a very large extent, is determined by the specific factors at play in each research situation. Do not worry if the situation in which you are involved causes you to design a research process whose order is different from the one used in this text. Imagine that each of the chapters of this book is the equivalent of a child's play block with a single letter printed upon it. This book has used those blocks to "spell" a certain "word". You do not have to "spell" the identical "*word*"—the "word" you construct will be the one most appropriate for the circumstances in which you find yourself. To pursue the analogy a little further, it can be stated that, just as in a written language, there are rules of syntax and codes of practice in the sense of style, so for marketing research there are rules of "syntax" and recommendations as to "style". Such rules and recommendations will be pointed out when appropriate.

It is rare for a textbook to be written in isolation, and this one is no exception. It is, therefore, a great pleasure to be able to place on record my sincere thanks to the following people for their help, guidance and encouragement whilst this book was being written: to all those students who have politely sat through my lectures while the basic "product" was being tested; to my colleagues in the Department of Marketing in the University of Strathclyde, Ken Deans, Christina Graham, Susan Hart, Annie Muss, Stephen Tagg and Alan Wilson; to Christine Reid of the Business Information Centre at the Strathclyde Graduate Business School; to Andrea Gillick who has coped heroically with what I laughingly call my handwriting; to Jennifer Pegg, my editor at Academic Press.

To these, and to untold others, I owe a debt of thanks which can only be acknowledged, never repaid.

CHAPTER ONE

Research for Marketing

Introduction   1
The evolution of business management   1
Turbulent business environments   4
Summary   8
References   8

Introduction

In almost all fields of human endeavour, there is a limit to what can be achieved both physically and mentally by an individual acting alone. If the activity in which that individual is engaged increases in size or in complexity, then individuals must band together to carry out in concert what they cannot succeed in doing if they continue to work independently; they form an organisation. These organisations exist in the arts, in the sciences, for the armed forces and for industry, commerce and finance with their constituent members numbering from two to, theoretically, infinity. One factor though is common to all organisations: whatever the end result they seek, if they are not to degenerate rapidly into an anarchic mess then they must be led, directed or managed. A skeleton and musculature (individuals) require a corporate central nervous system (management) to control and coordinate seemingly separate bodily (organisational) parts in order to achieve some predetermined aim.

The managements of organisations, particularly those concerned with business and industry, are not, however, pulled fully-formed from the top-hat of a professor of strategic management in the University of Life—they are the result of an almost Darwinian process of evolution.

The evolution of business management

The year 1776 saw not only the Declaration of Independence of what was shortly to become the United States of America, but also the publication of Adam Smith's great book *The Wealth of Nations*. Among many other ideas, Smith's work contains his theory on the "Division of Labour". Smith suggested that instead of each worker carrying out every process in the manufacture and packaging of pins, individual workers should only carry out one of those steps. The increased quantity of work would result, he said, because "... first, to the increase of dexterity in every particular workman; secondly, to the saving of time which is commonly lost in passing from one species of work to another; and lastly, to the invention of a great number of machines which facilitate and abridge labour and enable one man to do the work of many". One such "machine" was the vastly more efficient steam-engine of Smith's fellow Scot, James Watt; his innovation (an adaptation of an earlier machine invented by Newcomen) was a machine which represented a more reliable alternative to the current somewhat capricious power sources which depended upon wind or water. Watt's machine, apart from its power, had the great advantage over the other two main sources of power that it could be sited at will, with very few constraints. This counteracted one of the main drawbacks of mechanical energy, from whatever power source, Watt's engines included, and that is that it is very difficult, with any degree of efficiency, to transmit mechanical power over anything but the shortest of distances. Thus to make optimum use of the energy of Watt's innovation, workers had to be assembled in close proximity to it: this, added to Smith's ideas concerning the specialisation of the labour force, provided the essentials, though in a crude form, of a factory system.

The aim of these units of manufacture whether they operated in iron and steel, textiles, mining or "cheap tin trays" was commercial advance. And this, as Chambers (1961) has said, was made possible by the introduction of a series of technological innovations which enabled the factory owners to service the demands of a widening cross-section of the market by the progressive reduc-tion of the price of the product relative to its quality. Goods which, because of their almost "made to measure" mode of production, had previously been highly priced and therefore only within the grasp of those in the higher income brackets, could now be produced at much lower cost and were, consequently, available for purchase by a much larger percentage of the population.

With increased sales and revenues, factories were able to expand and to afford bigger, more powerful and more efficient sources of power, employ a larger workforce and to increase, substantially, their output. Increased affluence in the general population meant that levels of nutrition, housing and medical care were raised. This resulted in a level of mortality, which, though horribly high by our standards, was markedly better than what had been the norm heretofore. The rapid growth in population and in expendable income meant that though factory output was expanding, it could not do so quickly enough to satisfy all the demand.

Through to the end of the 19th century, in what is now called the developed world, an expanding range and volume of output, an ever increasing "cascade" of technological innovations and a seemingly insatiable consumer demand continued. The latter situation, that of increasing demand, ensured the efforts of those responsible for the management of industry were concentrated into more and more efficient modes of production. This trajectory of increasing output through the use of advancing technology put at the service of mass manufacture reached its high-point in Henry Ford's famous and arrogant dictum of "... you can have any colour, as long as it's black", though as Baker (1985) points out, "... when Henry Ford first produced the Model T, he was exactly in tune with the needs of the market".

During the 1920s and the 1930s, however, changes in the environment in which mass manufacture operated began to have an impact. As more countries developed industrially (one must remember that machine tools and industrial machinery were exported as well as finished products) the levels of competition were raised higher and higher, which soon led to a new situation: in many markets, supply began to exceed demand. This factor, together with changes in consumer demand patterns, led to a move away from a policy of product standardisation, to one of product differentiation. The changes in consumer demand sprang from the growing affluence and experience of the public. With increased levels of affluence the public did not need to devote such a high fraction of their incomes to the purchase of basic commodities, and they were increasingly unwilling to make do with basic goods only Many of the goods and services that they were purchasing were, by now, no longer first-time buys; they had bought them on previous occasions. They had gained skills, experience and discrimination in their use, which gave them the confidence, backed up with increased discretionary levels of income, to demand more sophisticated, better made and better value goods. The general public, arguably for the first time, were in a position to deny the manufacturer of basic goods and services the ability to "fob" them off only with products which they, the manufacturers, were willing to supply.

In the United States, increasing affluence and increasing frustration with the basic facilities offered by the Model T Ford caused its sales to fall. General Motors then moved from a production-led way of carrying out its business to one that included listening more to what the market was saying; they introduced an annual change of model. Ford, meanwhile, having failed with the attempted introduction of a standard Model A car was forced to follow the example of General Motors and move towards a more differentiated product policy. As Albert Sloan (1965) is quoted as saying, "Mr Ford failed to realise that it was not necessary for new cars to meet the need for basic transportation". This shift from a production to a more market-led orientation was curtailed, or certainly slowed, by World War II. But once the growth that had been lost due to the war had recovered, and the necessary reconstruction was well advanced, it continued to move business from "an internally focused, introverted perspective to an open extroverted one" (Ansoff, 1984). What finally propelled many of those firms, which had been obstinately clinging to a production orientation, to a market-led stance were the effects of the new technologies which had seen their advent as part of the research to support the war effort. From about the middle of the 1950s, the almost smooth, evolutionary path of development which had been followed for most of the previous century was being disrupted by the "accelerating and cumulating events which began to change the boundaries, the structure and the dynamics of the business environment. Firms were increasingly being confronted with novel, unexpected challenges" (Ansoff, 1984). This was an era which Drucker (1961) called "The Age of Discontinuity". But Ansoff (1984) argues that just as the move from a production to a marketing orientation found many firms lacking in the enthusiasm to shift, so has the change from a market orientation to, what he calls, the "Post-industrial Era" been resisted by many business organisations. It is, he notes, not just a question any more of a company seeking to devote its attention to a search for and a satisfaction of the demands of the market. Ansoff counsels that now both technological and political changes must be incorporated into the management information system of the firm and that firms cannot, any longer, sustain a system, as they have done in the past, whereby they merely extrapolated from previous experience to help guide them in future operations.

Turbulent business environments

The Shorter Oxford English Dictionary defines an environment as "conditions or influences under which any persons or living thing lives or is developed". Webster's Dictionary adds that it is "the whole complex of climatic, edaphic and biotic factors that act upon an organisation or an ecological community and ultimately determine its form and survival". In terms of the business organisation Glueck and Jauch (1984) say it "... includes factors outside the firm which can lead to opportunities for or threats to the firm". Stanford (1979) says that the environment is everything outside the limits of the organisation. Hall (1972) and Osborn and Hunt (1974) have suggested that it might, conceptually, be more useful to think of the environment in two ways:

(1) The general/societal environment which affects all organisations within the boundaries of a given system. Kast and Rosensweig (1985) include the following as components of the general/societal environment: cultural; technological; educational; political; legal; natural resources; demographic; sociological; and economic.

(2) The task environment which is specific to the organisation under study. Duncan (1972) has delineated the components of the task environment as consisting of those pertaining; to customers, to suppliers, to competitors and to socio-political forces.

The division of the environment into general/societal and task sub-systems is but one way in which organisational theorists have chosen to regard the environment. But whatever classification is chosen, and there are many others too, one thing can be guaranteed and that is that the environment will exhibit some form of turbulence.

Emery and Trist (1965) say that volatile high technology and unpredictable competitive circumstances are characteristic of turbulent environments. Brownlie (1984) says that turbulence is responsible for the "irregularity and unpredictability" of environmental changes. And, finally, Ansoff (1984) says that in turbulent environments "the challenges [to an organisation] become progressively more numerous, more complex and they develop faster and with an increased likelihood of strategic surprises". Taking the lead from many writers on the object of strategic management, it soon becomes clear that the key characteristics of turbulent environments are volatility, irregularity, unpredictability, novelty, complexity and the high degree to which it contains "danger".

No organisation, however tightly its exact functions and objectives are bound to itself, can be said to exist in a single component of the environment—let alone in a vacuum. Companies operating, for example, on the "cutting edge" of high technology cannot be said to exist solely in that technological sub-component; social, political, geographical, financial and legal forces will all, to a greater or lesser extent, impinge upon the organisation and the way in which it is managed and the way in which it can operate and progress.

Environmental forces have a direct impact upon an organisation, which, if the company is wise and capable of learning, will be allowed by the company, partially, to "dictate" the way in which the management should be organised. In the animal kingdom, many organisms, as a result of evolutionary (environmental) forces have developed all five senses, though it is likely that this development will have been disproportionate. One or two senses are likely to have evolved to a much higher level of sensitivity and discrimination than the others, because of specific threats that exist in the particular environment in which they live: nocturnal animals have evolved huge eyes to cope with low levels of light intensity and the creatures of the ocean deeps, where there is little or no light, have evolved incredibly sensitive pressure detectors to sense the approach of predators or of luncheon! The most successful organisms in the animal kingdom, however, have developed all five senses to the same high levels of resolution and sensitivity. This has enabled them to meet the multitudinous threats which exist within their environments with great success; it has also enabled them to profit from the opportunities which come their way—they have become more prominent "actors" upon the world "stage". The point to note from this example is that the more dynamic and turbulent is the habitat of an organism/organisation, the more complex, discriminating and sensitive are the sensory systems that are needed to cope with the concomitantly high levels of "danger".

In terms of business organisations, functional departments have (or should have) been established to deal with environmental signals. Animals' eyes sense light, ears sound, noses/tongues smell, fingers/paws touch; for a firm, the marketing department should be the equivalent of the senses; the body that picks up the signals from outside the organisational boundaries.

No living organism can live in a vacuum, and since business organisations can be considered to have had a birth, to grow, to mature and, maybe, to die (receivership and bankruptcy), they may also be thought of as having life. Organisms take in water, nutrients, oxygen and light and give out heat and waste products. Business organisations take in nutrients (gas, electricity) basic substrates, labour and give out waste products, finished products and, with prudent management, profits. Both types of organisations, living and business, can be considered as "open systems" with a constant transfer of substances, energy and signals across the organisation's boundaries. But from this point, it becomes increasingly difficult to pursue the analogy between living organisms and business organisations, the difficulty arising from the way in which each type of system is organised.

Those organisations in the top branches of the evolutionary tree have exceedingly sophisticated control mechanisms—a nervous system. This, in the most advanced members of the animal kingdom, comprises three parts: the central nervous system, the peripheral nervous system and the autonomic nervous system. As one descends the evolutionary tree in the direction of single-cell organisms, the degree of sophistication of the nervous system diminishes. At the most basic level of life, there is little but a set of feed-back "loops", "programmed" to maintain the well-being of the cell. If there is, for example, too much activity in their immediate habitat, the organism's sensory system detects this and directs that the organism should move away from this source of discomfort or danger. The sum total of all these feed-back "loops" could be called, in a very general sense, instinct. But even this innate quality, which causes an organism to act in a certain way if exposed to stimuli in a relatively predictable manner, is denied the business organisation.

No firm/company springs fully formed and fully equipped from the head of its founder. It is not automatically furnished with a complete organisational "nervous system", there are no corporate "eyes" or "auditory systems"—there is no structural sense of smell—all have to be created. It is the function and use of such a set of organisational senses—marketing research—which is the subject of this work. For without such a functional department no organisation, particularly those created to operate in the spheres of business, finance and commerce, would be able to sense and evaluate those threats which have to be avoided or rendered harmless, or those opportunities which have to be captured. Doubtless, for a while, they will be able to survive merely by reacting to events in their surroundings, but even with such a system as that, the use of the word "react" tacitly admits to a need for some type of detection apparatus to be in place. However, in dynamic and turbulent environments, reaction is an insufficiently rigorous and far-sighted style of management. The need to be able to detect, measure, assess, evaluate and act becomes paramount. If an organisation is only capable of reacting to external changes, then it denies itself the opportunity, to a certain extent, to help shape the external environment, one which the organisation would prefer to inhabit, rather than one which it must accept.

But the question of shaping environments as organisations would like is a strategic matter; what concerns us here is the step before that: the gathering of the information on which those strategic decisions are based.

Without valid and reliable visual, auditory, olfactory and tactile systems, a cat out hunting, or a mouse determined to avoid being hunted, would have no secure basis on which to make decisions concerned with their external environment. Inputs from the senses must be sufficiently detailed and accurate in their representation of reality for the cat and for the mouse to be able to make potentially life-threatening decisions. The senses do not make those decisions; in biological terms, they are said to be made by the higher centres. But the first and vital step in the process is the gathering of appropriate, valid data.

Marketing research should seek to do the same: provide valid and appropriate data on which the "higher centres" of management can act for the well-being of the entire organisation, not just for the present but for the future too.

In the earliest days of urban trading, a market was a place where people met to buy and sell merchandise. The products on sale were likely to have been, predominantly, of an agricultural nature: grains, vegetables, fruit, cheese, milk. By the 14th/15th century, the marketplace would have evolved into something with which many modern-day shoppers could now identify. To the commodity type of products, would have been added a small number of finished or semi-finished items that today would probably be called crafts: woven goods, metal-work, ceramics etc.

Now while it is possible that the weavers, blacksmiths and potters, for example, would produce common, everyday items for stock, it is probable that anything more complicated/expensive would have been made on an ad-hoc, commissioned basis.

Imagine this situation: we are in a small marketplace where Hengis, and his wife, run a pottery business. One market day, their old friend Hereward says to the potter "Hey Hengis! I need a dish to hold milk for cheese making. Make me one about three feet in diameter and nine inches deep."

Hengis then quotes a delivery date and price; they haggle. Finally they agree on a time for delivery of the finished good and a price. Hengis gets his profit and Hereward gets his pot; they are both satisfied with the deal.

There, in marketing terms, is an almost ideal situation. Hengis knows Hereward, the type of pot he requires and the general level of price he can afford to pay. Hereward knows Hengis of old and is sure that he will get a good pot at a reasonable price.

But as the marketplace, as a site for the business, and markets evolved, the distance between producer and consumer increased. The consumers' experience and powers of discrimination increased as did the level of their disposable incomes. This, together with the application of technology to systems of manufacture and the increased efficiency in modes of transport, further distanced the two parties in the exchange process. In the present age, with the advent of multinational corporations, the gap is as wide as it can be.

Or it would be if it were not for the influence of marketing research. Marketing research is a collection of "tools" of assessment, evaluation and measurement which seeks to reduce the "distance" between a product's manufacturer and consumer; primarily through the supply, to the manufacturer, of pertinent information concerning the customer. And remember, a "product" can be anything from a nuclear reactor to a packet of needles—via insurance policies, oven gloves and holidays on the Greek island of Rhodes!

Without reliable, valid data pertaining to consumers' current likes/dislikes and future aspirations, those that set out to satisfy a demand will be condemned to sell what they can make.

Marketing would have them make what they can sell.

Summary

Companies currently have to operate in highly complex, dangerous environments. Technologically induced discontinuities, the division of consumers into even smaller, and more specialised, segments and the internationalisation of business, have all combined to place "barriers" between a product's end-user and those who seek to service the demand of that end-user.

The combined environmental forces incident upon an organisation are now so strong that a company cannot ignore them; reactive management will no longer suffice, proactive management rules. The "senses" of the organisation, should seek to provide a steady stream of reliable, valid and appropriate data to help the managers of organisations as they pilot their vessels through the "shoals and reefs" of their environment.

References

Ansoff H. I. (1984) *Implanting Strategic Management*, Prentice-Hall, Englewood Cliffs, New Jersey.

Baker M. J. (1985) *Marketing and Management Strategy*, Macmillan, London.

Brownlie D. (1984) Integrating R&D Planning and Business Strategy, University of Strathclyde, Working Paper WP 84/1.

Chambers J. D. (1961) *The Workshop of the World*, University Press, London, Oxford.

Drucker P. (1961) *The Practice of Management*, Mercury Books, London.

Duncan R. B. (1972) Characteristics of organisational environments and perceived environmental uncertainty. *Administrative Science Quarterly*, **17**, 313–327.

Emery F. E. and Trist E. L. (1965) The causal texture of organisational environments, *Human Relations*, February, pp. 21–32.

Glueck W. F. and Jauch L. R. (1984) *Business Policy and Strategic Management*, McGraw-Hill, New York.

Hall R. D. (1972) *Organisations, Structures and Processes*, Prentice-Hall, Englewood Cliffs, New Jersey.

Kast F. E. and Rosensweig J. E. (1985) *Organisation and Management; A Systems Approach and Contingency Approach*, McGraw-Hill, New York.

Osborn R. N. and Hunt J. G. (1974) Environmental and organisational effectiveness. *Administrative Science Quarterly*, **19**, 232–246.

Sloan A. P. (1965) *My Years with General Motors*, Pan Books, London.

Stanford M. J. (1979) *Management Policy*, Macmillan, New York.

CHAPTER TWO

The Process of Research

Introduction	10
Problem-solving involving research	13
Marketing research and problem-solving	13
(1) Set the objectives of the research	15
(2) Define the research problem	16
(3) Assessment of the value of the research	18
(4) Construct the research proposal	19
(5) Specify the data collection methods	22
(6) Select the techniques of measurement	26
(7) Select the sample	27
(8) Collection of data	28
(9) Analysis of the results	28
(10) Presentation of the final report	29
Summary	29
References	30

Introduction

If a collection of individuals has been brought together to form an organisation, they have usually been gathered together to perform some function which would not have been possible for those individuals to carry out alone. This being the case, if that organisation is not going to start in chaos (let alone descend into such a state) then there must be some overall control. Individuals, in general, do not have the ability, instinctively, to know what should be done, in what order and who should be responsible for each particular section of the overall effort—this is always accepting, of course, that each individual knows what the aim of the organisation is!

Someone must be in a position to decide the overall objectives of the organisation, to make a priority ranking of what has to be carried out, and to coordinate the various parts of that system so that the designated objectives are attained. So that, like an animal's locomotion, the sub-systems of neural control, musculature and the skeleton work synergistically and not in opposition. Imagine the case of a mouse who becomes aware that it is being stalked by a large ginger tomcat.

Alas, this particular mouse has no overall neural control; each of its four limbs has a "brain" of its own. One leg decides to bolt down a convenient hole, another decides to run up a tree, the third .... no, it is too ridiculous to continue, but the point has substance. In any collection of individuals, whether it be orchestral players, rugby players or members of an insurance company, the left hand (or paw) must know what the right is doing.

But assuming that an organisation does have a central system of control, we can draw something further from the example of the cat and mouse which is useful. And that is that the moment the mouse sensed the cat, it realised there was a problem that required a fairly rapid, substantial and "correct" response if its own well-being was to be guaranteed.

The cat and mouse example provides another lesson, and that is that the mouse had an overall objective—to live! Without an overall objective a "living" organisation (a cat or a mouse, for example) just as much as a business, artistic or financial organisation, would find it difficult, if not impossible, to make any sense of the environment.

With objective A, an event in the external environment might be seen as a life-threatening problem; with objective B, the self-same event, with equal validity, may be viewed as the opportunity of a lifetime. Thus an organisation must refer back constantly to the reason, the mission, why it was brought into existence in the first place and why it has subsequently been sustained. Having an overall objective/mission enables an organisation to make an assessment as to the change it has detected in the environment: is it an opportunity or a threat? Its next step is to decide on the urgency with which the problem/ opportunity has to be faced. Then, it must decide upon the range of alternative responses, to select one (having made some fairly detailed evaluation as to both its effect and the consequences of *not* putting it into effect) and then act upon it. The final step is to monitor that chosen course of action. It may be possible for the response to run along exactly as intended—which is good, but unlikely. It is far more probable that some type of modification will be required. As the organisation gains more experience in working in that particular field of operation, so will there be a rise in experience/discrimination, which will make the task of deciding whether to modify or not that much easier. Once the response has been completed, whether it was to avoid a threat or capture an opportunity, managements of wise organisations will need to evaluate the new situation in which they find themselves. Has the problem indeed been solved, the threat avoided, the opportunity taken? Whatever the outcome, one can guarantee that it will not be a static situation, and it is prudent to repeat the process of environmental scanning, evaluation, assessment and response again.

It should never stop. Mice do not shut down their brains just because the cat from next door was once avoided!

The sequence of this process may be represented thus:

Organisational definition of overall objectives

↓

Sense/define problem/opportunity

↓

Decide upon response

↓

Implement response

↓

Assess the new situation

The type of situation just described is the most basic of problem-solving arrangements. It could apply just as well to the purchase of a new tie or shirt, or when looking at the menu in a restaurant. It can also apply in the more complex situations found in business environments.

In such a case, the situation is much the same, though there are some differences in matters of degree rather than substance. When we select a new tie or shirt or a plate of whelks, we do so because the choice we make is to please ourselves. And the consequences of "wrong" choice are little more than not looking like a *Vogue* fashion plate or a serious stomach-ache! In business, choices are not (or should not be) made for personal, subjective reasons; we are not pleasing ourselves, but acting on behalf of a whole range of interested parties. The consequences of a "wrong" choice, too, are commensurately greater.

Our poor mouse has only two responses on sighting the cat: flight or fight. This latter option is not advisable, so it must flee. Our choice from a menu is restricted both by what is on offer ("Sorry sir, the Caramel Cream is off") and by our own likes and dislikes. In neither case, mouse/cat or menu, is there a need, or perhaps time, to research alternatives or to weigh too seriously the consequences of each available alternative action. Faced with a threat forty times their own body weight most mice are not famous for the precision and elegance of their deductive logic. In the majority of situations in which a business organisation might find itself, it is likely that there will be a wide range of available choices of action. The concept of "corporate instinct" is a nonsense and, because of the consequent cost of failure, subjectivity should have very little influence.

Business organisations, because of the dynamic nature of the environment in which they operate or into which they hope to develop, are increasingly finding themselves in novel, dangerous situations. Instinct and subjective assessment, though undeniably of some use, would be hard-pressed to cope with the full gamut of the complexities inherent in these previously unexperienced circumstances. By the nature of novelty, dependable valid knowledge, experience and confidence will be at minimal levels. Thus, in these circumstances, instinct and subjectively filtered experience, which are so useful in those cases where there is secure knowledge and valid experience, must be replaced by an objective, rigorous search for reliable, truthful data. This will enable the company to move successfully through the problem-solving sequence that has been described.

Problem-solving involving research

As in all formally constituted organisations, there is a need for an overall objective. And there is also a powerful requirement to search out information which will enable company managers to make the appropriate decisions. To sense and describe the problem/opportunity, there is a need for research to help define the boundaries of the environment in which judgements are to take place and to define, in managerial terms, the situation inside those boundaries.

To list and select alternative responses to the situation also requires research; this will need to be more focused than in the previous stage. More focused because the opportunity costs of "getting it wrong" are greater, and also because we now have the ability, which we should take, to dig deeper into the subject; this can be done because of the foundations which were laid down in the problem-definition stage. To decide on the final response requires the most detailed and rigorous research of all—this is the point to which all the research, deliberations and thought have been leading.

During the time that the response is being implemented, whatever action is taking place, that action will need to be monitored—further research, though of a different nature to that previously described. And, at the end of all this work, the company will find itself in a new situation. A further assessment will need to be made. Have the research objectives been reached? Was the original conception of the problem/opportunity valid? Does the new situation require a further response?

Here, not only research is important, but measurement too. The process of problem-solving involving research may be presented as shown in Scheme 1.

Marketing research and problem-solving

In this chapter so far, problem-solving in complex environments has been described only in fairly general terms. The process could almost just as well apply to mice, selecting a dish in a restuarant or, in very general terms, to a business organisation.

Definition of objectives
↓
Sense/define problems/opportunities ⟵ background and environmental
research
↓
List and select alternative responses ⟵ focused research
↓
Decide on a response ⟵————— Rigorous, focused research
↓
Implement response
↓⟵———————— Monitoring research
Assessment of the new situation

Scheme 1

It is fitting that this chapter should now focus, more specifically, on the role of marketing research in problem-solving exercises.

The steps are broadly as they have already been presented, but as marketing research is the *raison d'être* of this work, they will be given here in greater detail.

The sequence of steps for marketing research may be presented in the following manner:

Set the objectives of the research
↓
Define the research problem
↓
Assess the value of the research
↓
Construct the research proposal
↓
Specify data collection method(s)
↓
Specify technique(s) of measurement
↓
Select the sample
↓
Data collection
↓
Analysis of results
↓
Presentation of final report

(1) Set the objectives of the research

The identification of opportunities or threats is a major responsibility of any business organisation's management. Problems which are out in the open and which are already causing the organisation difficulties are events over which marketing research can have little influence other than measuring, evaluating and assessing such problems. Such a situation is a testament to the failure of the company's system of environmental scanning—its process of monitoring. The most a company can do in such a case is to react, with the aim of ameliorating the more dangerous effects. Marketing research should reduce the need for a company to have to react, by making the organisation proactive, i.e. by sensitising management to oncoming threats and opportunities in a timely way such that steps can be taken to avoid those threats or to take maximum advantage of the opportunities.

The above is a very general description of marketing research being used in its broadest sense; many people may not agree with this, and would perhaps tend to call such a system of data gathering, environmental scanning. But there is little substance in the difference between environmental scanning and marketing research, more one of degree. Both processes seek to look out from within the boundaries of the organisation into their surroundings. In environmental scanning the "horizon" of research would usually be far in the distance or in the future. In marketing research the point of regard would usually tend to be closer in time and place to the company, the investigation being concentrated on some specific event or situation.

In either case, the research will need to be coordinated and it will need to be directed to some end. Without a fixed overt objective, coordination and direction of purpose are very difficult, because an absence of a context, which would be a consequence of research without objectives, renders the assessment of data, its reliability and validity, practically impossible.

Case study: setting research objectives

Tagg, Berry and Wheeler plc is an old established distiller and bottler of industrial gases. Up until the late 1980s, it was an expanding and moderately profitable enterprise which had established and maintained contacts with a wide range of industrial users in close geographical proximity to its factory. Since that time, however, it steadily lost one after another of its important customers to a large multinational organisation who opened a plant in their area in 1989.

Feeling the need for data which could be used as a basis for a re-formulated marketing strategy, Tagg et al. decided to promote John Smith, a relatively inexperienced marketing executive, to the post of Director of Marketing Research. At a stormy meeting between members of the board and the new Research Director, the three founding members of the organisation stated their thoughts as to the cause of falling sales as follows:

Tagg: "I think that our lack of profitability is due to too high production costs; if we rationalise our distillation processes, this will enable us to cut prices. The high cost of our product makes us vulnerable to competitive forces."

Berry: "Without question, the cause of our dwindling customer-base is that both the quality and the range of our products are not as good as our major competitors—both of these factors need to be investigated."

Wheeler: "It is nothing to do with production costs or the quality and/or range of the products. The real reason for our decline is that the whole country is in the grip of a general recession—every company's in the same boat."

As a relative newcomer to the company and as a very inexperienced marketing research worker, Smith found that he was unable to reconcile the conflicting views of the three senior board members; each insisted that his own theory be investigated.

Smith carried out their bidding. He mounted a reasonably well-thought-through survey only to find that he had generated thoroughly inconclusive data which was found to be almost totally useless as a basis on which to found a new marketing strategy.

Moral: without a rigorous assessment of the situation in which the research is to be conducted, and without a clear set of unambiguous research objectives which are mutually acceptable both to all those that commission marketing research and to those that have to carry it out, any research is doomed to failure.

(2) Define the research problem

Step 1, above, is the equivalent of a physician making an acknowledgement that one of his/her patients is generally unwell. Following from that observation there is a need for tests to be administered in order to help refine the diagnosis. The doctor could ask the patient to describe the feelings that they have; these are symptoms and are subjective. The doctor could also make an assessment of the problem by looking at the patient; these are signs and are objective (or should be).

In many cases, a combination of signs and symptoms is sufficient for an adequate diagnosis to be made. But if they are not, then the doctor will need to order tests. And here we arrive at Step 2 in the research sequence—the definition of the research problem. It is a critical step, as it designates the areas of research and the types of data that are required. To revert back to the medical analogy for a moment, it would be quite useless if, after the patient complained of a severe stomach-ache, the physician were to order that the patient's feet be X-rayed! So, definition of the research problem is very important.

However, this is, in many situations, a far from easy task, but is one which *must* be undertaken; without this step, the research can proceed no further if it is to provide valid and useful results. In complex, novel situations, actually defining what is the cause of the problem or the site of an opportunity may be similar to getting lost on a foreign motoring holiday. Roads are unfamiliar, street signs mean little or nothing, passers-by don't seem to speak any recognisable language—and after half an hour of this, even one's own ability to distinguish left from right is brought into question. In such a situation, it is too easy to make snap decisions. It is possible that on mature consideration, and with data from some appropriate exploratory research, the first analysis of the situation may turn out to be quite mistaken. Because of the importance of this stage in the research process, it is imperative that not only is a "true" image of the problem brought into focus, but also, in a more general sense, an accurate assessment is made of the environment in which the problem/opportunity exists: as has been noted before, the context of the research process is of great importance.

It is possible that sufficient information already lies within the organisation such that this question of problem definition may be adequately answered. Frequently this is not the case and so exploratory research will have to be undertaken. It is not possible here to prescribe the nature of that research as each problem is situation-specific and each case must be judged on the nature of that problem, the degree of importance that it holds for the company and the degree of expertise, in that particular field, of the marketing research consultant. What should be emphasised, however, is that the end result of this step must be a valid understanding and definition of the problem/opportunity that has to be undertaken, together with an accurate assessment of the environment in which any subsequent research will take place.

Where complex and new situations are being faced by both the research's commissioners and the marketing research organisation, an initial analysis of the environment, in which the problem/opportunity is thought to lie, may reveal a confused and conflicting mass of variables. Before proceeding further, it is necessary that this confusion be resolved. If not, then it will be difficult to be sure that the research which is ultimately stipulated will be appropriate to the objectives of the investigation. One way to cut through the complexities and make sense of this tangle of variables is to construct a model of the situation. Even one built on a simple, modest scale will ensure a more reliable assessment of the situation. From such a model, researchers will be able to put forward a hypothesis, or hypotheses, i.e. possible ways in which the research question(s) may be answered.

For example, when trying to estimate possible future sales after the introduction of a new model of microwave egg poacher, the hypotheses might include:

(1) High sales will depend upon a low price.

(2) High sales will be dependent upon an extensive distribution system.

(3) High sales will require an extensive advertising and promotional strategy.

Exploratory research may reveal that the third hypothesis is the one that holds the greatest potential to produce meaningful and useful results—results which will fully satisfy the overall demands of the research project. Conversely, it may be that exploratory research suggests that all three hypotheses are of importance. In such situations, it is the duty of the marketing consultant, in consultation with the organisation's management, to devise a research proposal which will provide adequate data to test each of them.

Schematically, Step 2 may be presented as below:

Overall research objective

↓ ←—— Exploratory research

Definition of the research problem

External expert advice ——→ ↓ ←—— Exploratory research

Development of the hypothesis

↓

Research proposal

The end result of this, Step 2, process will lead to the construction of the research proposal (Step 4). But before that stage is reached, an assessment needs to be made of the value of the research.

(3) Assessment of the value of the research

This is an important process.

In an ideal world every organisation would commission marketing research agencies to investigate every single problem or opportunity which they have to face. But ideal worlds, outside Hollywood, do not exist; everything has a value and everything has a price. The latter is a fixed quantity, the former depends upon many factors. Information which to one company may be of immense value to another company may be just so much dross.

After the research problem has been defined, a cost–benefit exercise should be conducted. Factors which help to determine the value of the desired information include:

(a) The degree of newness and hence uncertainty in that particular environment.

(b) The degree of complexity of the environment.

(c) The strategic importance and cost of making the wrong decision(s).

(d) The degree of importance which the company attaches to the decision(s) that have to be made.

The higher the level of importance which the company associates with each of these factors, the greater the value of the information resulting from the research project; the lower the level, the lesser the value.

The cost of a research project should never be allowed to rise above the value of the results.

(4) Construct the research proposal

If, for a moment, a research project is thought of as being similar to the construction of a building, then the stage of problem definition—Step 2—is equivalent to the laying down of the foundations; on that everything else will have to rest. Thus it is essential, *vital*, to ensure that the piles go deep into the ground, that they are correctly positioned, cover a large enough area and are strong enough to support the superstructure.

The first item of that superstructure is the steelwork, the girders and pillars: they represent the equivalent of the research proposal. But it should be noted that this administrative "steelwork" is going to have to be able to do something which, apart from natural pliancy, would be most unwelcome in a real building; it is going to have to be quite flexible.

Marketing research is not a one-way street. Once a project has been started, it is most unusual for an investigation to proceed in an orderly manner from start to finish exactly as planned. It does not have to resemble the short-sighted cyclist who, having accidently got his bicycle wheels trapped in the tram-tracks, has to go all the way to the terminus before they can be freed!

Marketing research is a learning process. Not just as a result of the entire process; but stage by stage as the rolling-stone of the process gathers the "moss" of data and experience. Data and experience which will enable those in command of the project to assess the quality and appropriateness of the data which is being generated. If, as a result of a certain amount of research, it is apparent that the definition of the research problem is unfocused or inappropriate, or that the research objectives will not be achieved if the current style or direction of the project is pursued, then the current research process must cease. Those in charge of the investigation must then make an assessment as to the cause of the problem, redefine the research problem/objectives in such a manner that it will enable the project to proceed, but this time in a direction which *will* enable the research objectives to be reached.

Individuals and organisations must be prepared to admit that all may not always go exactly to plan and that the system should be flexible enough to be able to benefit, in the later stages of the research, from the experience gained at the beginning.

Information needs

When an opportunity or threat is detected in a company's environment, it is the function of management to place the company in the optimal position to make the most of the former and to reduce, as much as possible, the effects of the latter. Research cannot, of itself, carry out this positioning; that is a strategic management function. What marketing research can do is to provide valid, reliable information that will allow the company's administration to take the necessary decisions with the confidence that the opportunity or threat has been accurately depicted together with all the relevant variables.

Translated into visual terms, the company needs to know that what it is seeing is a true, life-like representation of the situation and not a distorted cartoon-like image.

Marketing research can be used to help construct that picture, but it can do so only if at the problem definition stage of the project there has been an unambiguous request for data relevant to the situation under investigation, data which will be useful to those empowered to take decisions.

It is important for both client and researcher, that there should be close agreement on what, exactly, are to be the constituents of the research proposal. Thus it is recommended that when the proposal has been agreed, it should be written down and signed by both parties.

This is a useful exercise in that (a) it more clearly focuses attention on the problem and encourages mature consideration at a critical phase of the research process (one which may have serious consequences if it is improperly thought through), (b) in the course of a long and complicated research project it acts as a guide and reference-point, one that will keep all the involved parties within mutually acceptable limits, (c) it is useful when analysing and interpreting the data to have a document which specifically details the aims and objectives of the research.

But again, one must be conscious of the need for a certain amount of flexibility. As Luck and Rubin (1987) say "the original [research] designs and guides, but does not dictate the conduct of the research".

Categories of research

Research, in any sphere of investigation, may be sub-divided into three main categories: exploratory, descriptive and causal. Each has its advantages and disadvantages and in marketing research terms, each finds its optimal use in certain types of situation. As the spectrum of research category is traversed from exploratory, through descriptive, to causal, there tends to be an increasing degree of formality, and a decreasing degree of flexibility, in the way in which the research can be carried out.

Exploratory research may be used to uncover the variables at work in a situation, descriptive research to describe them, and causal research to establish the manner in which those variables are related to one other.

(i) Exploratory research

Exploratory research is the investigator's equivalent of dipping an elbow in the bath water in an attempt to avoid poaching the infant. It is most useful in the preliminary stages of a research project when the levels of uncertainty and of general ignorance of the subject in question are at their highest. Exploratory research is characterised by a large degree of flexibility; a lack of formal structure and of any drive to measure. The flexibility arises from a need to learn from the experience of the investigation and from the need to avoid being blinkered by any preconceived notions. The lack of formal structure permits researchers to "follow their noses" and their instincts.

Information may be derived from secondary sources of data and from personnel with an expert knowledge of the situation under investigation. Information may also be derived from mini-samples and small-scale experiments.

The main aim of this exploratory research is to uncover the boundaries of the environment in which the problems, opportunities or situations of interest are likely to reside and to uncover the salient variables that may be found there and which are relevant to the research project.

Other benefits of exploratory research include the opportunity to become familiarised with any temporal/seasonal effects which may occur (for example, when investigating the sales of ice-cream, the time of the year should be taken into account), the chance to identify the major "actors" and personalities of the environment and the possibility to start learning any language, dialect or jargon which may be used. And, in a practical sense, it will enable workers to make an assessment of how easy/difficult it will be to conduct research in that particular circumstance.

(ii) Descriptive research

If the main purpose of exploratory research, as detailed above, is to uncover the salient variables that are at play in the situation of interest, then the purpose of descriptive research is to provide an accurate and valid depiction of those variables; if exploratory finds something of interest and points the camera, the descriptive research takes the photograph. Descriptive research is probably the most commonly used form of research.

It might be used to investigate the market share of a company's products, or sales in a product category. The demographic characteristics of a target market might be detailed, or the distribution system in a target market might be investigated, or the distribution networks of a rival could be looked at.

Descriptive research does not try to uncover any causal links between variables—just to describe them. Data may be obtained from many sources, but usually the bulk of it will come from secondary sources of data and from surveys.

In some situations a combination of exploratory and descriptive research may provide sufficient data for the objectives of the research to be fulfilled.

However, in some cases, a mere description of the variables that are relevant and active may not satisfy the research demands. Where it is deemed necessary to prove that variable *A* causes or affects variable *B*, causal research should be employed.

(iii) Causal research

Descriptive research can only provide a photograph of, for example, two variables *A* and *B*. This will be a static representation; it does not contain a dynamic component which would enable one to say what the nature of that relationship was, to discover this dynamic element, causal research is used.

Causal research could be used, for example, to determine the relationship between sales and advertising, between market share and price, or between packaging and repeat purchases.

There are three main states which enable a researcher to infer a causal relationship between variables.

State One. There are sufficient grounds to infer that variable *A* causes an effect in variable *B*, if it is discovered, for example, that a multicoloured package is associated with raised sales figures and that a monochrome package tends to be associated with lower sales. Then it is possible to infer a causal relationship between package design and sales. But note, this relationship is not proven—all that has been done is that an inference has been drawn.

State Two. There are sufficient grounds to suggest that the effect in variable *B* was caused by the preceding action of variable *A*. If variable *B* alters before the actions of variable *A* have their impact, then no causal relationship between them can be inferred.

State Three. Practically, this case is the most difficult one to prove. State Three is the case where, having removed the effects of all other sources of action, there remains only the relationship between variables *A* and *B*. It can be seen, in reality, that it is practically impossible to be absolutely sure that this *is* the case. However, a combination of expertise, experience and common sense does enable the eradication of the most overt sources of "contamination", thus enabling a causal relationship to be established with dependable degrees of confidence.

(5) Specify the data collection methods

Having decided on the research objectives and the research proposal, it is now time to stipulate the method(s) of data collection. There is no hard and fast rule which says that only a single method may be employed or that a multimethod approach is absolutely obligatory; method or methods are chosen that will amply fulfil the demands of the research objectives. Remember—flexibility!

It is the function of marketing research to interpret the research objectives such that the appropriate data is collected. The data should be valid and reliable, easily and speedily obtained, affordable and relevant to the situation in question. There are an almost infinite variety of data sources. To make the situation more tractable, it is usual to aggregate them into two main groupings: secondary and primary sources.

Secondary data

Secondary data is data that has already been collected for some purpose other than the one under consideration. The data may lie within the company (internal data), and comprises such information as sales invoices, advertising/media costs, distribution data and previous market research reports. Data may also lie outside the organisation's boundaries (external data), and may include government publications, syndicated research, trade/professional association reports etc.

Primary data

Primary data is data which is collected specifically to answer the question(s) posed by the current research objectives. If secondary data is compared to an off-the-peg suit of clothes, then primary data is bespoke—made-to-measure.

All the employable means of obtaining primary data will be discussed in detail in later chapters, for the moment, primary data methods will be broken down as follows.

(i) Survey research

This includes structured or semi-structured data collection methods, with the information being collected from a census of the population of interest or from a representative sample of that population.

Personal interviews. Direct contact between researcher and respondent in the latter's home/office, central location or the street.

Mail interviews. Indirect contact between researcher and respondent via the postal system.

Telephone interviews. Semi-direct contact between researcher and respondent by means of a telephone.

Computer interviews. Indirect contact between researcher and respondent, where the data is directly keyed into a computer, in response to questions displayed on the computer screen.

(ii) Qualitative research

This takes the form of unstructured interviews and exercises, usually with small sample sizes, and is used to generate ideas and/or hypotheses and to investigate respondent's beliefs, feelings and attitudes in a way which may not be possible, or not nearly so effective, if they were to be asked to respond to direct questioning.

Depth interviews. Unstructured, free-flowing discussions on a one-to-one basis, intended to generate data which is deep and rich and which are conducted in an atmosphere free of peer-pressure, the need to conform to social mores and fear of ridicule.

Group discussions. A small group of respondents, usually numbering between 6 and 10, who engage in a wide-ranging investigation of a predetermined topic. The dynamics of the interaction between individual group members is of great interest.

Projective techniques. Methods by which respondents' feelings, beliefs and attitudes, which cannot be accessed by direct questioning, are allowed to be articulated via the projection of those feelings etc., on to objects and/or third parties.

(iii) Experimental research

Experimentation involves the manipulation of an independent variable or variables to test and measure the effect on the dependent variable. It is mostly used to investigate and quantify causal relationships.

Field experiments. The test is conducted in the respondent's home or office, on the assumption that under such circumstances they will react less to the fact that they are being tested and will, therefore, act more naturally.

Laboratory experiments. The test is conducted in an artificial setting, a laboratory for example, in an attempt to reduce the effects of variables outside the direct area of interest.

(iv) Observation

In some cases, it is preferable to observe respondents' behaviour rather than to interview them on that behaviour. It may be used to investigate people's current behaviour and the *results* of past behaviour. In rare cases it may be the only research method available to collect data, but it is more frequently used as an adjunct to other types of research.

The major categories of observations are as follows.

The audit. The premises of the respondent, home or office are investigated to uncover the extent of ownership of certain products/brands. This method may also be termed indirect observation.

Direct observation. Direct observation, by a researcher, of the behaviour of the respondent. If direct observational techniques are to be used as part of the research project, then the data must be visually overt. Thus "internal" variables, such as feelings, beliefs and attitudes, are not suitable topics for this technique. The event being observed can only occupy a short period of time (observing the purchase of a door-mat is acceptable, observing the purchase of the entire house is not). The event being observed must also be frequently performed: to have to wait too long for the occurrence would make the research cost-ineffective.

Recording devices. A number of devices are used for recording both micro and macro behaviour. The former tend to be used in laboratory settings and the latter in natural locations.

Laboratory settings. *Psychogalvanometers*: humans tend to perspire more when excited; therefore, after exposure to, say, an advertisement, the subject's response can be estimated by measuring the perspiration rate. Psychogalvanometers are the measuring instruments.

Eye cameras: these may be used to superimpose onto an image of an advertisement, for example, the pattern of the respondent's eye movements—the movements which occur when the image is viewed. This allows an assessment to be made of those parts of the image which attract most attention and those which suffer relative neglect.

Pupilometric cameras: physiologists have found a link between the diameter of a pupil and the degree of visual stimulation which the visual system is deriving from an image. Pupilometric cameras record and measure the movements of a respondent's pupils.

Natural settings. For those types of behaviour which are not suitable for recording and measurement in a laboratory setting, an assessment must be made in a natural setting. For this the main device is the video or movie camera. Cameras, of whatever technological basis, are positioned so that the required behaviour may be recorded for later analysis.

(6) Select the techniques of measurement

Measurement has been defined as the "assignment of numbers to objects to represent amounts or degrees of a property possessed by all the objects" Torgerson (1958). These numbers may then be analysed so that questions concerning that "property" may be answered.

Measurement is a fundamental part of marketing research. Managers are constantly demanding that various aspects of a market, of an environment or of a product/brand are measured. It might be the demographic constitution of a target market, the attitudes of that target market to certain aspects of a product, i.e. its functional features, price, advertising or packaging; or it might be the forces which condition a potential consumer's movement towards or away from that product.

The process by which the factors under investigation are turned into quantified data is called measurement. Thus, not only should there be an unambiguous statement of the problem to be researched, but there should also be an operational definition of what exactly is to be measured.

Measurement requires that an appropriate scale of measurement be used and that the "amounts or degrees of a property", i.e. the property's characteristics, are placed on this scale of measurement. The scale of measurement must be appropriate so that it is able to measure the characteristic(s) of interest. A ruler is used to transcribe the characteristic of dimension into numbers, and a thermometer is used to transcribe the characteristic of a body's thermal energy; both are instruments of measurement, but they are not interchangeable; each is used in the appropriate circumstance.

In marketing research the scale of measurement chosen is dependent partly upon the type of data collection method being used and partly upon the type of data required to fulfil the objectives of the research.

The two main methods of measurement in marketing research are questionnaires and attitude scales.

Questionnaires

Questionnaires are structured or semi-structured lists of questions, both open and closed, which are asked directly of the respondent and which may be used to investigate attitudes, beliefs, feelings, behaviour, knowledge and demographic characteristics.

Attitude scales

Nominal scales. Objects are placed in a category because they are identified with respect to some predetermined variable, e.g. age, sex, ownership of an E-type Jaguar. This is the scale used for classification.

Ordinal scales. Objects are ranked in an order depending upon the amount of a variable which is associated with that object or which it possesses. "Miss World" competitors are ranked on an ordinal scale, and so are candidates in marketing research examinations.

Interval scales. These use equal units of measurement with an arbitrary zero point. Addition and subtraction of scale scores are permitted, but division is not since that process assumes the adoption of a fixed position for the zero point. Thus, though it is possible to say that the difference between scale points 10 and 20 is identical to the difference between scale points 70 and 80, it is not permissible to say that a scale score of 80 is four times larger than one of 20.

Ratio scales. With a ratio scale, there is a predetermined zero point. They are similar to scales used in everyday life to measure, for example, height and weight. All arithmetic processes are allowed, thus in this case, it *is* possible to say that a scale score of 80 is four times larger than a scale score of 20. Just as it is possible to say that a 10 lb bag of potatoes is five times heavier than a 2 lb bag.

(7) Select the sample

It is rare that the market researcher has the time, the funds or the number of personnel necessary to conduct a census of each member of the population in which he/she has an interest, except where that population is relatively small; for example, when conducting research in industrial markets or amongst crowned heads of European countries. Besides, because of the problems that are associated with a census, which will be described in Chapter Four, researchers may prefer to use sampling techniques. The word population is used in marketing research in its statistical sense, and refers to all those cases/situations/people which contain variable(s) in which the research has an interest. Populations may, for example, comprise women in social classes A and B1 or they may be industrial buyers for firms which manufacture electrical spark-plugs.

It is usual in marketing research, rather than conducting a census, to extract a sample from the population, and to let that sample stand as proxy for the whole of the population of cases/situations/people with which they share the characteristic(s) of interest.

Sampling may be broken down into two main classes, probability and non-probability techniques. Each will be dealt with in greater detail in Chapter Four.

As with many other marketing tools, the style of sampling that is used in a particular situation cannot be chosen in a vacuum; it is dependent on the research objectives, the data requirements, the time and financial resources available, the degree of complexity in the environment, the degree of accuracy which the results are required to possess, and the variability of the population.

Probability techniques:
    Simple random sampling
    Stratified random sampling
    Cluster sampling
    Multi-stage sampling

Non-probability-techniques:
    Convenience sampling
    Judgement sampling
    Quota sampling
    Purposive sampling

(8) Collection of data

This is when talk stops and the data is actually collected.

(9) Analysis of the results

Data generated by the research process will not, in itself, answer the research problems that the project was mounted to investigate. The data will need to be processed, from sets of numbers or from collections of qualitative statements, into a form which can be clearly communicated to all interested parties and which will display, explain and allow to be discussed the significant variables which pertain to the research objectives.

It is not possible to prescribe here what exactly should be the types of analysis that each research project should undergo. But it can be said that certain types or levels of analysis are only possible if the data has been collected in a certain way and has been measured using certain instruments and scales of measurement. Therefore, it is essential that the researcher, prior to the selection of the sampling technique and the instruments of measurement, and before the collection of the data begins, should decide upon the information requirements and the manner in which the data is to be analysed. If this is not done, then much valuable time, energy, and funds will have been wasted. For example, it is of little use trying to analyse, using advanced statistics, data which has been generated using non-probability sampling techniques.

(10) Presentation of the final report

In concert, at the outset of the project, the client and the consultant should jointly agree upon the research objectives and the research proposal. In presenting the final report, the consultant must ensure that all the requirements that were decided upon are addressed. The report should also include an executive summary of the findings, a description of the environment in which the research took place, the assumptions (if any) that were made in order for the research to proceed, and the research design (together with the salient factors that led to that particular choice).

At the commencement of the work, client and consultant should also have agreed as to whether the report should present only the results of the study or include an evaluation of those results too. Secondary sources of data should be included, together with the reasons why, if any, data was discarded.

A further and most important factor should be borne in mind when writing research reports, and that is that they are meant to communicate data and answers to those who have commissioned the research—commissioners who, in general, are not marketing specialists.

The writers, therefore, should not take the report as an opportunity to dazzle readers with a display of the full gamut of their technical erudition and grasp of research jargon. It is rarely helpful, for example, for a reader to have to wade through pages on the theory of canonical correlation when all they want to know is what happens to sales if they double the price of their products. Technically unversed managers may not have a great interest in how samples were chosen, whether ratio or nominal scales were used or the types of data analysis that were employed. They are, however, interested in valid, reliable, understandable data which will enable them to take those complex decisions (concern with which initially prompted the research) with the confidence that they are now "fully in the picture".

Keep the style of writing clear and to the point. "A nod is as good as a wink to a blind horse" is surely preferable to saying that a forward inclination of the cranium is the equivalent of a transitory occlusion of the palpebral fissure to an equine quadruped devoid of visual perception!

Summary

The ten steps in the research process that have been discussed are not meant to be rigidly prescriptive—they are but a guide; though they can be followed exactly if the research objectives and the situation so dictate. A further point to note is that although the points/steps have been presented in a strictly linear form, in a real situation they might not occur in quite such a convenient order. It may be that the sampling techniques and the data collection methods are chosen almost simultaneously and that both are chosen in the light of the data requirements and the type(s) of analysis which are needed to render the required results. There will be many feed-back loops in a practical research study—research hardly ever runs on a track with well-oiled wheels.

Marketing research is more like a taxi-cab—it will go anywhere you want (providing you have the fare) but the cab-driver must know how to drive, must have a working knowledge of the Highway Code, and the passenger and the driver must agree at the outset as to the final destination.

References

Luck D. J. and Rubin D. S. (1987) *Marketing Research*, Prentice-Hall, Englewood Cliffs, New Jersey, 7th edition.
Torgerson W. S. (1958) *Theory and Methods of Scaling*, John Wiley, New York.

CHAPTER THREE

Secondary Data—Uses and Limitations

Introduction   31

Use of secondary data   32

Advantages of secondary data   35

Disadvantages of secondary data   35

The sequence in which secondary research is used   37

Internal sources of data   39

External sources of data   40

Summary   43

References   44

Introduction

If a family has decided to visit a newly established neighbourhood restaurant or go to the latest musical, because of the expense involved, it is usual, before committing themselves to the unknown, to carry out a little investigation. They might turn to the local or national press to look up the reviews, or they might also ask the opinion of friends who have already paid a visit. What they have been doing on a very small, though no less valid, scale is the subject of this chapter; they have been conducting secondary research.

Associated with the definition of any research project should be an explicit statement of both the data that will be necessary to fulfil the requirements of the research objectives and the way in which the data is to be collected. But tailor-made research which is conducted with the aim of answering the specific objectives of the current research—primary research—is costly and time-consuming. The research may also, in the initial stages of the project, especially when the situation contains large degrees of complexity and novelty, not be orientated in quite the most optimal direction. To achieve that aim, experience and guidance are needed, factors which, because of the newness of the situation, may not be too much in evidence in either the commissioning organisation or the research consultancy. In such situations, therefore, rather than blindly stumbling through the jungle of ignorance, it is fitting that use be made of those sources of data and of those people who do have the experience and knowledge and who can offer the necessary guidance.

It is certainly quicker and cheaper to read someone else's research reports than to reproduce their investigation. Proponents of the use of secondary data might ask "Why bother to employ an architect when there are so many house designs so readily available?" No one would disagree with that, providing that the plans which are available will render the type of house for which the prospective client is looking. So, secondary data cannot provide the answers to all the questions that research workers need; there are disadvantages but, with prudence, they can be overcome.

The following chapter discusses both the advantages and disadvantages of secondary data; it also places its use within the context of the overall research project.

Use of secondary data

Research which has been carried out by someone else for another purpose is classed as secondary data. Research which has been designed by ourselves to answer specific research questions is called primary research.

We are currently in the middle of an explosion of data: newspapers, journals, magazines, government and research agencies, television, radio are all issuing vast amounts of facts, figures and comment. There is also an extraordinary array of hardware with which to analyse and display such data: computers, facsimile machines, electronic mail, compact disc recorders etc. There is no shortage of raw material on which to work nor of ways in which access to it may be gained. Data, of an almost infinite variety, complexity and usefulness, lies within and without the boundaries of organizations; a bewildering amount. How then does one start and what "filters" are available to reduce the seemingly overwhelming mass of facts and figures to something more tractable?

As has been detailed in Chapter Two, as the sequence of steps in the research process is traversed, there should be an increasing need to focus, in a more detailed manner, on the exact type of data that is required. If the research objectives and proposal have been unambiguously constructed, then they should contain practical insights into the type of data that will be necessary to satisfy the overall objectives of the research. Secondary research, or desk research as it is sometimes termed, should take place early on in the process, and should aim to secure reliable, valid information. Secondary data, according to Newson–Smith (1988), can:

(a) provide a backdrop to primary research,

(b) act as a substitute for field research,

(c) be used as a technique in itself,

(d) be used in acquisition studies.

Each one will now be examined in more detail.

(i) Provide a backdrop to primary research

As has been stressed on several previous occasions, the context in which research takes place is of the utmost importance. Without a context, facts, opinions, trends etc., cannot be evaluated properly, and it becomes increasingly difficult to relate what may rapidly become a meaningless jumble of data to the project in hand.

If a market research agency, or someone from a large organisation's marketing research department, is working in an environment or in a marketing situation with which they are unfamiliar, there will be a natural tendency to proceed slowly and with care: to research, first, the subject in journals, newspapers, previously published market research reports or to make use of those who have expert knowledge of the particular field of study. Secondary data sources, whether "organic" or inorganic, will prevent unnecessary primary research.

If there is an extant research report, journal article or other published material which adequately covers the topic of interest, then why repeat it? Even if it does not exactly fit all the research project's objectives, which is likely, then it will, at least, provide guidance as to the likely sources of data and the magnitude of the problems that might be encountered should primary research, ultimately, be thought necessary.

Given that it is likely that some sort of sampling of the target population will have to take place, secondary research can also be useful in suggesting practical ways in which the variables which are pertinent to that population may be defined and made operational. If researchers are entering a market segment or situation for the first time, secondary data may reveal who are the important "players", the size of the market, the types of opportunities and threats which are likely to exist there and the active trends.

(ii) As a substitute for field research

Given the unlikely and wholly theoretical situation where primary research costs nothing in time or money, then every company would surely prefer to have its problems investigated by specifically designed, tailor-made research projects. But, there is no such ideal in the world of marketing research, there is always a cost, which means that the most must be made of what is available.

Secondary research is most useful, here, in that previously published data may exactly answer all the questions to which the company would like answers. Perhaps not every single last question will be answered, but sufficient data may be available to eradicate the need to mount a primary research programme. This is an occasion on which a cost–benefit analysis needs to be made, weighing the benefits to be gained from secondary data which is already available against the additional costs which would be incurred as a result of having to carry out primary research.

One situation where secondary data is unlikely to be able to provide most of the required information is where the constitution of a marketing-mix is being investigated. Too much of such a situation is so situation-specific as to be an unlikely subject for research by a third party. Here, organisations must bite the bullet and proceed to gather primary research, though desk research may prove useful in pointing out those variables which would be of interest in classifying market segments or consumer/industrial trends.

(iii) As a technique in itself

As Baker (1991) points out, there are some types of research programme which may only be realistically carried out by the use of secondary research. And as such, secondary data must be considered as a technique in its own right. The example Baker quotes is where an attempt is being made to establish trends in the behaviour of a market. Longitudinal studies are unrealistic for a one-off study, which means that one must rely on published historical data. A further point, he notes, is that much published data concerned with the structure and performance of a market is compiled by means of censuses, a method which can be superior to sampling—the technique which would be the likely procedure in a field research study. Secondary data may also be used as a way of describing the situation and the boundaries in which the primary research is to be set.

(iv) Acquisition studies

One of the most popular strategic options for a company, in recent times, has been that of acquisition. It is, however, an operation full of risks and problems, not the least of which is the desire of the "predator" to keep as quiet as possible to avoid startling the "prey". Field research into the target company, with all its attendant publicity, is an obvious way to announce one's presence—the organisational equivalent of a huntsman treading on and snapping a branch.

In acquisition studies, data may be gathered under two main headings:

Company description. Company history, financial structure and performance, production techniques, employee make-up etc.

Products and markets. Competitor activity, product policy, advertising, marketing etc.

Most of the above data may be gleaned from published sources: company reports, the trade press, newspapers, government statistics etc. Outside acquisition studies, Baker (1991) points out, such secondary data would also be useful to a company when conducting competitor analysis, but it would appear that this resource is made use of by surprisingly few organisations.

Advantages of secondary data

Green, Tull and Albaum (1988) provide the following advantages which arise from the use of secondary sources of data.

(1) Secondary data may solve the problem, obliterating the need for primary research altogether, therefore saving time.

(2) Because it is usually easier to search out secondary data sources than it is to mount a primary research programme, considerable cost savings may be made.

(3) Secondary data may not, in some cases, answer all the questions posed by the research objectives, but it is still a useful exercise in that it can:

(a) aid in problem definition and the generation of hypotheses concerned with its resolution; it can expose pertinent variables and ways in which they are related;

(b) guide researchers in their primary data collection; it will show how previous researchers have tackled similar problems—their good points and, maybe, where they encountered problems and the ways in which they were overcome/reduced;

(c) be used as a basis for classification which will then enable primary data to be made congruent with past studies such that trends may be displayed;

(d) help in the definition of the target population and of the variables which may be used in the determination of appropriate samples.

Disadvantages of secondary data

Given all the claims that appear to have been made on behalf of secondary research, one might be forgiven for speculating as to why anyone should actually carry out primary research.

But as might be expected, there are disadvantages in its use. So, before secondary data is used, the researcher must ask the following questions:

(1) Is the secondary data relevant?

- Does the published data fit the requirements of the present research objectives?
- Do the classifications of the published data fit in with the needs of the current project?
- Are the units of measurement congruent with the demands of the investigation in hand?

(2) Is the secondary data too costly to acquire?

Usually secondary data will cost considerably less to acquire than mounting a primary research project. However, some specialised marketing research reports may cost several thousand pounds. A cost–benefit analysis will be needed to determine the relative benefits to be derived from such an expenditure versus those to be gained from bespoke primary research.

(3) Is the secondary data available?

Does the data actually exist? For many situations or product-specific cases, there is no secondary data. Given that the data does exist, is it possible to gain access to it at a price less than it would cost to carry out primary research?

(4) Is there a possibility that the secondary data is biased?

Researchers must attempt to determine who collected the published data and for what reason. If it was gathered and published to serve some situation in which either/both researchers and commissioners had an interest, then it should be carefully examined for bias.

Bias may arise at all levels of a research project. In order to gauge whether it is present, and if so in what quantities, it is useful if a copy of the original secondary data can be obtained. (Certainly much better than merely working from selected quotes in other people's work.) Obvious sources of bias, such as questionnaire wording, may then be examined.

(5) Is the secondary data accurate?

While obvious inaccuracies should cause few problems of detection, the main difficulty arises in trying to make an assessment of *how* accurate the remainder of the data is. Weiers (1988) suggests that the following check-list be used.

- Was the sample representative?
- Was the questionnaire or other measurement instrument(s) properly constructed?
- Were possible biases in response or in non-response corrected and accounted for?
- Was the data properly analysed using appropriate statistical techniques?
- Was a sufficiently large sample used?
- Does the report include the raw data?
- To what degree were the field-workers supervised?

To this may be added a further point: if all the raw data is not included in the report, does it detail the amount of data which was discarded and the criteria which were used to reject it?

In order to complete the check-list, it is therefore considered vital that the original reports be examined, and that the minimum use be made of reports in which the original is quoted second- or third-hand.

(6) Is the data sufficient?

The secondary data may meet all of the criteria set out above and yet may not be sufficient to answer all the questions in the research objectives. If it is not sufficient, then the consultant must consider moving on to a primary research process.

Case study: uses of secondary data

In international marketing, before proceeding with the creation of a multi-country advertising campaign, it is essential to investigate, via secondary sources of data, the regulations concerned with advertising for each of the countries it is intended to target.

For example, while comparative advertising is encouraged in the United States, in France and Germany it is banned. In Italy, direct comparisons are banned too, though substantiated indirect comparative advertising may be pursued. In Austria direct advertising to children is illegal, in Italy children cannot be shown eating and in France pre-broadcast screening of commercials is a requirement. In Italy and Switzerland advertising of all tobacco products is banned in all media as are drugs and medicine in the latter. (Dunn and Barban, 1978.)

The sequence in which secondary research is used

Figure 3.1 shows the position that secondary data occupies in the overall

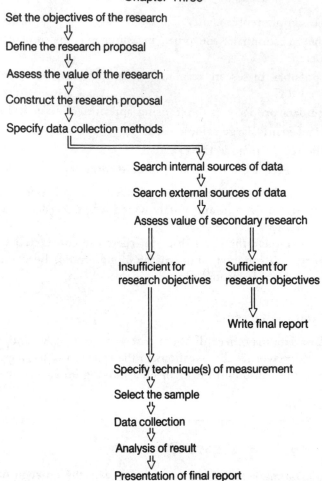

Figure 3.1. The position of secondary data in the overall research sequence.

research sequence; it also shows the sequence of steps which should be followed when using secondary sources of data.

An important issue in the use of secondary sources of data is that an attempt be made to specify, as accurately as possible (given the amount of information that is known concerning the research situation), what the data requirements of the project are. The volume of secondary data available is vast, and without some guidance it is easy to gather too much that is of only peripheral relevance. Sensible advice is given by Luck and Rubin (1987) when they say "a good rule in all research is parsimony: using only meaningful data".

As much useful data lies within the boundaries of the company it is a sensible idea to begin the search for data with internal sources; why bother going to the expense and trouble of finding and gaining access to external sources if the project's data requirements may be satisfied within the firm? And it is becoming increasingly likely that with a more widespread use of MIS, Management Information Systems, functional departments will have the desired data in a form suitable for the investigation's analysis.

If the internal sources of data do not meet all the data requirements then the research must move on to external sources. Stoll and Stewart (1984) recommend that directories, catalogues and indexes are consulted before books, abstracts and periodicals.

It is also important to remember the expertise of librarians; they are especially skilled in the techniques of data search and may save the project a considerable amount of time.

Internal sources of data

All companies collect data in one form or another, for one purpose or another. Invoices, bills, sales records, guarantee cards, sales force reports, records of product repairs etc. In most organisations this data is a much underused resource. Accounts data tends to remain within the boundaries of the accounts department; similarly, sales records and reports tend to stay within the confines of the sales department. There is much intra-departmental analysis of this data, but rarely much inter-departmental synthesis, except in those firms which are small enough to have friendly, informal communications. For example, it would be useful for a marketing department to know the geographical and demographic breakdown of its customers, an analysis which would not be too difficult if, as a matter of course, they had ready access to customers' self-returned guarantee cards.

As much data is gathered, for use and analysis, by functional department, it tends to be in a form which those departments have stipulated, and, as it stands, may not be of much use to the marketing research department. However, with the advent and increasing proliferation of computerised MIS, such a disadvantage could be readily overcome.

Internal sources of data may be divided as follows:

Accounts. Contains information on:
    Customer's name and location
    Type and quantity of product purchased
    Costs of sales, advertising etc.

Sales records. Contains information on:
    Markets
    Products
    Distribution systems

The majority of companies operating a system of sales records usually do so as a way of administering the salesforce: whose function, in the main, is *not* to act as a collector of basic data for the marketing research department. This is unfortunate, as the members of the salesforce are the company personnel who, more than any other group, come face to face with the customer. Thought should be given to incorporating a reporting system whereby the salesforce's expertise and knowledge of the customers can be recorded in such a manner as to be useful to the company's MIS.

Other reports. Contain information on:
   Trade associations and trade fairs
   Exhibitions
   Customers complaint letters
   Previous marketing research reports
   Conferences

External sources of data

The amount of information outside the boundaries of an organisation is vast. So where can a start be made?

If the topic of the investigation is not familiar to the researcher, probably the best approach is via those directories which give a guide to sources of secondary data (Directories of Directories!); these, at least, will give an indication as to the general direction in which to proceed.

It is always better to start off with the general and "funnel" down towards the specific. From the "Directory of Directories" one may work from general industry data, via specific industry data, to specific company/market data.

Tull and Hawkins (1988) assemble sources of secondary data into several main groups:

   Directories
   Computerised databases
   Associations
   Government agencies
   Syndicated services
   Other published sources
   External experts

Before each of these groups is discussed, it should be emphasised that it is not the intention to provide a detailed analysis of all known external sources of secondary data.

It is therefore the aim to give a flavour of each grouping, not a banquet!

Directories

These are good as a starting point, especially in unfamiliar situations. They can provide information on industries and markets, location and size of manufacturers, together with their products, sales, profits. Examples include:

Extel Handbook of Market Leaders
Jordan Industrial Sector Surveys
Kelly's Business Directory
Kompass
Sell's Directory of Products and Services
Times 1000 Leading Companies in Britain & Overseas
Extel European Companies Service
Moody's Industrial Manual
Who owns Whom: North America

Computerised databases

Computer technology now allows the storage, cataloguing and retrieval of data in a rapid and efficient manner. It requires the researcher's computer to be linked, usually by a modem, to the database's computer. In absolute terms it is quite an "expensive" system, but again, the word "quite" is relative; the costs of retrieval will need to be balanced against the benefits of the time saved and the width/depth of material that can be scanned.

European databases include:

European Kompass Online
Financial Times Company Information
Hoppenstedt Austria/Germany/Netherlands
Jordanwatch
PTS Prompt
Reuters Textline

Because of the cost of using computerised databases, it is advisable when first using such a system, to make use of the expertise of a trained operator, at least until experience is gained.

Associations

There are many associations covering industrial, commercial, financial and other professional bodies, all of which publish, in one form or another, data of interest to their members, data which can prove of enormous interest to those involved in the marketing research process.

However, a point which users should bear in mind is that many associations are acting as spokesmen for their industry or grouping. The information which they publish will, for obvious reasons, try to show their members and their professions in the best of lights. The data which they contain should therefore be treated with a certain degree of caution.

Professional publications include the Directory of British Associations. In this can be found information pertaining to, for example:

> British Association of Ski Instructors
> Highland Cattle Society
> National Hairdressers Federation
> Women's Squash Racquets Association.

Government agencies

All governments collect and publish vast amounts of data from the national level, via that of the region, down to the urban and rural level; this provides an enormous resource for those involved in marketing research. One of the main drawbacks with using government generated data is, in part, its enormous size.

In the UK, useful starting points include *Government Statistics, a Brief Guide to Sources* and the *Guide to Official Statistics*. These will give an indication as to where investigators should start looking when commencing their research into particular areas of interest, each government department collecting its own data.

There are far too many sources to be able to mention them all here, but Baker (1991) lists two main groups of data which may be consulted with reference to marketing and social change; these include:

Marketing:
> Business Monitor
> Housing and Construction Statistics
> Ministry of Agriculture Information Notice
> Family Expenditure Survey
> Census of Population
> Regional Trends
> National Food Survey

Social change:
> Social Trends on:
> General Household Survey
> OPCS Monitor

Syndicated services

Syndicated research is carried out by commercial research companies on industrial and consumer markets. The resulting data is then available for sale to that research organisation's clients; the data is, usually, not confidential and/or client-specific. This is a large subject and will be dealt with in some detail in Chapter Five.

Other published sources

Included in this grouping are such publications as journals, books, university/college publications and newspapers.

Their bulk is great, and finding a "way in" to this treasure trove is a major problem. One of the most "user-friendly" methods would be to carry out a computer search making use of the skills of an expert librarian—someone who would be able to guide the investigator.

There are also hard copy directories of abstracts which help in cutting down the research time. These include:

Business Periodicals Index
An Bar Management Services Abstracts
Research Index
ABI/Inform

External experts

These "organic" sources of secondary data could also be considered part of primary research, but here they are treated as those who, because of their expertise, position and contacts, have the ability to provide the research worker with the most apt and up-to-date information.

Of course, the information they give may be prone to a certain amount of subjectivity, but, at least, it will give assistance in tracking down useful sources of data. These may then be used in assessing the validity of the information given by the experts.

Summary

This chapter has presented the subject of secondary data, its place within an overall research design and its advantages and disadvantages. An indication has also been given as to the likeliest places in which it may be found.

It is not the intention to give the impression that secondary research is the answer to every researcher's prayers. Secondary data can be of great assistance, and, in a few cases, may fully answer all the questions posed in the research objectives. But it can only be of assistance if it is in existence and if it is available and accessible. If secondary data does not exist, or if it only partially fulfils the objectives of the research project, then those involved with the investigation must turn to primary research to answer the necessary questions.

References

Baker M. J. (1990) *Research for Marketing*, Macmillan, London.

Dunn S. W. and Barban A. (1978) *Advertising*, Dryden Press, London, 4th edition.

Green P. E., Tull D. S. and Albaum G. (1988) *Research for Marketing Decisions*, Prentice-Hall, Englewood Cliffs, New Jersey, 5th edition.

Luck D. J. and Rubin D. S. (1987) *Marketing Research*, Prentice-Hall, Englewood Cliffs, New Jersey, 7th edition.

Newson-Smith N. (1988) In *Consumer Market Research Handbook* (edited by R. Worcester and J. Downham), McGraw-Hill, London, 3rd edition.

Stoll M. and Stewart D. W. (1984) *Secondary Research: Information Sources and Methods*, Sage Publications, Beverley Hills, California.

Tull D. A. and Hawkins D. I. (1990) *Marketing Research: Measurement and Method*, Macmillan, New York, 5th edition.

Weiers R. M. (1988) *Marketing Research*, Prentice-Hall, Englewood Cliffs, New Jersey, 2nd edition.

CHAPTER FOUR

The Process of Sampling

Introduction   45
Census versus sample   46
Terminology   49
The process of sampling   50
(1) Define the population   50
(2) Define a frame for the population   51
(3) Select a sampling unit   52
(4) Choice of a sampling method   53
(5) Decide on the size of the sample   61
(6) Define the sampling plan   65
(7) Select the sample   65
Summary   66
References   67

Introduction

It is almost true to say, to paraphrase Descartes, 'I sample, therefore I am'. Sampling is a fact of life; all life—there is no escape.

Not only do we sample, but we ourselves are sampled. Opinion pollsters sample the public as to their voting intentions, chefs dip their fingers into a saucepan to determine the seasoning of a boeuf bourguignon, whisky distillers sample their products every so often to check on the maturing process. Without the ability to sample, a great many research projects could not take place. Sometimes it is possible and necessary to conduct a census of the population, for national statistics for example, or in industrial marketing research where there is only a small population. But in the majority of research situations it is neither practical nor possible to conduct a census, sampling thus being the only viable alternative.

It is not the main intention of this work to delve too deeply into the use of statistics in marketing research. However, interested readers will find in the Appendix a short explanation of how statistics may be used to generalise about a population based on the results of a single sample.

Census versus sample

It is neither necessary nor useful to be too dirigiste about the choice between census and sample. Each situation must be judged solely on its own merits. Below are presented four factors, cost, time, accuracy and what has been called the destructive nature of measurement; each of these will need to be considered when making the choice between census and sample

Cost

It is obviously less costly to sample one house than to interview every household in the country. If one requires information about schoolchildren's attitudes towards a certain television programme, then it is less costly to speak to 500 of the under 18-year-old population than to speak to them all.

However, if one requires information concerning motor car manufacturers or symphony orchestras, then it would be possible to conduct a census in these situations as there are far smaller populations than in the ones quoted previously.

In deciding between a census and a sample, one must always consider the value of the information that is to be obtained; price in itself is of too crude a nature to be the sole determinant. If the cost of a census is less than the value of the information which will result, then a census is the obvious method to adopt. If the cost of a census is greater than the value of the information, then one must turn to sampling—the need for the information still being present. Usually the choice is quite clear cut; in all but the smallest of populations it is very likely that the choice of sampling will predominate, given that budgetary considerations are a very important constraint on research.

Time

In an ideal world, marketing research consultants would have infinitely large budgets, infinitely large numbers of staff and an infinite time period in which to complete the project—an unlikely situation.

In many cases, the commissioners of the research require that the project be brought to a speedy conclusion—if not earlier!

A census, in general terms, is a very large undertaking, the quantity of data generated being vast. In turbulent, dynamic environments, by the time the results of such a census would be ready, the situation which provided the *raison d'être* for the project may very well have changed totally; a threat may have made a disastrous impact on the firm, or a profitable opportunity may have been lost.

It is usual for a sample to be drawn more quickly than a census.

Accuracy

The accuracy of a measure is the degree or the level of precision with which that measure is able to represent a parameter. In sampling, accuracy is a measure of the "fit" between the dimensions of the characteristic as revealed by the sample compared to the dimensions of that characteristic as it exists in the population.

In marketing research, accuracy is affected, partially, by two factors: sampling error which is associated with the drawing of a sample and non-sampling error or bias.

Sampling error

This is the error that is caused by selecting a probability sample from a population which is not representative of that population. For example, it is possible to draw a sample of 250 students from a music college all of whom are students of the 'cello; this is obviously not representative of the population of the conservatoire as a whole. Sampling error may be reduced by increasing the size of the sample. Probability sampling also allows for the use of statistical techniques to estimate the size of the sampling error.

Non-sampling error

Non-sampling errors comprise all those errors in a marketing research project apart from those that have their source in sampling error. Non-sampling error may be either systematic or random.

If a census of the population is taken, there can be no error arising from the way in which the individual elements are selected. There is no preferential or even random selection, all appropriately qualified members of the population are included. There is no sample—therefore there can be no sampling error.

However, sampling error is not the only source of contamination which can affect the results of the research; there is non-sampling error too.

Non-sampling error can reduce the accuracy and therefore the validity of a census and a sample. Non-sampling error can grow so large in a census that, in some cases, a more accurate representation of what is happening in the population can be derived from a sample—but only if non-sampling error is likely to be less than any sampling error.

For example, if a questionnaire contains an error or if the questionnaire is consistently misinterpreted, then the larger the sample the more will the error be compounded—it will grow larger. And for a given population, a census is the largest "sample" that can be drawn.

There is also the question of non-response: if a questionnaire is not returned by a certain number of respondents, or if some of the respondents refuse to undergo an interview, how do we know that those respondents who refuse to cooperate are not different from those respondents who do return their questionnaires or do agree to be interviewed? The larger the non-response, the greater will be the inaccuracy of the results.

With a census a great number of people are involved: interviewers, administrators, computer operators etc. Human beings are fallible, mistakes are made, inferences can be drawn which are not necessarily true, responses can be interpreted that do not validly reflect the truth. And the control of the project becomes more and more difficult as the size increases.

Samples drawn from a population are smaller than a census drawn from the same population. This means that the opportunities to "compound" errors are reduced and that control over the project may be more rigidly enforced.

It is for these reasons that a sample may give a more accurate measurement than a census when investigating the same population.

The destructive nature of measurement

Our chef from the introduction to this chapter could not conduct a "census" of the contents of his saucepan of boeuf bourguignon—if he did, what would his guests eat? The whisky distiller could not take a census of his products to see if they were up to standard—a pleasant thought though that may be to some. If he did, he would have no product to sell, and the police might then be interested in obtaining a sample from him!

In many cases, taking a census destroys, which means that a sample is the only alternative way of obtaining the required data. For example, if one wanted to measure a population's attitude to something then by conducting a census, all of the population would be alerted to that "something" which might alter their attitude by having their attention brought to it. That population would have been altered by the act of measurement; their "innocence" of that "something" would have been destroyed for ever and they would be different as a result. Therefore, they could not be asked a question on that topic again without taking into account the fact that measurement (and an alteration) had already taken place. This incidentally, in some specific cases, is a recommendation for sampling; by using only a sample of the population for measurement, only part of the population's "innocence" would be destroyed. If it was necessary to have to return to that population, a different sample could be drawn, none of whom had been surveyed before and who would, therefore, still be in a "state of grace".

Measurement may not always be destructive. One can test-drive motor cars prior to making a purchase decision without destroying the cars, and in such cases, questions of cost, time and accuracy apart, a census which does not destroy is theoretically possible.

But for fireworks—stick to sampling!

Terminology

In the foregoing, several words have been used which are in common, everyday use. However, in sampling, these words have specialized, technical meanings which are slightly different from the way they are used in normal conversation. To remove any confusion and ambiguity, let us have a short story to show how these technical words should be used correctly in the context of marketing research.

Once upon a time in the South Pacific, there were two islands, Rogers and Hammerstein.

On Rogers, the King decrees that there will be a census of all the 100,000 population. Hammerstein, naturally, feels obliged to do something similar, but due to the fact that they are heavily in debt to the World Bank, they can only afford a fraction of the expense that their neighbours are prepared to spend. Therefore, Hammerstein's King orders that only 10,000 of his population will be questioned. This is only 10% of the population and is called a sample.

The King of Rogers is very musical, but to his horror the census discovers that only 30% of his population know the words to "There is nothing like a dame". This figure of 30% is called a parameter and only applies to the characteristics of a population.

The King of Hammerstein finds that only 6% of his sample know the words to "There is nothing like a dame"—not such a musical nation. In such a situation, 6% is called a statistic and it may only be used to describe the characteristics of a sample.

The King of Hammerstein is now in a position to be able to make two statements based on the results of his sample.

(1) "Only 6% of my sample can remember the lyrics to my favourite song." This is a descriptive statement; it is only describing what has been discovered—nothing more.

or, he could say

(2) "Only 6% of the nation can remember the words to my favourite song." This is an inferential statement. It is inferential because the King is generalising that the characteristic of interest (the ability to remember the lyrics of a song) held by the sample is also held, to the same degree, by the island's population.

Having laid down some of the basic concepts of sampling, let us now consider in detail the way in which it is organised within the overall context of a marketing research project.

The process of sampling

The various stages in the process of sampling may be listed thus:

(1) Define the population.

(2) Define a frame for that population.

(3) Select a sampling unit.

(4) Choose a method of selecting that sample.

    (a) Probability

    (b) Non-probability

(5) Decide on the size of the sample.

(6) Define the sampling plan.

(7) Select the sample.

(1) Define the population

The objectives of the research should have detailed those sources from which the research project is going to have to collect data. Consequently, the attributes of the population in which the project has an interest must be described in terms which are unambiguous and clear to all those involved in the research project.

To remove any lack of clarity it is usual to define a population using the following terms:

Element. That body concerning which we require information and which will provide a basic unit for analysis. In marketing research, the element may be, for example, a person, a family or a factory.

Unit. The way in which access may be gained to the element. In some cases, for example, when we define the element as an 18-year-old student, the element and unit are the same as we can access the unit directly; this is called single-stage sampling. However, if we define the element as an 18-year-old student who lives in a Hall of Residence, then this would be a two-stage sampling process, as the element is the student and the Hall of Residence is the unit.

Extent. The geographical boundaries inside which the research is to be conducted.

Time. The temporal boundaries inside which the research is to be conducted.

Population definition is far from easy. One must ensure that within the definition that is chosen, all the people, the factors and variables which have a role to play in the situation under investigation are included. Too "tight" a definition of the population might exclude a number of key factors etc., which should be included; this will result in bias. Too "loose" a definition might include factors, variables and people who do not have a direct influence on the researched situation; this too will result in the introduction of unwanted error.

As situations become increasingly complex, with more and more factors, variables and people becoming involved in the subject of the study, the greater becomes the difficulty in being able, accurately, to define the population. Here is an excellent example where exploratory research can be of assistance; it can help define the boundaries of the population and the important factors that are at work within those boundaries and which consequently have to be included in the definition of the population.

(2) Define a frame for the population

A sampling frame is a way of establishing the boundaries of the population which will contain all the elements and units necessary to fulfil the objectives of the research. Sampling frames are not required for non-probability sampling techniques, but for probability-based techniques they are essential, as these latter methods are based on the fact that each element must have a known chance of selection. If elements are excluded, or if they are included more than once, then an element would have, respectively, no chance of selection or twice (or more) the chance of being selected. Such inaccuracies are termed frame error.

Thus a sampling frame should have the following characteristics:

(a) Each element should be included only once.

(b) No element should be excluded.

(c) The frame should cover the whole of the population.

(d) The information which is used to construct the frame should be up to date and accurate, i.e. only those elements which truly meet the research's objectives should be included.

(e) The frame should be convenient to use.

From this rather stringent list of conditions, it can easily be seen that the search for a perfect sampling frame could rapidly turn into another of the modern equivalents of the medieval pursuit of the unicorn!

It is theoretically possible for the population to be defined, to be followed by a search for the appropriate sampling frame. In practice, however, it is usually the case that because of the operational difficulties in finding a perfect, or even an adequate, sampling frame, sampling frames are allowed to define the population.

Telephone directories are often used as sampling frames, so let them stand as an example of some of the difficulties which may be encountered.

(a) Some subscribers may be ex-directory.

(b) Some subscribers may be included more than once.

(c) Some subscribers may have moved house and changed their number(s).

(d) Some numbers may be included from outside the geographical area which the directory is supposed, exclusively, to be covering.

(3) Select a sampling unit

The sampling unit is the entity which holds the element(s) of the target population which are to be sampled.

In some cases the unit and the element may be the same. For example, if we want to sample students from a university's first year intake, then we might be able to contact them directly; sample unit and element are identical in this case.

However, it might not be possible to contact them directly, in which case it might be easier or preferable to contact them where they live and to interview them there; here, sample unit and sample element are not the same. The unit is their home/hall of residence but the element remains the same; it is still the first year university student.

The way in which the sampling unit is selected depends upon various factors including the sampling frame and project design.

(a) Sampling frame
If a complete, accurate and reliable list of elements is easily obtained, then that would suggest that the research should be able to sample them directly; i.e. sample unit and element are identical. If such a list is not available, then one may have to use the place of work or residence as the basic sampling unit. For example, if one wanted to question all the head chefs currently working in France, it is most unlikely that there will be a list of such personnel. But it is very likely that there will be lists of the hotels and restaurants where they work. In this case the unit (the hotel etc.) is not the same as the element (the chef).

(b) Project design
Telephone interviewing requires that the sampling unit contains a telephone number. Mail questionnaires require that the sampling unit contains an address, where access to the element may be gained.

(4) Choice of a sampling method

Sampling is the process by which a certain number of units are selected from the population. Broadly speaking, there are two main types of sampling: probability and non-probability techniques.

Probability sampling techniques:

(a) Simple random

(b) Stratified random

(c) Cluster

(d) Multi-stage

Non-probability sampling techniques:

(a) Convenience

(b) Purposive

(c) Quota

(d) Judgement

Probability sampling techniques

The units which constitute a probability sample are selected by chance, with each unit having a known chance of selection (Tull and Hawkins, 1990).

The sample that is drawn is, hopefully, representative of the entire population in which we have an interest. However, it can never be an exact replica of that population. Probability sampling, by applying the rules of probability allows a generalisation to be made about a population and gives a method by which to calculate the degree of confidence which we can impart to the results of the sample. An added advantage of probability sampling is that as each unit in the sample has a known chance of selection there can be no bias resulting from the way in which the sampling process was carried out; any bias which does occur will have its source in frame error and/or non-sampling error. Sample error, in the case of a probability sample, arises from the variability of the population and/or the size of the sample.

(d) Simple random sampling
This is the most basic of the probability techniques.

Premium Bonds in the United Kingdom (a type of lottery) are drawn by simple random sampling. When a bond is bought, its number is programmed into a computer. Each month the machine selects, by the generation of random numbers, a predetermined quantity of bonds which are then assigned monetary values as prizes. Each number in the computer is included only once; otherwise some bond holders would stand an unfairly increased chance of winning. Each bond thus has an equal and a known chance of selection.

Other methods of simple random sampling include the use of random number tables. These are tables constructed by computer which, at random, selects numbers between zero and nine. Since each number is selected randomly, the numbers that are selected can have no influence on any succeeding number selection.

In marketing research, random number tables may be used, as an example, in the following manner.

A bank wishes to sample 10,000 of its credit card holders. Each credit card holder can be identified by the nine figure number on the card. The researcher could thus turn, at random, to any page in a book of random numbers and start counting off blocks of nine digits, each block of numbers could correspond to a credit card (some combinations, of course, will generate numbers which are not the equivalent of a credit card—these can be discarded) and the holder can be identified easily. The sample would have been selected randomly and each of those customers selected would have a known and equal chance of selection.

There is also systematic random sampling. Supposing that a project required that a sample of 100 units was required from a population of 8000. The population would be divided by the required sample size, e.g.

$$\frac{8000}{100} = 80$$

80 is called the sampling interval (and 1/80 is called the sampling fraction). A number between 1 and 80 is selected at random to commence the process. From that number onwards, every 80th unit would be sampled.

If the randomly chosen number was, say, 26, then the first sampling units would be 106 and the next 186, 266 and so on.

Advantages. It may be carried out with relative simplicity and as the selection process is being carried out in a random manner, obeying the laws of probability, estimates may be made of the sample error which will enable inferences to be made about the population within known intervals of confidence.

Disadvantages. The major disadvantage of simple random sampling is that it may produce samples which are highly unrepresentative and thus do not reflect the characteristics that are held by the population.

Suppose a sample of 500 medically qualified personnel is drawn, using simple random sampling, from the lists of the General Medical Council. It is possible (but unlikely) that all 500 of the sample are ophthalmologists; inferring from this sample would suggest that all those on the GMC are ophthalmologists. This is known not to be the case and can be verified merely by scanning the full list. A further example: suppose a sample of a population is taken and the variable that is being measured is highly variable; it could be annual income, the number of compact discs that individuals own or the size of a firm's workforce. Certainly, using random sampling the size of the standard error can be calculated. The larger the dispersion of the sample, the larger will be the standard error. Distribution curves for samples which have wide dispersions (and, consequently, large standard errors) will tend to be short and flat—the "beret" shape.

For such a flattened curve, + or − one standard error covers a very wide range of values; this means that even though the standard error can be calculated, it is of very limited use because its size is so large.

Simple random sampling cannot make any attempt to counteract the population's variability and such a situation can introduce a high degree of sample error to the sampling process. For a more detailed discussion of the use of statistics in marketing research, please see Appendix One.

The sample variability can, to some extent, be reduced by the use of stratified random sampling.

(b) Stratified random sampling

Stratified random sampling accepts that a population has a high degree of variability and tries to ensure that the different segments of the population are represented in the sample in the same proportions as they occur in that population. If they are adequately represented in the sample, then the sample error will be reduced (the distribution curve will be of the "dunce's cap" variety) and generalisations about the population can be made, based on the sample, with a high degree of confidence. The basis of stratified random sampling is the concept of stratification.

In stratification, the population is divided into mutually exclusive strata—sampling units can only appear once, otherwise they would not have an equal chance of selection. One must also ensure that all sample units are included in a strata; if any unit is omitted then it will not have a known chance of selection. In effect, stratified random sampling adopts the position that each stratum is a population in its own right; random sampling then takes place within each stratum. And as long as each sampling unit is selected by chance, then the laws of probability are being followed.

Stratifiers may be geographical, demographic, or any other variable that is appropriate to the research in hand. The aim of stratification is to try to get sample units inside each stratum which are alike as possible while, simultaneously, attempting to keep each stratum as different from each other with respect to the stratifier. Having a great number of strata does ensure that there is a high degree of similarity amongst the sample units inside a stratum, but it usually means that the differences between strata are reduced.

Proportionate and disproportionate stratified random sampling. Having divided the population into various strata, a decision has to be made about the type of sampling process that is going to be followed.

Proportionate sampling is where the proportion of a characteristic possessed by the population is reflected by the sample having the same proportion. For example, if 19.7% of a population are members of sports clubs then 19.7% of the sample should also be members of sports clubs.

Disproportionate sampling occurs when the proportion of a characteristic as possessed by the population is *not* reflected to the same extent in the proportion of the sample.

If one is conducting research into the purchase, for example, of thermal underwear, it may be thought a reasonable assumption that as a greater quantity of such items are bought by the 65 + year-old stratum than any other age stratum, then more of them should be sampled. If proportionate sampling had been used, then the number of units in the 65 + age group would be too small a basis on which to generalise about the entire population. Disproportionate sampling may also be used if there is great variability within a stratum; it is therefore useful to over-represent that stratum in the sample. A high degree of intra-stratum variability makes for problems when it comes to ensuring representativeness, a problem which would be greater if proportionate random sampling had been used.

You will have noticed that this deliberate enlargement or diminution in the size of certain strata does not obey the laws of probability in that it is now no longer the case that all sample units have an equal chance of selection. This is true, but the chance of selection is still known; thus probability laws are still in operation and when calculating results, appropriate weightings can be applied which will correct the "distortions" that have been imposed on the process of selection.

Stratified random sampling has the advantage, as do all forms of probability sampling, that it enables estimates to be made of sample error. To this may be added a further plus-point: because stratified random sampling has the ability to reduce the effects of large sample variability, the size of the potential sampling error may be reduced.

The major disadvantage of this technique is that the ability to divide up the sample into meaningful strata depends on finding stratifiers that are relevant to the research project. As the process of stratification can only be carried out using variables for which the distribution is known in the population, the technique may not be as flexible as it first appears, in that the most commonly available figures for the distribution of characteristics in the population may only be demographic and these may not be relevant to the research study. Stratification may also make the sampling process more costly as (a) the process requires a separate sampling frame for each stratum and (b) the process may select sampling units which are geographically widely dispersed. One method to circumvent this, latter, disadvantage, is cluster sampling.

(c) Cluster sampling

In this process, the population is again divided into sub-groups, though they are called clusters rather than strata. Each cluster should contain sampling units which are as alike as possible with respect to certain characteristics, with clusters, simultaneously, being as different from each other; they should be "mutually exclusive" (i.e. they do not overlap) and "collectively exhaustive" (i.e. all units are included) (Weiers, 1988).

Next, a random selection of *clusters* is made. The final stage involves taking, from the selected clusters, a random sample of units or a census—though it is usually the former.

In area cluster sampling, geographical location is the variable used as the stratifier to divide the population into clusters. Thus the United Kingdom might be divided into various regions: Strathclyde, West Midlands, Greater Manchester etc. A number of these areas (clusters) are then selected at random. Suppose that the three regions chosen at random are Grampian, Lothian and East Anglia. The next step, is to select a sample from inside each of these three clusters or to conduct a census inside each of these selected clusters. The laws of probability are being followed—all elements have a known and equal chance of selection, which means that an estimate of sample error can be made. It can also be seen that the sampling units are quite narrowly dispersed—an advantage in that it will help cut costs, travelling expenses being much reduced.

The main disadvantage with cluster sampling is that problems may occur if the clusters are too "tightly" defined; i.e. if only very small geographical areas are sampled, there may be a reduction in the sampling process's statistical efficiency. For example, in one small geographical area, there may be a tendency for it to house a population with similar incomes, types of accommodation, social classifications and levels of education. And as each cluster is supposed to contain a more or less homogeneous set of units, it is counter-productive to use a larger sample to obtain a more representative result. Though statistical efficiency suffers in cluster sampling, the economic efficiency is much improved.

(d) Multi-stage sampling

If a population is widely dispersed with respect to some characteristic, especially geographical location, it is often appropriate to use a multi-stage sampling technique. And if it is required to make some estimation of the sampling error, then the laws of probability must be applied.

The cluster sampling technique described above is a single-stage process; multi-stage sampling is a form of cluster sampling, but more than one stage is involved.

If the clusters to be sampled are of greatly varying size, then it is appropriate that the sampling process be carried out under a system called probability proportionate to size (PPS). Thus a cluster, which can be a county, a region, a city or town, which is twice as large as all the others in the population will have twice the chance of selection.

Let us look at an example to make the process clearer.

We wish to take a sample of 100 dentists in the United Kingdom.

First, the country is divided up into regions as before and a number of them are chosen at random with a probability proportionate to the population of their dentists. Thus Greater London with X times the population of the Hebrides will have X times the chance of selection. Five regions are chosen by this method.

Second, inside each of these five regions, four cities are selected at random with a probability proportionate to their size. Thus Glasgow with a population of 500 dentists has five times the chance of selection of Ipswich which has only 100 dentists. Thus, in total, at this second stage, 20 cities have been chosen.

Third, from each city five dentists are chosen at random.

We have selected our 100 dentists as required and they have been chosen by a probability technique, but they are only dispersed through 20 cities, as opposed to being spread all over the country as might have happened if they had been chosen by simple random sampling.

It is important to note that stratified sampling and multi-stage sampling are quite different. In stratified sampling the population is divided into sub-groups (strata) *all* of which are sampled. Multi-stage sampling also divides the population into sub-groups (clusters) but only a *few* of them are sampled. Stratified random sampling is usually carried out for the purpose of reducing sample variability and hence sample error. The use of multi-stage sampling tends to be motivated by reasons of cost and labour saving.

Multi-stage sampling's disadvantages are similar to those of cluster sampling in that the system may become very cumbersome and sample error may be increased by the selection of clusters where the sampling units have great homogeneity, i.e. by the choice of small areas of a city.

A great advantage of both cluster and multi-stage sampling techniques is that it may enable a probability sampling technique to be used on a population for which, at the macro-level, there is no adequate sampling frame. It is difficult to discover a sampling frame that would adequately cover an entire country. By using cluster or multi-stage sampling techniques, which reduces the geographical areas to be sampled, the chances of finding a usable sampling frame at the micro-level are increased: city maps and electoral rolls being commonly available.

Non-probability sampling techniques

Probability sampling techniques use the laws of probability; as each sampling unit has a known chance of selection, estimates may be made of the size of the sampling error. With non-probability sampling, the chances of selection are not known; therefore the ability to generalise about a population, based on the results of a sample, are much reduced. Non-probability sampling does not require the use of a sampling frame; thus the project's costs may be reduced.

The sample is chosen at the convenience of the research consultant or to fulfil the demands of some predetermined purpose. If the sampling is carried out badly, however, Aaker and Day (1990) say that the results of non-probability sampling may contain "biases and uncertainties that make them worse than no information at all".

(a) Convenience sampling

The most important factor that is considered in this style of sampling is that the operation should be convenient to those carrying out the research. A university lecturer might like to gauge student reaction to his latest "block buster" text on marketing research, so he asks his Master's level degree students. Such a sample might contain unknown and unknowable amounts of error and/or bias. The lecturer might have no idea as to the representativeness of this class versus the national population of students. And because the laws of probability were not followed, no estimation may be made of the size of the sample error. Convenience sampling can be carried out quickly and with minimal cost. As such, it is normally used only in the exploratory stages of a research project; it can be helpful in providing a "feel" for the subject to be investigated.

(b) Judgement sampling

In judgement sampling an attempt is made to ensure that the sample is more representative than it was in the previous example of convenience sampling. Consultants use their experience, or they make use of the services of experts in appropriate fields to make an assessment and then a choice of the sampling units on the basis of their relevance to the research project. If one were having to conduct a survey in, for example, the chemical industry, then expert advice could be taken or one's own judgement exercised, as to those individual companies which should be included in the sample.

If the population is small and the knowledge, expertise and judgement of those making the selection of the sampling units is good, judgement sampling can result in a sample which has less variable error than would a sample chosen by simple random sampling, although this can never be proved conclusively. However, as samples get larger and/or the population is of some complexity, judgement sampling becomes less reliable compared with those techniques which have the advantage of being based on the laws of probability.

(c) Purposive sampling

Sampling units under this system are not chosen with the main aim that they should be representative of the population; the basis of this sampling technique is that the sample members should meet certain conditions which are thought appropriate to the successful completion of the investigation.

For example, a project might have as its objective the launch of a new type of running shoe. Therefore, a purposive sample of the top 250 runners in the country might be selected and their reactions to the new type of shoe measured.

(d) Quota sampling

None of the three methods of non-probability sampling methods that have been outlined so far make any attempt to be representative of the population. Indeed, purposive sampling seems, almost, to relish the rejection of such a criterion.

In quota sampling there is an attempt to mirror in the sample the characteristics of interest in the same proportion as they occur in the population. If, for example, it is decided to extract a quota sample from the population to test a new Sunday newspaper, then such variables as age, sex, social class and income levels might be used to segment the population such that each age group, sex, social class and income level were represented in the same proportions in the sample as they are in the population.

Quota controls should be easy to use, available and current, and should not result in too many "cells". Perhaps most importantly, they should be relevant to the characteristics that are the subject of the study. It is of limited use, for example, to the objectives of the research to use quota controls for age, income and ethnic origin just because they are freely available, if the characteristics in question are not related to any of the above controls.

Quota sampling has the advantage of being cheaper than probability sampling techniques, quick to carry out and relatively easy to administer. It may also proceed without the need for a sampling frame.

The disadvantages arise from interviewer bias in the selection of sampling units to fill each quota "cell". A further disadvantage comes from the potential mis-match between the controls that are picked to set up the quotas and the characteristics which are being measured; it is also often difficult to discover, and to make work, quota controls which can accommodate the high degree of variability which may exist in a population. And, as with all the other non-probability sampling techniques, the method does not allow an estimation to be made as to the size of the sample error.

It is important not to confuse quota sampling with stratified sampling. The major difference between them is that in the former the interviewer/researcher selects the sample element, in the latter the selection process is carried out by random selection.

Probability or non-probability sampling?

Both types of sampling technique have advantages and disadvantages; each method may be more appropriate than the others given the existence of certain conditions.

Tull and Hawkins (1990) provide the following list of factors to be borne in mind when making the choice.

(a) Type of information needed: are proportions and/or averages required, or are projectable totals needed?

(b) Size of error-tolerance the problem will admit: are highly accurate estimates of population values required?

(c) How large might non-sampling error be? What size of error due to frame choice, non-response, measurement and population specifications is likely?

(d) Population variability: will the population be homogeneous or heterogeneous in relation to the characteristics of interest?

(e) What are the likely costs of error? What will be the costs if the results obtained are above/below the error tolerance?

Tull and Hawkins say that "...the need for projectable totals, low allowable errors, high population heterogeneity, small non-sampling errors and high expected costs of error favour the use of probability sampling".

(5) Decide on the size of the sample

An important question that the researcher must answer is: how large a sample should be taken from the population?

Sample size primarily depends upon the degree of accuracy that is needed, i.e. how representative is the sample of the population with respect to the characteristic/variables of interest.

The accuracy will depend upon two characteristics of that population for which the sample is to stand proxy:

(a) Degree of variability in the population: populations which have high degrees of heterogeneity require larger samples than those populations which are more homogeneous.

(b) The presence of population sub-groups: the sample must be large enough to allow a valid analysis of any sub-groups that may be present in the population.

As with much else in marketing research, the choice of the size of the sample is a matter of compromise. Obviously, all constraints aside, researchers would prefer to conduct a census (given an absence of non-sampling error) rather than have to take a sample, but constraints are usually all too present. Sample size estimation attempts to gain the maximum benefit with the minimum of disadvantage.

Luck and Rubin (1987) claim that the determination of sample size is as much of an art as questionnaire design development. In deciding on the trade-off between, for example, increasing sample size to reduce sample error and increasing the cost, or reducing the budget with the consequent potential problem of increasing the size of the sampling error, both qualitative and quantitative factors must be considered.

Five of the most commonly used methods of sample size estimation will now be presented.

(i) Judgement

This method relies on the judgement/experience of the research consultant. "Judgement" may also imply that the sample size is decided in a quite arbitrary manner which ignores many of the factors such as cost, value and required level of accuracy, which should be considered.

This is a method to be used when all other avenues have been tried.

(ii) What can be afforded?

Not only must the cost of the sampling be considered, but also the costs associated with the rest of the project: data analysis, the salaries of the field workers, telephones etc.

What is missing from this way of estimating the size of the sample is a consideration of the value of the information to be collected. Cost in itself is a poor guide in deciding the sample size. For example, a small sample may be much more useful, though of a higher cost per unit, than a large sample, if the information so gathered is of high value.

(iii) What did other projects do?

It is possible to use a sample size similar to that used by other researchers looking at the same or a closely related topic. This assumes, of course, that the other projects used samples of optimal sizes and that they too were faced with broadly similar constraints.

Other research project's samples sizes may be useful as a guide, but should not be the sole basis on which to decide one's own sample size.

(iv) Required size per cell

This method can be used for both quota sampling and stratified random sampling.

It is usual to have to accept a minimum of 30 units per "cell" in stratified random sampling before any statistical analysis can be carried out.

Thus, if a sample is to be made up on 3 age groups, 2 income brackets and 3 geographical areas, the number of cells will be $3 \times 2 \times 3 = 18$.

Eighteen cells with a minimum of 30 sample units per cell gives a minimum sample size of 540 respondents.

This figure of 30 units per cell is usually adhered to in quota sampling, even though there is to be no statistical analysis.

(v) Statistical methods

The accuracy of a sample, i.e. the degree to which it is a truthful representation of the population for some chosen characteristic, is not related to the size of that population but to the size of the sample and the variability of the population from which the sample is to be selected.

Statistics can be used to calculate the confidence level or the degree of confidence which can be associated with the results of a sample.

It is known that:

> 68% of sample values will lie within the range + or − one standard error of the mean.

> 95% of sample values will lie within the range + or − two standard errors of the mean.

> 98% of sample values will lie within the range + or − three standard errors of the mean.

Before an estimation can be made of the size of the sample, it is necessary for those involved with the research to ask three questions:

(a) How accurate do we need the estimate to be?

(b) How confident do we need to be?

(c) How dispersed is the population, i.e. what is its standard deviation?

The formula that links these three questions is:

$$\text{Level of confidence} = \frac{\text{required level of accuracy}}{\text{standard error}}$$

(formula 1)

This may be rearranged as follows:

$$\text{Standard error} = \frac{\text{required level of accuracy}}{\text{level of confidence}}$$

(formula 2)

Standard error is given by the formula:

$$\text{Standard error} = \frac{\sigma}{\sqrt{N}}$$

where σ = standard deviation and N = size of sample.

Thus formula 2 becomes

$$\frac{\sigma}{\sqrt{N}} = \frac{\text{required level of accuracy}}{\text{level of confidence}}$$

The first two of the questions to be answered, level of accuracy and level of confidence, will be answered by the use of experience, judgement and the needs of the research. The third question, that concerning the standard deviation of the population, can be answered either by consulting secondary data, e.g. government statistics etc., or, if there is no secondary data, by mounting a small exploratory survey to sample the population, from which the standard deviation may be calculated. From this "mini-survey" the actual sample size can be determined.

Here is a worked example to show how the theory works in practice.

Suppose it is wished to find out the size of the sample necessary to estimate the mean height of university students to within + or − 4 cm at a confidence level of 95%.

We consult government statistics and discover that the standard deviation for such a population's height is 20 cm.

Using the formula:

$$\frac{\sigma}{\sqrt{N}} = \frac{\text{required level of accuracy}}{\text{level of confidence}}$$

Putting in the figures:

$$\frac{20}{\sqrt{N}} = \frac{4}{2}$$

$$\sqrt{N} = \frac{20 \times 2}{4}$$

$$\sqrt{N} = 10$$

$$N = 100$$

We would require a sample of 100 students.

There are many other statistical techniques which can be used, using such concepts as the significance of the results and the correlation between variables, events or other sets of data.

It is not the intention that this text should proceed any further down those particular statistical paths. Interested students will be able to pursue their interests in this subject in greater depth in volumes more specifically devoted to the subject.

(6) Define the sampling plan

This step involves making operational all those decisions that have been taken to date. Two prime objectives should be considered while this process is in train:

(1) That the maximum amount of relevant information is gathered from those who meet the specifications of the sample.

(2) That an attempt be made to reduce all possible errors to a minimum.

The main methods of collecting primary data are observation, personal interview, mail survey and telephone interview. Now while it may be possible to have left the decision about the type of data gathering method to be used until this point, in practice the decision will already have been taken. Without some preliminary policy concerning data gathering in general, it would not have been easy to proceed as far as this point; that type of decision may have had to be made or will have been made at the start of the project. Data necessary to fulfil the specific demands of the research objectives may only be able to be collected in certain ways.

But having arrived at a broad decision regarding data gathering, the sampling plan must now turn the intention to act into action itself.

The sampling plan may need to decide such questions as:

(1) What is a household?

(2) How is the head of a household to be defined?

(3) What do we do if a questionnaire is returned because the addressee has moved?

(4) What do we do if a telephone interviewee slams down the phone having answered only 50% of the questionnaire?

The sampling plan will need to decide the policy for the way in which the sampling process is to be administered.

(7) Select the sample

The moment of truth! The sample is selected: the "phoney war" is over.

Case study: the use of survey measurement and sampling in an industrial context

XYZ Plastics Ltd (a disguised company) has a turnover of approximately £15 million per annum, and specialises in the manufacture of plastic pipes and fittings for use in the motor car/commercial vehicle industry. Its product range covers pipes for hot and cold liquid/gases, for ventilation and for electrical conduits.

The company, recently, has been suffering from a reduced level of business activity. In the main this is due to a combination of:

(a) a general economic down-turn which has had a severe effect upon the volume car/vehicle market,

(b) the development of the home car repair business which is reducing the volume of trade in XYZ's traditional markets, i.e. repairs conducted in garages,

(c) improved selling efforts by XYZ's traditional competitors,

(d) the entry of low-priced competitive goods into the market.

Internally, the company decided that a market research study was necessary, and that its overall objectives should be to indicate the company's strengths and weaknesses vis-à-vis its competitors, so as to provide data on which to base a new marketing strategy. In consultation with their appointed marketing research agency, the research proposal that was mutually agreed upon decided to investigate the following areas of interest:

(1) the image of the company in the market,

(2) their competitive position against:
   (a) established competitors,
   (b) new, low-priced products,

(3) the perceived range and quality of their products,

(4) their customers' degree of company and brand loyalty,

(5) the strengths and weaknesses of the company's marketing mix,

(6) the trends active in their preferred mode of distribution.

The company agreed with the research agency that a sample of approximately 300 respondents would be chosen on a basis of proportionate random sampling, using size of purchasing company as the stratifier. There was also to be a further sample of 50 respondents, chosen again by proportionate random sampling of the personnel, in the end-user markets, who carry out the function of product specification; size of company was here, too, used as the stratifier.

Even though there was a wide geographical spread of the respondents, the type of information that it was necessary to collect dictated that personal interviews, based on semi-structured questionnaires, be used. Though some of the information to be collected was of a factual nature, the majority of it comprised opinion and attitude measurement. This fact, together with the opportunity to discuss on an in-depth basis and to probe respondents' answers, convinced the research agency that the value of the data would far exceed the high costs necessary to collect that data.

Summary

Except in rare cases, where populations are small for example, it is usual in marketing research to draw a sample from a population rather than to conduct a census.

The chapter has discussed the process of sampling and the way in which sampling fits in with the other components of the research project.

Probability and non-probability sampling techniques have been displayed, together with a short explanation of some basic statistical methods. The chapter concludes with a discussion of ways in which sample sizes may be determined.

The decision as to the type of sampling technique to be utilised and the size of the sample is conditioned, to a very large extent, by the need to keep the size of the sample error as small as possible. Probability versus non-probability techniques, large samples versus small samples—such choices will involve a certain amount of compromise. Compromises are never easy to make and, if in doubt as to the choice between competing alternatives, researchers should be guided by the notion that the best (or least worst) option is the one that renders the most reliable and valid representation of the population of interest.

References

Aaker D. A. and Day G. S. (1990) *Marketing Research*, John Wiley and Sons, New York.

Luck D. J. and Rubin D. S. (1987) *Marketing Research*, Prentice-Hall, Englewood Cliffs, New Jersey, 7th edition.

Tull D. S. and Hawkins D. I. (1990) *Marketing Research: Measurement and Method*, Macmillan, New York, 5th edition.

Weiers R. M. (1988) *Market Research*, Prentice-Hall, Englewood Cliffs, New Jersey, 2nd edition.

CHAPTER FIVE

Survey and Panel/Syndicated Research

Introduction	68
Methods and applications in survey research	69
Error in survey research	71
Methods of data collection in survey research	74
Non-response in survey research	81
Summary: survey methods	83
Panel/syndicated marketing research	84
Omnibus surveys	89
Summary: panel/syndicated marketing research	89
References	90

Introduction

If it is decided that individuals are likely to hold information necessary to answer questions posed by the research objective, then there are two basic methods of obtaining that data: we can ask the individuals appropriate questions or their behaviour may be observed. The latter type of research will be discussed in Chapter Seven; the former, which is usually called survey research, is the topic of this chapter.

Questioning respondents is a widely used research method and, to many, it is seen as the only type of marketing research. Respondents, who may be children, industrial buyers, heads of households or consumers of chocolate eggs, are asked questions through face-to-face confrontations or via the telephone or the postal system—mail questionnaires.

However, although survey research is a quick, efficient and cost-effective way of gaining the required data, it is not a straightforward method. Without skill, tact and expertise the results may easily become contaminated with bias and error. Questions of bias will be discussed, as will the errors that arise from non-response.

The final section of this chapter will discuss panel/syndicated research.

Methods and applications in survey research

In the interactive style of survey (personal interview, mail and telephone questionnaire), as opposed to the observational style, there is a requirement for an active response, either written or verbal, by the respondent to the questioner/questionnaire.

The three main types of communication process between questioner and respondent are:

(1) face to face interview,

(2) telephone interview,

(3) completion of mail questionnaire.

Whichever method is chosen, the decision will rarely be reached in a clear-cut manner. The majority of marketing research situations are not seen in terms of well focused black and white images—usually middling shades of grey are the best that can be hoped for. Each survey method has its advantages and disadvantages, and the skill of the researcher is utilised in optimising the chosen survey method with the multiple and maybe ambiguous demands of the research situation. Aaker and Day (1990) say that while each situation is unique the following list, broadly speaking, represents the major factors which have to be considered when making a choice of survey method:

(a) available budget,

(b) nature of the problem and the complexity of the data requirements,

(c) need for accuracy,

(d) constraints of time.

The advantages and disadvantages of each survey method will be discussed in detail later in the chapter.

It is not wished to convey the impression that the researcher is limited only to a single choice of survey method; many research projects could not be carried out if this were the case. In some situations, because of the factors in play, it is necessary to use a mixture of methods; this allows the disadvantages of one method to be ameliorated by the advantages of another method. Again, one must remember that the "rules" of marketing research are there merely for guidance; they may be bent or even broken, but make sure that it is for a good reason. Flexibility of approach, conditioned by the situation-specifics, is likely to improve the reliability and the validity of the results by reducing the ingress of errors and bias.

What types of data are particularly suited to gathering by survey methods?

As Kinnear and Taylor (1991) point out, much of marketing research is concerned with gathering data today, so that future objectives may be reached.

The types of data which are most useful in forecasting the future behaviour of markets may be grouped under four main headings: behaviour (past and present), attitudes and opinions, respondent variables and knowledge.

(1) Behaviour, past and present

Common sense tells us that the evidence of historical actions will be a useful guide as to possible future behaviour. In mathematics, a commonly used technique is that of extrapolation, whereby a ruler is placed along the known points of a graph to give an indication as to where the future points are likely to lie. In marketing research, the equivalent of the points of the graph are the answers to such questions as: what products were bought? how often? bought by whom? for whom? where were they purchased? in what quantities? Such questions have been found to be useful predictors of possible future actions. But it is important that pertinent variables are used when seeking data which is to be used in forecasting. It is of little use measuring the past behaviour concerned with educational achievements, for example, in order to predict the type of motor car a person may purchase. That is, it will be futile if there is no proven link between educational levels and motor car preference.

(2) Attitudes and opinions

Topics such as opinion and especially attitude loom large in marketing research. Attitudes are often used as a way of segmenting a market; they are also an important factor when seeking to evaluate and assess the effectiveness of an advertisement or an advertising campaign. This importance arises because of the assumed links between attitudes and behaviour. Those concerned with marketing research are thus often called upon to measure attitudes and changes in attitudes.

Attitudes and their measurement are important—so important that they will take up a substantial portion of Chapters Eight and Nine.

(3) Respondent variables

Respondents may be classified against a variety of variables; such variables include the demographic (age, sex etc.) socio-economic (income, class etc.), psychological and, those concerned with life-style—a psychographic variable. The classifications of such variables can be used to stratify samples and as predictors of possible future actions.

(4) Knowledge

Surveys may be used to determine whether or not respondents have knowledge/experience of some fact/situation; the extent of that knowledge/experience may then be measured.

Error in survey research

One of Lady Bracknell's memorable lines in "The Importance of Being Earnest" is that the truth is rarely pure and never simple. There you have the problems, in a nutshell, of working with people. And, above all, working with people is what is being done when conducting survey research. Nothing, it would appear, could be more simple than to ask a question and to receive and note a reply: WRONG!

Errors, if care is not taken, will spring up like weeds in the middle of a lawn, without the gardener (marketing researcher) being able to predict their size and location.

It is a very rare situation for a survey research project to be free from error.

Any marketing research study must accept that part of the function of the research design is to minimise error. The three main types of error that can appear in survey research are sampling error, response error and non-response error; the latter two examples are sometimes called non-sampling error.

Diagrammatically they may be represented thus:

Total error = sampling error + non-sampling error
                          ↑   ↑
                     Response   Non-response
                     error   error

Each of them will now be discussed.

Sampling error

Sampling error arises when the probability sample that is drawn from a population is not representative of that population. If a sample of 100 people is drawn from the population of Berlin and all of that sample is composed of female drivers then that sample is obviously not representative of the population of the city.

That is an exaggerated case; in more real-life situations, the non-representative nature of the sample is not nearly so blatant, which is what makes sampling error such a dangerous factor. Sampling error size depends upon the variability of the population and the size of the sample. The more homogeneous a population, the smaller is the chance of sampling error; i.e., the less variable the population is, the more likely it is that a sample will include a majority of those that are average. If the population was 100% homogeneous, then a sample of 1 would suffice. Also, the larger the sample, the less likely is the chance of error, i.e., the larger the sample, the more probable it is that the sample will include a wider range of the population's variability. This is obvious if it is remembered that with a census of the population (the largest "sample" that can be drawn from one population) there can be no sampling error.

Response error

Response error can occur even with a census and is due to the "contamination" of the process of communication between interviewer and respondent. Some of this contamination may arise because of a respondent's refusal to respond; for those that do agree to take part in the survey, distortions in the communication process may arise because they are unable to respond or because they are unwilling to respond to some or part of the survey instrument.

Inability to respond

Ignorance. Respondents are not in possession of the answer. Therefore, try not to ask questions of those unqualified to answer.

Forgetfulness. Respondents might have been capable of giving the answer once, but they have forgotten it. Try to confine the questions to events/ situations of the recent past or to use a method of "jogging" their memories without introducing interviewer bias; e.g. use a check-list or cue-card.

Inarticulate. Respondents could answer, but they do not have the ability to frame an adequate answer; this is especially prevalent when asking questions concerned with beliefs, feelings, motivation and attitudes. Questions concerning such topics are best dealt with using data collection methods such as projective techniques, which will be covered in Chapter Seven.

Unwillingness to respond

Aaker and Day (1990) provide the following list of reasons why respondents may be unwilling to answer some/all of the questions in a survey.

Privacy. Certain questions, concerned with topics such as income, or sex or, in some cases, age, will seem to some respondents an invasion of privacy.

Try to reassure respondents that such data is vital to the survey and that details will be treated in the strictest confidence.

Time pressure. If the interview is a long one (or if it is perceived as being long) then there may be a tendency for fatigue and boredom to increase as the interview proceeds. In order to speed up the survey process, respondents may resort to giving the first answer that they think of in the hope of hastening the end of the interview.

When piloting the survey try to establish the average time for which an acceptable level of interest can be maintained. Better a short interview, free of this type of measurement error, than a longer one containing error because of ennui.

Prestige. Human nature being what it is, it is quite understandable that respondents will try to present themselves to an interviewer (a stranger) in the best possible light.

Questions regarding income, social class, educational achievements may well receive answers that are biased "upwards" to increase the "image" of the respondent. Also, questions which are concerned with social behaviour may tend to receive answers which suggest that the respondent adheres to the norms of acceptable behaviour even when they do not do so. Questions on social issues should be framed such that the respondent can answer truthfully without "losing face".

Courtesy. Respondents may be tempted to give the answer that they think the interviewer wishes to hear, in the hope that they (the respondent) will not appear uncooperative.

Uninformed error. Respondents give an answer to a question even though they are completely ignorant of the topic of enquiry; they guess, which will introduce error.

Response style. This effect occurs in questions which have a good/bad or positive/negative response element. Certain respondents have a tendency to opt for a particular style of response irrespective of the context of the question; i.e. certain respondents have a tendency to select positive or good responses over negative or bad responses.

Non-response error

If, for the purposes of a survey, a sample of 500 individuals has been selected as being representative of a population, but only 200 actually agree to take part, then those 200 respondents can no longer be regarded as representative of the entire population. The error which has arisen is called non-response error.

The two main reasons for non-response are:

(1) refusal to take part in the survey, and

(2) the "not at home" situation.

For case 1

Ways of reducing the number of refusals may be found in the previous sections concerned with a potential respondent's inability and/or unwillingness to respond. For example, respondents must be reassured as to the confidentiality of their answers, the short time it will take to answer the questions, the value that the survey attaches to the respondent's answers etc.

For case 2

The most commonly used method to reduce the effects of the "not at homes" is that of the call-back. Respondents can also be contacted prior to the personal or telephone interview to arrange a convenient time for the interview to take place. For mail questionnaires, self-addressed and stamped envelopes can be included for the return of the questionnaires to the research organisation.

There is no single, guaranteed way in which research workers can increase the response rates of a survey, as each separate survey, and the environment in which it takes place, is unique. Experience of survey research techniques will obviously give an indication of what will and what will not work in certain types of situation. To gain that experience research workers should be prepared to experiment and to learn from their mistakes/errors of judgement and from those of others.

Methods of data collection in survey research

The choice of the data collection method is one of great importance and one that is seldom obvious. The difficulty in the choice arises from the combined effects of the situation-specific characteristics and the fact that each method of data collection has its individual advantages and disadvantages. It is very difficult to generalise, in abstract, about which method, or which combination of methods, is to be preferred in certain circumstances; many of the skills of the researcher are used at this point of the project in adapting the vagaries of each data collection method to the special circumstances of the current survey.

The survey methods which will be discussed are the personal interview, the telephone interview and the mail questionnaire.

The personal interview

The two main characteristics which are used to classify an interview are structure and directness.

Structure. The degree of formality which allows or denies the interviewer the opportunity to adapt the questionnaire to each situation when faced with individual respondents, all of whom possess a unique set of characteristics.

Directness. The degree to which the respondent is aware of the purpose(s) of the research.

The four types of interview which can occur are:

(1) structured and direct,

(2) unstructured and direct,

(3) structured and indirect,

(4) unstructured and indirect.

Cases 2 and 3 will be dealt with in Chapter Seven when qualitative research techniques are discussed.

Case 4 is rarely used in marketing research; it is more usually confined to the realms of psychoanalysis.

Case 1 the structured–direct is the method most often used in survey research and will now be investigated in detail.

Advantages of the personal interview

(1) The face to face situation allows the interviewer to do much to reduce respondent anxiety and allay potential embarrassment, therefore increasing the response rate and decreasing the potential for measurement error.

(2) It is a very flexible method in that routing of questions is very easy. For example, if question A asks "Have you heard of brand X", and the questionnaire then says "If YES go to question B, if NO go to question C", the experienced interviewer can do this with ease. Certainly more easily than respondents can do it if they are having to read the routing instructions, as would happen with mail questionnaires.

(3) Interviewers can ask, within narrow limits, for a respondent's answer to be made more clear.

(4) The questions are given in a fixed order with a fixed wording, and the answers are also recorded in a standard manner. All of these facts help reduce the variability that might be introduced if there were to be more than one interviewer working on the study, each one of whom was asking questions and recording answers in a way peculiar to themselves.

(5) Standardised questions and ways of recording the responses mean that less skilled interviewers may be used, thus reducing the costs of the project.

(6) As the interview will be in a face-to-face situation, pictures, signs or objects (products etc.) may be used to refresh a respondent's memory or to demonstrate some action.

Disadvantages of the personal interview

(1) It is time consuming.

(2) Cost per completed interview is high, especially when compared with mail and telephone survey methods.

(3) There may be difficulties in arriving at the "correct" questionnaire design (a problem which will be faced in Chapter Six).

(4) Because interviewers are not given very much latitude to explain, questions must be kept relatively simple, and simple questions may not permit the survey to gather data of much depth and richness.

(5) Questions usually have to be "closed" because of the difficulties in recording and coding the answers to "open" questions.

(6) Because of the fixed formal structure of the interview, examiners cannot probe behind respondents' answers to gain further understanding of vague or ambiguous replies.

Despite all these disadvantages, the personal interview is one of the most popular of data collection methods. It can take place in almost any geographical site; the most commonly used one has given the method a second name—the mall interview or the mall intercept. (But beware, the type of people who visit a shopping mall/arcade may not be representative of the entire population in which your study has an interest.)

To gain the trust of the respondents, the interviewer should be well groomed, friendly and willing to take the time to reassure potential respondents that the survey is of some importance and that their responses will make a valuable and valued contribution to the study.

The telephone interview

An increasingly popular alternative to the personal interview is the telephone interview. The advantages and disadvantages will be discussed shortly, but two recent innovations concerned with the topic should be mentioned first.

(1) Random digit dialling
In probability sampling, one of the drawbacks already discussed was the problem of using telephone directories as sampling frames. By using random digit dialling the disadvantages of a respondent's number not being listed (and therefore making the directory/frame incomplete) are circumvented. It does not, of course, eliminate the problem of potential respondents who are not connected to the telephone system.

For a given location, the usual procedure is to dial the area code and then to use random numbers to generate the final four numbers. The problem of trying to dial non-existent numbers may be reduced by using "plus-one" dialling (Weiers, 1988). Here, a number is selected by conventional sampling techniques from the telephone directory—the number then has 1 added to it before dialling. The resulting number is more likely to be a working number than one generated randomly, as the existence of the first number increases the chances of the second being viable.

(2) Computer assisted telephone interviewing (CATI)

In this system, the telephone interviewer reads the questions from a monitor and then directly inputs the respondents' answers into the computer. This holds considerable advantages for those questionnaires that have complex routing instructions, the computer being programmed automatically to make the necessary decisions.

It also means that questions may easily be changed with little inconvenience, certainly an improvement over having to reprint a large number of paper questionnaires.

One final advantage is that as a result of the answers being keyed directly into the computer, an analysis of the survey can be produced at any time during the "run" of the survey.

Advantages of telephone interviewing

(1) Low cost per completed interview, especially compared with the personal interview.

(2) Convenient: calls may be made from a central location causing a reduction in the need to travel, saving cost and time.

(3) Because of the concentration of the interviewers at a single, central location, administrative control becomes easier and more economical. This is also useful in reducing bias and interviewer error.

(4) It is a method which provides much quicker results than the mail questionnaire and the personal interview.

(5) It provides the opportunity to draw a sample from a wide geographical spread.

Disadvantages of telephone interviewing

(1) It is difficult, in the short duration of a telephone call, to establish a friendly, working rapport with the respondents, which means that they may not feel fully at ease.

(2) Respondents can easily terminate the interview; thus questions must be short, easy to understand and be able to engage and retain the respondent's interest.

(3) Telephones have become a favoured medium for selling purposes. Thus respondents may not be willing to give the interviewer any time at all because of the fear of being "sold something".

(4) Even with the advances of plus-one and random digit dialling, the sample contacted using the medium of the telephone may not be representative. Not everyone is connected to the system, though this is becoming less of a problem as time goes on.

(5) Because of the purely aural nature of the communication process, the ability to use visual clues/aids to refresh memories or to demonstrate products is denied the interviewer.

Interviewer error

In personal and telephone interviews there is direct contact between interviewer and respondent. Response errors have already been described, but another source of error also needs to be aired and that source is located in the interviewers themselves.

Kinnear and Taylor (1991) list four main categories of interviewer error: interviewer/respondent rapport, asking the questions, recording responses and cheating.

(a) Interviewer/respondent rapport
Being interviewed as part of a marketing research survey is a far from common experience for the majority of the population. In such a novel situation, the interviewers become an important role-model in the way the respondent thinks that they should act. The greater the similarity in dress, accent, demeanour etc., between respondent and interviewer the more likely it is that the rapport will be good, which means that there will be an increased probability of more valid, reliable results. If the interviewer does not look sympathetic, then it is easy to understand if the respondent does not approach the questioning process in an appropriate frame of mind. A Saville Row besuited, clip-board wielding interviewer with an Oxford accent would not be viewed by the "regulars" at a working man's club with much sympathy.

(b) Asking the questions
Interviewers must:

(1) Read out the questions exactly as they appear on the questionnaire in a clear voice without mistakes and stumbling.

(2) Read out the questions in the order in which they appear on the questionnaire. Standard question sequence is very important.

(3) Read out all the questions on the schedule.

(4) Probe, if necessary, to get the respondent to react to the question. If the respondent does not understand the question then the interviewer must explain the difficulty in a way which does not introduce bias into the

subsequent answer, i.e. without suggesting to the respondent the type(s) of answer that they should give.

(5) Pronounce every question with the same stress and intonation; even subtle alterations can radically alter the sense of a question. (Try repeating the words of Cole Porter's song "What is this thing called love?" with a stress on a different word at each repetition.)

(c) Recording responses

The way in which the interviewer records the respondent's answers may be a further source of error. If the interviewer paraphrases or shortens or misquotes the true answer, then bias has been introduced. The greater the difference between what is said and what is recorded, the greater the potential size of the error.

(d) Cheating

Because of the inability to supervise, exactly, every single interchange between respondent and interviewer, there are many opportunities for the interviewer to cheat. Cheating may take the form of:

(1) not asking certain questions that are thought by the interviewer to be embarrassing, they then provide the "answers" themselves;

(2) not selecting a "correct" respondent type when sampling and "just going for the next person that comes around the corner";

(3) sitting in a cafe and filling in all the questionnaires themselves.

Cheating, except in the most blatant form, is difficult to detect. Good training and close overall supervision helps prevent it in the first place, as does the use of only skilled, reputable interviewers. But if the cheating is of the Case 1 type, then detection is hard. Some research organisations try to re-interview a certain percentage of the respondents in an attempt to validate their results.

The mail questionnaire

If the size of the interviewer-induced error is likely to be large or its magnitude cannot be predicted with any degree of accuracy and if costs are an important factor when deciding on the data collection method, then mail questionnaires should be given serious consideration.

In a mail survey there is no third party between the respondent and the answer they give, in that it is a self-completed questionnaire. As there is no one to explain ambiguity or to clear up any difficulty in comprehending the questions, the wording and the sequence of the questions needs to be carefully thought through prior to their use. The ability to probe, to "get behind" unclear answers, is also denied the researcher using this method.

Advantages of the mail questionnaire

(1) It allows a reduction in the size of the field staff to a minimum and thus reduces the effects of an interviewer as a source of error.

(2) Cost per completed questionnaire is low if response rates are high.

(3) The relatively anonymous way in which the data is collected may give respondents the confidence to give answers of an embarrassing nature. Other survey methods deny them this because of the higher degrees of social interchange between interviewer and respondent.

(4) The ability, economically, to cover extremely wide geographical areas, which, in turn, may help to generate a more representative sample.

(5) Because of the problems associated with gaining access to respondents when using personal interview or telephone interview techniques, the mail questionnaire may "open up" new segments of the population for survey research.

(6) Respondents have the opportunity, when filling in a mail questionnaire, to do so using their own time-scale This removes pressure; it also allows them to consult records, invoices etc., if the questions are of a technical nature or if the research requires very accurate answers.

Disadvantages of the mail questionnaire

(1) There is a lack of secure knowledge as to who, exactly, fills in the questionnaire. Even when they are addressed to named individuals, there is nothing the researcher can do to prevent others from completing the questionnaire.

(2) Due to the fact that all the questions may be read before they are answered, the ability to move from the general to the specific in a controlled sequence is removed. Respondents can see at a glance where the questions are leading.

(3) As there is no interviewer to act as an interpreter/explainer, complicated questions which are not understood may either be omitted altogether or their answer may merely be guessed.

(4) Questionnaires which are long, or which appear to be long, will tend to increase the non-response rates. This may become manifest in two ways:

   (a) questionnaires which are actually long or perceptively long will not be attempted at all;

   (b) questionnaires of a "reasonable" length may be started, but towards the end, when respondents become increasingly tired, may have questions omitted.

(5) High non-response rates mean that the costs per completed questionnaire can become high.

Non-response in survey research

Non-response in survey research is a problem, particularly where those who do respond are likely to be different in some way from those who do not respond. The easiest way to reduce the effects of this situation is to try and increase the percentages of those who do respond.

Reducing non-response for personal and telephone surveys

(1) Both of these survey methods rely heavily on the quality of the interaction between respondent and interviewer; voice to voice in the case of the telephone. Interviewers who appear/sound pleasant, interesting and interested in the respondent, and who convincingly persuade the respondents that their views are important to the research, will reap the benefits in lower rates of refusal.

(2) Refusals due to the "not at home" syndrome can be reduced by calling back.

(3) Respondents may be promised gifts and/or monetary reward.

Reducing non-response for mail surveys

Non-response with mail surveys is a particularly difficult problem and is probably the biggest drawback to this research method. There is a lack of "humanity" about the mail survey in that no interviewer's presence or voice is present to "personalise" the process. Therefore, the way in which the questionnaire appears and is presented is of the utmost importance; the questionnaire is the only contact between the two parties in the research interchange.

(1) Prior to the dispatch of the questionnaire, respondents can be contacted and asked if they would be prepared to aid the study by filling in a questionnaire.

(2) In place of the verbal introduction to the research that can be given with personal and telephone surveys, the inclusion of a covering letter may act as an "overture" to the "first act" of the questionnaire proper. It can be used to explain the purpose and context of the research and to put the respondent in the appropriate frame of mind.

(3) Include a stamped, self-addressed envelope for ease of questionnaire return.

(4) Provide a gift or monetary incentive upon completion of questionnaire.

(5) Address the respondents by name and not as "The Occupant" or "To whom it may concern". For the latter, most people would reply that "it doesn't concern me!"

This may not only increase the response rates, it may also encourage the named person to fill in the questionnaire personally, rather than "farming it out" to some other member of the firm's administration or to a junior member of the family.

(6) Name, if possible, not only the organisation that is conducting the research, but also the name of those who have commissioned it—the sponsor.

(7) Offer, to those respondents who indicate an interest, the opportunity to receive a copy of the survey's final results.

(8) Non-respondents can be contacted by mail or telephone and encouraged to return their completed questionnaires.

Estimating the bias due to non-response

If, after valiant efforts, the response rate to the survey is still low, then the researcher can make some estimation as to the possible size of the error that has been introduced by comparing the differences in results between respondents and non-respondents. (It is possible that though there is a percentage of the population who do not respond, there is no resulting bias, i.e. both respondents and non-respondents are the same; this is possible, but not likely.)

There are two important and useful ways in which the differences between respondents and non-respondents may be estimated; sub-sampling and trend analysis.

Sub-sampling
From those that did not respond to the initial survey, a sub-sample is drawn so that the survey can gather data to enable the researchers to make generalisations about the entire block of non-respondents.

This method, of course, assumes that respondents will be more receptive to the requests of a survey the second time around than they were on the first round.

Trend analysis
Armstrong and Overton (1977) assume that those respondents who are slow in returning the questionnaire, or who have responded only as a result of call-backs, are more like non-respondents than those who have responded quickly and who did not require "prodding". If the original mailed questionnaires are succeeded with "waves" of call-backs or follow-up mailings then the data

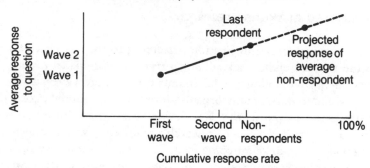

Figure 5.1. Projected response of average non-respondent. (From Aaker and Day, (1990), *Marketing Research*, 4th edition, John Wiley and Sons Inc., with permission).

from succeeding "waves" can be used to establish trends in the answer patterns.

Aaker and Day (1990) say that data from the waves, the trends, can be used in two ways:

(a) non-respondents can be assumed to have similar characteristics, to be like, the last respondent of the last "wave", or

(b) non-respondents can be assumed to have similar characteristics to an extrapolated respondent in the centre of the non-respondent group. This may be represented diagrammatically as in Figure 5.1.

Summary: survey methods

Surveys, whether by mail, via the telephone or conducted on a face-to-face basis, constitute some of the most widely employed and useful techniques in marketing research.

No single method will fit, absolutely, the unique demands of each research programme and great skill needs to be exercised, on behalf of the practitioner, in choosing the appropriate "blend" of methods, so that the disadvantage(s) of one method are neutralised or reduced by the advantage(s) of another method or other methods.

So far in Chapter Five, much time has been devoted to describing ways in which each individual survey method's disadvantages may be ameliorated; special attention should be paid to those problems which arise from the processes of interaction which take place either between respondent and researcher or between respondent and survey method.

Remember, above all, flexibility of approach. A stance which is vital if the research process is to reconcile successfully, the often conflicting demands of respondents and those who seek to understand or learn from them.

Panel/syndicated marketing research

Organisations which seek information pertaining to some aspect of a market
may decide to commission an ad hoc survey, tailor-made to the specific
demands of their own, unique, requirements for data. However, as this can be
a very costly undertaking, many organisations, before committing themselves
to such a course of events, may first decide to purchase information—syndicated research—from a specialist research agency etc., which collects data for
resale to a wide range of client companies. This information may fully answer
all the organisation's requirements for data, thus saving the considerable
outlays of time and money which can result from the commission of a
"bespoke" research project.

In syndicated research, the data is usually collected from a panel of respondents, which gives this style of investigation its other name: panel research.

A panel may consist of individuals, households, industrial buyers, firms etc.,
who agree to provide data to governmental bodies, commercial research firms,
universities etc., on a periodic basis.

Panel members may agree to provide information only when called upon to
do so. On the other hand, continuous panels provide data on a regular basis.
Data requirements may include information concerning consumer products,
industrial products and store audits. Because information is acquired over time,
from the same sample, the problems that arise from using discrete but equivalent samples, e.g. sampling errors, are reduced, which increases the reliability
of the resulting data.

Kinnear and Taylor (1991) have classified syndicated data sources into six
main groups: consumer data, retail data, wholesale data, industrial data,
advertising evaluation data, and media/audience data.

(i) Consumer data. Comprises data from consumers regarding purchases
and the circumstances surrounding such purchases. Data is grouped into sales
by brand, type, variety/flavour, price paid, quantities bought, where bought,
brand switching and demographic/socio-economic characteristics of those that
purchase.

Data may also be gathered concerning the attitudes and opinions of consumers towards a wide range of social, economic and political situations.
Trends in consumption patterns and in "life-styles" may also be investigated.

Buck (1976) found that consumer panel research could uncover significant
market segments for certain types of products, e.g. central heating units, 50%
of whose sales were accounted for, in a three month period, by only 2.5% of
the population: those with new homes, those who had recently moved house
and those who had recently married.

(ii) Retail data. Data collected from retail outlets, generally concentrating on the products/services sold and/or the characteristics of the retail outlets themselves.

(iii) Wholesale data. That data which is concerned with warehouse transactions; e.g. SAMI Inc in the United States monitors sales of brands in 425 product categories in 36 markets, data which client companies can use to analyse levels of sales, package size, impact of promotional activities and of competitor activities.

(iv) Industrial data. Though there are far fewer research agencies operating in this part of the market, compared with that for consumer goods, those that do, generate data which can be used to estimate sales prospects, identify sales territories, and establish sales potentials.

(v) Advertising evaluation data. Companies spend vast amounts of money on advertising. It is in their interests, therefore, to make some assessment as to the effectiveness of their advertising efforts. Data can be generated with which to gauge the effectiveness of a company's advertising and that of its main competitors.

(vi) Media/audience data. In advertising, it is an important function of the media planner to uncover media which have audience characteristics similar to the target market for whatever is being advertised.

Media planners also find it useful to know what competitors are spending on advertising, where they are spending this money and what media they are patronising.

Consumer panels

Consumer panels, in survey research, are the most common of all the types of continuous research. Panel members, who may be individuals or households, may be chosen by simple random sampling or, more usually, by stratified random sampling. This latter method is used so that the sample chosen is as representative of the general population with regard to such characteristics as demographic make-up, income levels and family structure as is possible. If people refuse/decline to serve on a sample after they have been selected, or when panel members drop out, they are replaced by a unit of similar characteristics.

Information may be gathered from the panel members in two main ways: (i) audits and (ii) diaries. While both are popular in Europe, the latter method tends to predominate in North America (Aaker and Day, 1990).

(i) Home audit

Members of staff of the research company organising the study visit the panellists' homes and physically check for the presence of those items being surveyed. Households/individuals are requested to retain the containers and/or wrappings of those product types purchased in the interim since the last audit. They may also be asked to complete a short questionnaire. Because of the way that the wrappers/containers are stored, this type of research is often called a dustbin or garbage audit.

(ii) Diaries

In this method, panellists complete some type of diary which records the purchases of the specified products, together with the frequency of purchase, the size of the package, the price paid, where purchased, and brand.

These diaries are usually collected by, or posted back to, the research organisation on a two-weekly or monthly basis.

It is common to reward panel members in some way, financially or with gifts.

Companies in the United Kingdom include the Attwood Consumer Panel, AGB Home Audit and the Taylor Nelson Family Food Panel. In the United States the most famous consumer panel is that organised by the AC Nielsen Company.

Case study: uses of survey research

In a national context
Each year, the Central Statistical Office publishes the "Family Expenditure Survey". For the 1990 survey, 10,000 households were asked to keep a spending diary for a two-week period.

The government uses this data to create the "representative basket of goods and services" from which the retail price index is calculated.

The data collected, which includes a notional amount devoted to housing, covers such areas of interest as numbers of cars possessed by household units, the ownership of consumer durables such as central heating units, washing machines, freezers/fridge-freezers etc. The survey also collects data on a family's expenditure on such items as food, motoring costs and fares, clothing, footwear, alcoholic drinks, tobacco products, cosmetics and charitable donations.

As the geographical position of each respondent unit is known, the data may be used to compare spending patterns between various parts of the country. The 1990 survey, for example, showed that average household spending varied from £203 per week in Northern Ireland to £273 in the London area; that the heaviest smokers were to be found in Scotland; that the biggest drinkers lived in the North-West of England; and that people from the Midlands spent the most on motoring.

Retail shop audit

One of the main problems for a manufacturer is to assess, as accurately as possible, consumer demand for their products. Merely looking at the amount of products leaving the factory gates does not accurately reflect consumer demand because of the way that products may be held up or expedited through the distribution system. For example, when a product is launched, there will be a large amount of the good leaving the manufacturers but, as it is a new product, little initially will be sold. If management looked only at what was leaving the factory, they would have a greatly inflated impression as to the product's sales.

Also, as the retail store audits investigate product types, it is possible for a client of the research company not only to track what is happening to their own products, but to also to look at the behaviour of their competitors' products. Thus market trends and market share data may be obtained as well as information on the types of outlets where their products and that of their competitor brands are being purchased; information that is invaluable in planning distribution strategies.

At set intervals, staff of the research company visit a sample of shops, audit the stock and record the details of any deliveries since the last audit; from this data they can calculate the sales for each product for the period between their visits.

Original inventory + deliveries – Final inventory = Sales

Retail stores are segmented according to their types—multiples, independents, department—and by volume of business. The auditors tend to concentrate on those shops which sell the biggest range of products in which the research organisation is interested. Hence, disproportionate stratified sampling may be used to select these outlets.

A recent advance in retail shop audits is the use of EPOS—electronic point of sale scanning.

Most consumer products are now marked with a unique bar code. These bar codes are "read" by laser scanners at the shop's tills, the information being transmitted to a central computing facility. Originally intended as a better way of organising stock control, EPOS is also proving useful in continuous marketing research.

Advantages of panel research

Because panel research provides a moving picture (a video) of a market situation rather than a fixed image (a snapshot) which occurs in a one-off survey situation, it is an excellent method for monitoring trends in, for example, brand switching, brand loyalty, repeat purchases, market size and market penetration. It is also useful in uncovering significant market segments and for experimentation. In the latter case, changes in one of the constituents of the marketing mix can be confined to one geographical area; the results of the alteration may then be compared with what is happening in another geographical area where no changes have been made—the control area.

(a) There is a reduced need to keep on generating samples.

(b) There are good reasons to believe that a higher response rate will be recorded when compared with the response rates of ad hoc. surveys. This means that fewer questionnaires have to be used and/or that fewer interviews have to be administered.

(c) The results of panel surveys are likely to be more accurate as respondents become used to the discipline of recording their purchase data.

(d) Data may be generated for a comparatively small outlay—certainly much less than it would cost to mount an ad hoc survey.

(e) Panel/syndicated research can provide useful data on competitor activity.

(f) Because it is a continuous research process, it is likely that it will provide data far more quickly than will an ad hoc survey.

Disadvantages of panel research

The main disadvantages of panel research lie with the sample itself.

(a) The lack of representativeness; once the initial sample has been selected, it is possible that the invitation to become a panel member may be turned down, thus "upsetting" the representativeness of the sample.

(b) The effects of those that drop out; over time it is also quite likely that a number of those panel members who do consent to become panel members will either drop out or will become less enthusiastic in accurately obeying the "rules".

For both (a) and (b) a major problem arises in finding replacement panel members who share similar characteristics with those that they are to replace.

(c) A related difficulty in regard to representativeness is the question of the replacement that has to take place when the panel members get too old. Not that being old is a disadvantage, but the research organisation has to maintain a panel that is representative, amongst other factors, of the demographic make-up of the general population.

(d) A question asked by Weiers (1988), and one which must be borne in mind by the organisers of the research, is: "Do panel members, who agree to join in with the research who have similar characteristics in relation to the general public, differ in some way from those who refuse to join the research?"

(e) Panel members may change their purchasing patterns as a result of being surveyed. This disadvantage may be reduced by a reasonably rapid turn-over of panellists, with, maybe, two years being the maximum that anyone can serve as a panellist.

(f) The data generated in panel/syndicated research is available to all those with the ability to pay. Thus no client of the research agency is purchasing a unique report.

Omnibus surveys

Several research agencies run continuous survey questionnaires. By using this method, client companies may obtain speedy results to some pressing data requirement needed at very short notice.

An omnibus survey is a questionnaire made up of several sets of questions, each set from a different client company. The costs of running the survey, interviewing etc., are then shared between all those contributing questions. Chisnall (1986), however, recommends that if a single client company's questions take more than ten minutes to deliver, then the company should seriously consider running an ad hoc survey of their own.

Questions can cover a wide range of interests, but they should be short, preferably closed, easily understood and easily answered.

Summary: panel/syndicated marketing research

Panel/syndicated research has, as do all other forms of marketing research, both advantages and disadvantages. Its major advantage is that it can provide a "moving picture" of a situation; an ideal research tool if the dynamic aspects of a research situation are an important consideration in meeting the overall objectives of the research.

It is also useful in rapidly generating results of a type which, for a single client company, could be more expensive and/or difficult to obtain.

References

Aaker D. A. and Day G. S. (1990) *Marketing Research*, John Wiley and Sons, New York, 5th edition.

Armstrong J. S. and Overton T. S. (1977) Estimating non-response bias in mail surveys, *Journal of Marketing Research*, August, 396–402.

Buck S. (1976) *Measuring Behaviour: using a panel can measure change very accurately*, AGB "Audit", Spring.

Chisnall P. M. (1986) *Marketing Research*, McGraw-Hill, Maidenhead, 3rd edition.

Kinnear T. C. and Taylor J. R. (1991) *Marketing Research: An Applied Approach*, McGraw-Hill, New York, 4th edition.

Weiers R. M. (1988) *Marketing Research*, Prentice-Hall, Englewood Cliffs, New Jersey, 2nd edition.

CHAPTER SIX

Questionnaire Design

Introduction   91
(1) Initial considerations   92
(2) Question content   93
(3) Question phrasing   97
(4) Types of response format   102
(5) Question sequence   106
(6) Questionnaire layout   107
(7) Pretest, revision and final version of the questionnaire   108
Reliability and validity in questionnaire design   109
Summary   111
References   111

Introduction

Unfortunately, it is not possible to write a prescription that will guarantee a perfect questionnaire; besides, perfection, in such a context, is a state few think capable of being reached. Good questionnaires, on the other hand, can be designed and good questionnaires are those that validly fulfil the objectives of the research with the minimum invasion of error and bias. But, even to construct a "good" questionnaire is a difficult task and, again, it is almost impossible to state, in abstract, exactly how it may be achieved—too many of the qualifying conditions are situation-specific. What can be done, however, is to give the reader the advice of those who have gained useful, practical experience through long exposure to the subject.

Questionnaires may be used in a variety of contexts in survey research: in mail surveys, telephone interviews, formal, structured interviews and also, but to a lesser extent, in self-administered and group-administered questionnaires. Whatever the context, the way in which the questionnaire is constructed is very broadly similar. Thus the advice which is about to be given is meant to apply in all circumstances; survey-specific variants will be detailed at the appropriate juncture.

A major problem with questionnaires is that though they are difficult to construct, the majority of those people who have never had to do so think that it is merely a case of typing out a list of questions. This is not the case. Much thought needs to go into the process, some of it before the questions are framed.

Tull and Hawkins (1990) provide an excellent set of steps on questionnaire design which it is intended to follow here; the sequence is:

(1) Initial considerations.

(2) Question content.

(3) Question phrasing.

(4) Types of response format.

(5) Question sequence.

(6) Questionnaire layout.

(7) Pretest, revision and final version of the questionnaire.

(1) Initial considerations

Like the legs of a kitchen stool, there are three initial considerations that need to be borne in mind when starting out on the construction of a questionnaire: the type of information that is required, the type/nature of the respondents who are to be surveyed, and the type(s) of method by which the survey is to be administered.

And like those culinary legs, all three considerations need to be of the same length and strength; if they are not, then like the stool, the questionnaire will "wobble". The ultimate intention should be to achieve the optimal degree of "fit" between the three basic considerations. It would be counterproductive to try to extract a certain type of information from a type of respondent who does not possess or have access to such data.

For example, it would be inappropriate to use a mail questionnaire to ask young people questions that require very complex answers, or to take up the valuable time of a "captain" of industry by asking basic questions by means of an administered questionnaire when that type of data would be much better gathered by another method. Researchers will need to go from consideration one, to two and then to three and then back around again as many times as it takes to get a satisfactory degree of congruency between each of them; this is an iterative process of cyclic evaluation.

The questionnaire must fully answer all the data requirements that have been encapsulated in the research objectives. To leave anything out would be negligent; to start to search for too much data would increase the cost of the study and may, because of its perceived length, deter some respondents from replying, thus increasing the non-response rate.

Thought should also be given to the respondent; whether they will be allowed to give their answers anonymously (whether they care) and whether the purpose of the research is to be announced.

(2) Question content

This step is concerned more with what type of data the question is meant to gather rather than with the way in which it gathers it—that function is the provenance of "question phrasing".

The function of the question content step is to ensure that the demands of the research objectives for specific data are met. One of the essential skills of those involved in questionnaire construction is the ability to design a research tool that will fulfil the data requirements.

When deciding on question content, five factors should be remembered:

(i) Is the question necessary?

If the answer to a question does not have any contribution to make in satisfying the objectives of the research, then omit the question.

(ii) Does the respondent comprehend the question?

Shaw said that Great Britain and the United States of America were divided by a common language; the same may perhaps be said about the gulf between interviewer and respondent.

The language of the question should be of the level of the respondent group being interviewed/questioned. Teenagers do not use the same language and words as managing directors, and vice versa. More of this topic will be considered in the section concerned with question phrasing.

(iii) Is the question sufficient to elicit the required data?

Questions, though relevant to the objectives of the research study, may not be able to generate the required data.

Much of this inability to generate what is wanted arises with questions that are phrased badly or are too ambiguous to render specific information. Double-barrelled questions are a common failing when students first attempt questionnaire construction:

For example, consider the question "Do you often go to the theatre and concerts?" A "yes" response does not indicate whether it is a "yes" to the theatre or a "yes" to the concerts.

If such a question, after piloting or consideration, is found to be insufficiently clear or focused to fulfil the data demands, then it is better to split the question into two parts, or more, so that all the information needs are met. Questions which require the respondent to "collect" data from different mental "files", such as asking a company manager "what was your total expenditure last year?"—which would involve him having to sum the figures from various functional departments—would perhaps be better answered if a set of separate questions concerned with each cost centre were to be asked.

In the question quoted at the start of this section the word "often" was used. To one respondent, that word might mean a frequency of, for example, once per week, while to another, it might be taken to mean nothing more than once every year.

Words describing frequency, such as "often", and of comparison, such as "slightly", "somewhat", have a wide range of interpretations. Thus great care needs to be exercised by those who construct questionnaires to ensure that all respondents share a common "standard" against which such words can be compared. If it is not possible to do this, then the questionnaire must explicitly state what is meant by such an expression; e.g. instead of asking "Do you often go to the cinema?", ask "Do you go to the cinema, (a) once a week, (b) once a month, (c) twice a year?"

(iv) Does the respondent have the necessary data to answer the question?

Relevance of the question to the research is not the sole influence on the content of the question; the ability of the respondent to answer will also play its part in deciding question content.

The ability of the respondent to answer will depend upon the following factors.

(a) Degree to which the respondent is informed

Few human beings like to admit that they do not know the answer to a question. In marketing research it is common and understandable that some respondents will not have heard of the topic on which they are being examined. It is equally understandable that they might try to "bluff" their way out of what, to them, is an embarrassing situation by guessing; these "answers" are a major source of measurement error in marketing research.

One method to try to cope with this source of error is to phrase the question in such a way that the interviewer does not appear to be suggesting that the respondent *should* know the answer.

Rather than ask "What is the interest rate on credit cards?" which implies that the respondent should have the data at their fingertips, it is better to ask, "Do you happen to know what the interest rate is on credit cards?"

If the answer to this is "yes", then a second question can be asked which enquires what that rate is. If the answer is "no" then the respondent will not be tempted to guess, as they should not feel as if they have been "boxed into a corner". A "no" answer does not contribute to measurement error in this context.

(b) The state of the respondent's memory

The more important an event is to a respondent, the more frequently it occurs, or the more recently it has taken place to the time of the interview, the more likely it is that the respondent's memory will be reliable.

But people do forget. Questions which require data pertaining to unimportant, infrequent events, or to occurrences some time in the past, are likely to tempt respondents to guess the answer. Researchers, therefore, should not place too much faith in a respondent's ability to reply, in such instances, with a high degree of reliability. Rather than allowing them to guess, which will introduce measurement error, it is better to use some method to "jog" their memories, but to do so in a manner that does not introduce interviewer bias.

Rather than asking a respondent to list the products they bought on their last shopping trip, which relies on their ability to remember a not very interesting or memorable event, it is better to use aided recall, i.e. to show the respondent a list of standard shopping items and ask them which of the products, if any, they bought on their last expedition to the supermarket.

(c) The articulateness of the respondent

A respondent's ability to articulate their answers, particularly those concerned with feelings, beliefs, opinions and motivations, will vary greatly. In many cases, even the most verbally adept may find it difficult to articulate a reliable reason or set of reasons why, for example, they purchase a certain brand of washing powder rather than another. Matters of fact require a lesser degree of articulacy than do those complex emotional patterns of beliefs, motivations and feelings which precede, for example, the purchase of a product or service.

If the data requirements of the study depend upon gaining such information (beliefs etc.), then those in charge of the project should perhaps consider other research methods better suited to uncovering such information; in-depth interviews and projective techniques, for example.

(v) Is the respondent willing/able to answer the questions?

Just because a person can do something, it does not mean that they will do it. Similarly, just because a respondent is able to provide an answer, there is no law that says he must.

A refusal to answer a question may take two forms:

(1) Refusal to answer one question or a number of questions on a questionnaire/interview; this is called item non-response.

(2) "Refusal" to answer by providing a "wrong" or distorted answer; this is called measurement error.

Three reasons are given by Kinnear and Taylor (1991) for this unwillingness to provide accurate answers: the situation is inappropriate for data disclosure, data disclosure would prove embarrassing to the respondent, data disclosure is a potential threat to the prestige of the respondent, i.e. the respondent by so doing would "lose face". To understand why respondents may be unwilling to respond to certain types of question, put yourself, for a moment, in the position of a respondent.

There you are, one Saturday morning, out in the High Street shopping, or your telephone rings just as your favourite television programme begins, or a big fat questionnaire plops onto your "welcome" mat. The man/woman with the clip-board or a disembodied, unknown voice at the other end of the line, in both cases perfect strangers, with hardly a good morning, suddenly starts asking questions concerned with your income or sexual orientation, whether you do or do not beat your spouse, whether you keep coal in the bath, what you think of the immigrant "problem"!

Is it surprising that many respondents "freeze" or refuse to cooperate?

These may be somewhat extreme examples, but the point is clear: interviewers *must* be sensitive to the feelings of the respondents.

No answer is better than a distorted answer, but best of all would be a truthful, accurate answer; how may this be achieved?

Certain techniques have been found to be of some help:

(a) Be absolutely certain that the question is necessary, particularly if it is anticipated that it may cause respondent embarrassment or anxiety. Questions which do this or cause loss of prestige may not only cause the respondent to omit that question, they may so anger the respondent that their cooperation on the remainder of the survey is immediately terminated.

(b) Try to reassure the respondent of the importance of the question and of the value which the study attaches to their answer.

(c) Use counter-biasing statement; i.e. begin the question with a statement which implies that the topic of which one speaks is common or quite usual. For example, "Many people are of the opinion that the Inland Revenue is run by descendants of Count Dracula. Do you happen to think this?"

(d) Third-party questions: imply that the behaviour in which you are interested is an attribute of a third party. The theory behind this is that the respondent will "project" his/her behaviour onto that third party. For example, instead of asking "Do you visit the Edinburgh Festival because the Festival Club has cheap whisky?", ask "Do you think that people visit the Edinburgh Festival because the Festival Club has cheap whisky?"

(e) Labelled response categories. Offer the respondent a card with a list of possible answers (identified by a letter or a number) to questions that are potentially embarrassing. To answer, the respondent then only has to read out the appropriate letter/number. Pilot studies, prior to the main study, will indicate the possible range of answers that can be expected.

(f) Prestige. With questions including an element of prestige, researchers should be aware of a tendency for many respondents to "trade up" their answers. Their claimed usage of products/services/objects which are generally seen as having a high prestige image will be increased, while their claimed usage of products/services/objects having a low prestige image will be down-graded. In terms of their professions, window cleaners may become transparent wall maintenance engineers and refuse collectors may become environmental recycling operatives!

There is also a natural (and understandable) tendency for respondents to gravitate towards behaviour patterns which are seen as being socially acceptable or desirable, even when they themselves do not back the responses they give to surveys with the appropriate actions. Many may claim to think that a 30 mile per hour speed limit is "a good thing" while actually roaring through the streets with scant regard to the rules of the Highway Code. For questions which include an element of prestige, researchers should avoid asking direct questions for fear of the above possible reactions. Instead, the use of such techniques as counter-biasing statements and third-party questions is recommended.

(3) Question phrasing

In the question phrasing stage of the questionnaire construction, the person responsible for the questionnaire has to translate the question content into useable form, i.e. they have to operationalise, in words, the data requirements. And it must be done in a way that renders the questions easy to understand, easy to answer and unambiguous. This may seem a straightforward task, but it is one which requires great care and sensitivity.

As Oppenheim (1984), in a text which is useful reading for those concerned with questionnaire design, says:

"In some ways the problem of question wording is a sampling problem. We are sampling a particular universe of content in the respondent's mind, for instance his attitude to Mexicans. We are not planning to obtain the whole of this universe of content, but only enough of it to enable us to outline its salient features, general direction, depth or intensity and, perhaps the presence or absence of specific items. Our questions must be adequate for this sampling process; they must not be too one-sided and they must make it easy for the respondent to respond fully."

It is clear from this that the wording of a question is of pivotal importance to the way in which the respondent translates the question into their own terms.

Sensitivity must be exercised over the choice of words, but again, it is not possible to write a prescription for the "right" way to phrase a question. But what can be done is to give a check-list of factors to consider when translating question content into words.

These factors include the following.

(i) Clear and simple words

If we speak to a native of Bologna, then the language we use, logically, is Italian; when in Rome—speak "Roman"! If we speak to a six-year-old child, then words of the complexity of, for example, hypothetical, carbon tetrachloride, antinomianism, are best avoided; a look of blank incomprehension would be the best response that could be expected. Why ask after a neighbour's domesticated canine quadruped if all you want to say is, "How's your dog?"

Find a style of language that is appropriate for the target population. Do not be condescending and speak "down" to them, or, on the other hand, assume that they are as well informed on a subject as you think you are, with the consequence that the majority of your questions go "right over their heads". If you are interviewing teenagers, then providing that both respondents and interviewers know the exact meaning, use street argot if necessary; it will simplify the communication process at the same time as presenting you in a sympathetic light. This may encourage a higher response and more accurate, valid answers.

(ii) Question length

Oppenheim (1984) suggests that a question should be no more than twenty words in length. Any longer than that and many respondents may lose all sense of it.

(iii) Ambiguous and vague words

Given the huge range of words and meanings in the English language, there are many opportunities for ambiguity and vagueness to become manifest. If the meaning of a question is not clear to a respondent, how are they supposed to be able to give a clear and unambiguous answer? If they have to guess at the question's meaning then measurement error will be introduced. A vague question will lead to a vague answer and in mail questionnaires the researcher will have to accept this as there is no opportunity to probe for clarity; this makes interpretation difficult and interviewer bias may creep in.

Payne (1951), in another text which should be compulsory reading for those involved in questionnaire design, said that the following six questions should be asked about every word in a question.

(1) Does it mean what we intend?

(2) Does it have any other meaning?

(3) If so, does the context make the meaning clear?

(4) Does it have more than one pronunciation?

(5) Is there a word of similar pronunciation with which it might be confused?

(6) Is there a simpler word or phrase available?

(iv) Biased words and leading questions

A biased word "is one which is emotionally coloured and suggests an automatic feeling of approval or disapproval, for instance Nazi, bosses, interference, motherly, starvation, strike-breakers... " (Oppenheim, 1984). Respondents, he says, are not really answering the question but are reacting to the biased word or phrase.

Consider the following two sentences:

(a) The head of the union threatened a strike if their pay claim was not met in full.

(b) The head of the union promised a strike if their pay claim was not met in full.

In objective terms both sentences have very much the same meaning, but in subjective/emotional terms they are quite far apart.

A word used in one context or to one group of people may be quite "neutral"; when used in another context or to another group of people it may appear highly coloured; a word can act like a chameleon and take on the characteristics of its surroundings.

This is a problem for those setting questionnaires. Suppose that the research worker is a member of a group to which a certain word is "neutral"; this is acceptable if the target population, to whom the questionnaire will be aimed, also thinks that the word is "neutral". It is an unacceptable choice if the target population thinks that the word is biased or if it causes a biased response. To ensure that this is not the case, a pilot test of the questionnaire is recommended.

Once the problem word has been pointed out, it is the researcher's responsibility to find a word that carries less, or better still, no emotional overtones for all the groups that will be questioned while still retaining its full, objective meaning.

Leading questions are those which either suggest the way in which the respondent should answer, or strongly suggest what the questioner's position on the subject is. For example: "All right-minded think that something should be done about our filthy street, do you?"

Questions which include "You don't happen to believe/think/act ... do you?" tend to lead to negative answers.

Questions which begin "Don't you think that...?" tend to receive positive answers.

Blatantly leading questions should be spotted without too much difficulty, but, inadvertently, many questions become "leading" by the lack of provision of an adequate set of alternative answers.

For example. "Do you prefer green beans with your meat course?" This gives no alternative way of replying. It would be better, instead, to ask "Do you have green vegetables with your meat course?" followed by a second question "Which green vegetable do you prefer?"

Leading questions can be made less "leading" by the inclusion of an appropriate number of alternative replies.

This topic will be discussed again later when question format is covered in "Types of response format".

(v) Double-barrelled questions

Do not ask two questions in one sentence. "What do you think of the price and the quality of this book?" This type of question is especially difficult to answer if the respondent has to choose from, say, only two responses; good and bad, yes or no etc. To what part of the question does the given answer refer?

Two questions require two independent sentences.

(vi) Negative questions

Questions which have a negative formulation, with which a respondent has to agree/disagree, can be confusing. And confusion leads to the respondent guessing and hence measurement error.

Question: "Marketing research is not interesting?"

1	2	3	4	5
Agree	Partially agree	No opinion	Partially disagree	Disagree

To tick box 5, "disagree", actually means that the respondent thinks that marketing research is interesting. An acceptable answer, if valid, but is it worth putting a respondent through the mental gymnastics it requires to "sort out" that question? It is better to phrase the question in a straightforward way and avoid possible errors.

Questions involving double negatives, unless absolutely necessary, should be treated with the greatest possible caution.

(vii) Questions containing estimates

Questions which ask respondents to make an estimate or to make generalisations are a great potential source of error. Respondents should not be put into a position where they have to guess at an answer. Estimates and generalisations encourage respondents to guess and should be avoided.

Instead of asking "How many bottles of beer do you think you drink a year?", ask "How many bottles of beer do you drink a week?" and do the small arithmetic calculation of multiplying by 52 yourself.

(viii) Hypothetical questions

Before including questions which commence with phrases such as "Would you like to...?" or "What would you do if...?" try and work out, exactly, what use is going to be made of the answer.

"Would you like a season ticket to La Scala?"

"What would you do if you discovered you were the sole heir to the fabled Trautman fortune?"

These types of question not only encourage respondents to guess, which is unfortunate, but implicitly goad them into wild speculation. Therefore, hypothetical questions are almost useless in generating valid, accurate data.

(ix) Implicit assumptions

Questions should not be asked as if all respondents had possession of all the relevant factors; common sense tells us that this is not the case. Some respondents are well informed and some not so well informed. In any case, questioners should not act as if they knew that all respondents were fully conversant with their (the question setters') thought processes while they were constructing the questionnaire.

Badly phrased questions which make an implicit assumption of a respondent's background knowledge will not produce valid, accurate results. They fail in their ability to generate useful responses because some respondents will make one assumption and others will make a second, and so on.

The question "Do you think that public transport should be free?" will evoke an answer depending upon the respondent's assumptions concerning the effects of free transport.

In the question "Do you think that public transport should be free if" ... (for example)... "...it reduced urban congestion?" the implicit assumptions in the first version of the question have been replaced by an explicit statement to which all respondents, now being fully informed as to the consequences of free public transport, can react.

Many questions included in questionnaires are flawed because they do not state the essential assumptions upon which the question is dependent, which can produce inflated or deflated responses.

The question "Are you in favour of enforcing all cars to be fitted with catalytic converters in order to help reduce atmospheric pollution?" would tend to produce a stronger positive response than it would if the implicit assumption "...even though it would also increase petrol consumption by 15%" had been added.

A note on phrasing probes/follow-up questions

On some structured or semi-structured questionnaires, after a question that invites an open-ended response, there might be an instruction to the interviewer, if the answer is unclear and requires clarification, to "probe".

It should be remembered that leading of the respondent and bias can occur in a "probe" follow-up just as in the main part of the survey. Perhaps they can occur more frequently; it is very difficult for the constructor of the questionnaire to know, in advance, the type of clarification that an answer will require. Thus the phrasing of the "probe" or follow-up question has to be left to the discretion of the interviewer. It is a far from easy task to think of a probe etc., on the spot, that is neither leading and free of any of the other types of error that have just been detailed.

(4) Types of response format

(i) Open-ended questions

Free responses
In open-ended questions, the question is followed by an unstructured answer, the respondent being allowed to reply using any words they so wish. The interviewer then has to record the response. Some respondents may wish to take the opportunity of a free response to expound at length about the topic in general which makes the interviewer's task very hard, if all the reply is to be recorded (as it should if bias due to the interviewer "editing" the response

is to be avoided). This potential problem may be reduced by phrasing the question in such a way that it is orientated directly at a specific topic rather than at a subject in general.

Projective techniques
These are undoubtedly a type of open-ended, free response answer format, but they are better discussed in the context of qualitative research (see Chapter Seven).

With the free response, open-ended type of question, it may be necessary to use probes/follow-up questions, and, therefore, the problems of leading questions and bias may intrude. Luck and Rubin (1987) suggest that interviewers should be provided with a formal/standardised wording for use when a probe or a follow-up question is found to be necessary.

(ii) Closed-ended questions

In a closed-ended question, the question is followed by a structured response.

Dichotomous questions
This is the most restrictive, the "tightest" response category and only allows the respondent a choice of two responses; yes/no, black/white, never on a Sunday/only on a Sunday etc.

They are excellent for those occasions where a fact is to be determined and where the views of the respondents are likely to be clear cut, or as one might say, black and white.

But in those situations where the issue is not quite so obviously polarised, dichotomous questions should be avoided as they may bias the respondents' answer by forcing them to make a choice between only two responses, when they would prefer to opt for an answer that does not lie at the extremes of the polarities.

The question "Are you going to rush out and buy the latest book on marketing research—Yes or No?", may compel a respondent to choose one answer or another, when what they really want to say is "Yes—if my grant arrives" or "No, I actually bought it yesterday".

The provision of response categories "Maybe", "Don't know" or "No opinion" does little to resolve the issue, but such "neutral" responses may be acceptable if they capture the true feelings of the respondent. Bias may arise, however, if, to avoid making a choice through reasons of embarrassment etc., the neutral response is chosen. If pilot studies reveal that many respondents really do hold a truly "neutral" position, then such an alternative should be included; if studies reveal that it is going to be used as a way of avoiding having to answer, then it should be dropped; the respondents are then "forced" to make a choice.

Dichotomous questions may be regarded as a sub-set of multiple choice questions.

Multiple choice questions

In multiple choice questions the respondent is presented with a "menu" of answers from which they can select the one that most closely approximates to their views. It is usual for a respondent to be allowed only a single choice on the assumption that a person will only hold a single opinion on a topic.

In cases where a respondent is likely to have views which do not fall conveniently into a dichotomous split, multiple choice questions are to be preferred. They are also easier to use for both respondent and interviewer, they reduce any bias which may be introduced by the varying degrees of the articulacy of respondents, they are more convenient to code and they remove the source of bias that occurs when an interviewer has to record a long response after having asked an open-ended question.

For example:
"For an evening's entertainment, which of the following would you prefer?"

_____ A visit to the theatre

_____ A visit to an opera

_____ A discotheque

_____ A restaurant meal

_____ Ten-pin bowling

Problems which arise from the use of multiple choice questions include (a) the number of responses to include in the "menu", (b) the bias that can arise from the position of such responses in the "menu", and (c) the question of whether the alternatives should be balanced or unbalanced.

(a) The number of responses. In order to capture, fully, a sample's range of possible responses, all possible responses should be included in the "menu" of alternatives; this is clearly impractical; think, for example, of the number of different car makes that are available?

Imagine the question, "What type of car do you own?" The list of alternatives would be prohibitively long and an edited list would necessarily exclude certain makes that some respondents might own, resulting in a "none of these" response which is clearly inaccurate. However, from your knowledge of normal distribution, you will know that the majority of respondents will own motor cars from a fairly limited range of manufacturers. Exploratory/secondary research will give the constructor of the questionnaire a good indication as to those makes which should be included in the "menu" of alternatives and which will capture the responses of the majority of those sampled. An "insurance policy" alternative answer of "any other makes, please specify" will ensure that all respondents have the opportunity to reply accurately.

(b) The position of the responses. In some cases, bias may arise when there is a preferential choice of one alternative over others, not because this is the respondent's choice which most accurately reflects the true state of affairs but because of the physical position of the alternative on the "menu". To reduce positional bias, different versions of the questionnaire can be prepared. One order of alternatives may give what will be called a "negative" bias, another order of alternatives a "positive" bias; their combined effect will be a reduction in the overall bias due to position. However, this type of bias can never be fully eradicated.

(c) Balanced versus unbalanced alternative responses. A balanced set of alternative responses would consist of something like the following, where there is an equal number of responses on each side of the centre/neutral point.

Question, "What do you think of marketing research theory?"

1	2	3	4	5
Very boring	Boring	Indifferent	Interesting	Very interesting

An unbalanced set of alternative responses could resemble the following, where there is an unbalanced set of responses; the alternatives are not equally displayed around the centre/neutral point.

Question, "What do you think of marketing research theory?"

1	2	3	4	5
Mind-bogglingly boring	Extremely boring	Very boring	Somewhat boring	Indifferent

Such a category of response should only be used if there is strong evidence, from secondary/exploratory research or from the questionnaire's pilot study, to suggest that this latter, unbalanced, case will be the one most likely to occur.

Check-lists
A check-list question is one where respondents are presented with a list of items from which they can select those that most closely approximate to their answer; they may pick one item or them all, if that is appropriate. An "insurance policy" question of "If not any of these, please state which" will cover the possibility that a pertinent alternative has not been provided. Check-lists are especially suited to the gathering of factual and demographic data.

Ranking
In a ranking question, the respondent is asked to make an assessment of the items on the list and then to rank them according to some predetermined criterion.

The disadvantages of this style of answer include the researcher:

(1) having to make the assumption that the respondent has an adequate knowledge of all the items on the list, and

(2) having to acknowledge the fact that ranking questions do not allow the respondent to express the amount by which each item is preferred. Because it is a straight first, second, third etc., system, the situation where the second item is three or four times more preferred to the third item remains hidden.

Scales
Scales have the advantage that they are able to turn what may be a qualitative response into a quantitative one. More attention is devoted to this topic in Chapter Nine.

(5) Question sequence

Again, there are no nostra, no prescriptions and no magic wands that can be waved to guarantee a well-sequenced questionnaire, free from all potential error. But there are guidelines that can be used to try to ensure that potential errors are reduced.

(a) Use the initial questions as an opera composer would use an overture; to engage interest, to reassure and to give a foretaste of what is to follow—but like a good composer, do not squander all your best tunes (questions) at once. Do not be tempted to dive into the heart of the questionnaire, with complex, intricate questions—those that should form the kernel of the study.

Respondents may be anxious about the interview situation and will need reassurance, something that they will not receive from difficult questions so early on in the interchange. If any of the initial questions are of a potentially embarrassing nature then they might meet a firm respondent refusal to answer; keep this type of question until much later in the questionnaire, by which time the interviewer should have built up a sufficiently good rapport with the respondent; the questions will then not appear so problematic.

Anxiety-inducing or potentially embarrassing questions may receive a refusal to answer; in extreme cases, they may cause enough affront to respondents that they refuse to answer any further questions. If these types of question are left until the end of the questionnaire and yet respondents still refuse to answer them, at least the majority of the questionnaire will have been completed and the item non-response rate will be low.

(b) Avoid questions which suggest the answer to subsequent questions as this will cause bias; i.e. do not put ideas into the minds of the respondents.

(c) Overall, the questions should move from the general to the specific. Topics should be grouped together and inside each grouping questions should move from the general to the specific. There should also be a logical flow from question to question and from topic to topic.

(d) Ensure that all questions relating to one topic are asked before moving on to another topic; asking questions in a "grasshopper" manner will make it difficult for the respondent to follow your train of thought; it will also make the analysis of the questionnaire unnecessarily complicated.

(6) Questionnaire layout

Administered questionnaires should be easy for the respondent to use; ease of use will enable the responses to be recorded with the minimum of error. Questionnaires that are to be used in a mail survey or in self-administered form should also be attractive as there will be no interviewer present to argue their case. A badly presented, messily printed questionnaire is just as likely to cause non-response or measurement error as badly constructed questions.

Design considerations include:

(a) Paper quality: use good quality paper, especially if the questionnaire is of the "stand alone" variety.

(b) Size: if a questionnaire is long, or if it appears long (even if it is not), it may discourage the respondent from even starting to answer the questionnaire. Therefore, try to keep the bulk of the questionnaire as low as possible, but do not feel tempted to reduce the size of the questionnaire by, for example, photo-reduction, if by so doing the print size is made so small as to make extended reading tiresome.

(c) Spacing: do not try and reduce the overall size of the work by squashing everything together. Use spacing (but not too much) to break up solid blocks of text.

(d) Type face: solid blocks of text may be made to appear less dense by using different type faces. Instructions are important, they can be made to stand out by the use of different styles of print type.

(e) Colour: to add interest, consider the use of different coloured inks. But careful choice is involved to ensure that the print is still easy to read, especially if coloured paper is also used.

(f) Routing/branching instructions: these guide the respondent through the questionnaire, and need to be precise and user-friendly; one should not need a PhD in computer programming to be able to work one's way through a series of questions. Instructions should be kept to a minimum; they should enable the respondent to move comfortably from one question to the next appropriate question. Routing and branching instructions should be robustly tested when the questionnaire is piloted, as they are often a source of great confusion.

(g) Responding: ensure that it is made clear how respondents should answer and that it is easy for them so to do. It helps if the response boxes are placed in the same position vis-à-vis each of the questions. This helps the respondent to answer all the questions because gaps may be seen easily.

(h) Open-ended questions: research suggests that the more lines that are offered to respondents for answering an open-ended question, the more they write. Calculate, therefore, the amount of space needed to capture the essentials of respondents' answers without encouraging them to write an essay. Remember, their answers will require analysis. This calculation can be helped by experimenting with different amounts of space when the questionnaire is piloted.

(7) Pretest, revision and final version of the questionnaire

It is almost impossible to produce a "perfect" questionnaire, at a first attempt. Questionnaires, when they are first drafted, are full of questions that are ambiguous, contain cumbersome double-negatives, are double-barrelled or are too vague. Instructions may be confusing, it may be too long and variables that should have been included may have been omitted.

To issue a questionnaire that has not been pretested is foolhardy.

The pretest is a way of uncovering faults before it is too late. It is also important in ensuring that the questionnaire will gather the information that it is intended to gather.

Questionnaires are not written for the benefit of those that devise them, they are written to gain information from the respondents. Therefore, it is to respondents that one should turn when it comes to pretesting questionnaires. A small sub-sample of the intended respondent group is chosen, perhaps 10 to 15. Try not to include only average respondents; those that lie to the extremes of the sample type may contribute much that is useful (Aaker and Day, 1990).

The pretest can be run as a debriefing session or by using the protocol method.

The debriefing method

The questionnaire is presented to the respondents in exactly the same manner as it would be in a real study. When the interview has been completed or when the questionnaire has been filled in, the respondents are examined on their thought processes while completing the questions and on whether there were any problems with such items as routing and branching instructions, comprehensibility of questions etc.

The protocol method

The protocol method involves the respondents "thinking aloud" as the interview progresses or as they fill in the questionnaire.

Comments from both types of pretest can then be used to refine the questions and the way in which the questionnaire is designed and presented. Those involved with the research should pay particular attention to such areas as whether:

(1) the meaning of the questions is clear,

(2) the questions are easy to answer,

(3) the questions flow logically from one to another,

(4) the routing/branching instructions are clear,

(5) the questionnaire is too long,

(6) the questionnaire engages and retains the respondents' interest.

Answers to these questions should to used to refine the questionnaire before it is issued in its final form. With complicated, technical questionnaires, it may be necessary to pretest several times over, the comments being used to refine the work after each occasion.

Reliability and validity in questionnaire design

Errors which arise from sampling, non-response and interviewer bias, for example, have been discussed at the appropriate points in the text, as have the problems which occur because of the characteristics of the respondents; inability to answer, unwillingness to answer, ignorance etc. The area of interest to be discussed now is that of reliability and validity in the use of questionnaire techniques.

The questionnaire may be used to measure facts and/or opinions; the question of reliability and validity for the latter subject will be covered in Chapter Nine; here, reliability and validity in the case of factual questions will be dealt with.

Reliability, as was stated in Chapter Two, refers to the consistency in reaching the same result when the measurement is made over and over again. Validity refers to the degree to which the question measures what it is supposed to be measuring. A valid measure will always be reliable, a reliable measure does not guarantee validity.

A car's speedometer which reads 10 m.p.h. too fast consistently shows a figure that is incorrect. When the car is moving at 40 m.p.h. the speedometer will always show 50 m.p.h.; in that sense it is reliable. But it is not valid; if it were, then it would show the true figure—40 m.p.h. A valid speedometer at 40 m.p.h. will always show 40 m.p.h.; it is both valid and reliable.

Pretesting, revision and further testing a questionnaire may very well refine the research tool and increase the reliability of its ability to measure consistently, but that does not necessarily mean that the validity will also be increased.

One way to ensure that an instrument really does measure what it is supposed to be measuring is to compare the results with a "yard-stick"—an external measurement. However, if such a comparison is to be made, researchers should ensure that the criteria that are chosen are appropriate. To help increase the reliability of a questionnaire when matters of fact are being measured, internal checks can be included. That is, questions concerned with the same fact/situation are scattered throughout the questionnaire, though they should not be so blatant as to appear in exactly the same form each time they are used.

A question "Did you buy any washing powder last week?" could be followed, several questions later, by "Which of the following items did you purchase last week?"; the respondent is then shown a cue-card with a list of standard shopping items, including washing powder.

Apparent inconsistencies, e.g. a person of 16 years claiming to have a very high income, can be resolved by careful and tactful cross-examination.

Reliability when questionnaires are used in panel research can be estimated by face-to-face interviews with a sub-sample of the respondents.

To estimate the validity of factual answers usually requires that the researcher consult other sources of information, secondary data or census reports. When the original survey method is a mail questionnaire, the validity may be checked by conducting a series of face-to-face interviews with a sub-sample of the respondents. This is done on the assumption (Belson, 1986) that a face-to-face interview will generate more valid data than a mail questionnaire.

A further point to be taken into account when considering validity and reliability is that of the use to which the results of the survey are to be put.

Oppenheim (1984) notes that some surveys are used for the purposes of prediction. A survey may have excellent validity, in the descriptive sense, at the time it was taken and yet have poor validity in its ability to predict an outcome accurately. Between the time of the respondents' measurements and the occurrence of the actual event, many factors may have had an impact. Valid descriptors often make poor predictors.

Summary

Questionnaire design is the art of the practical not of the perfect. With specific reference to the topic of the design process there are many limiting factors which have to be considered. General considerations to be borne in mind include the overall objectives of the research, the types of data analysis that are to be used, the budget and the time constraints; the design of the questionnaire has to fit in with all of these.

The notion that good questionnaire design can be guaranteed by the rigid pursuit of rules has, it is hoped, been removed. But good questionnaire design can be done. Be sure in your mind as to what the questionnaire is meant to do, use your common sense, and, above all, think the process through from the viewpoint of those people who will have to provide you with the necessary data—the respondents.

References

Aaker D. A. and Day G. S. (1990) *Marketing Research*, John Wiley and Sons, New York.

Belson W. A. (1986) *Validity in Survey Research*, Gower Publishing, Aldershot, Hants, and Brookfield, Vermont.

Kinnear, T. C. and Taylor J. R. (1991) *Marketing Research*, McGraw-Hill, New York, 3rd edition.

Luck D. J. and Rubin D. S. (1987) *Marketing Research*, Prentice-Hall, 7th edition.

Oppenheim A. N. (1984) *Questionnaire Design and Attitude Measurement*, Heinemann, London.

Payne S. L. (1951) *The Art of Asking Questions*, Princeton University Press, Princeton, New Jersey.

Tull D. S. and Hawkins D. I. (1990) *Marketing Research: Measurement and Method*, Macmillan, New York, 5th edition.

CHAPTER SEVEN

Qualitative Research

Introduction   112
Group discussions   114
Individual depth interviews   121
Projective techniques   125
Observation   130
References   133

Introduction

In Chapter Five, it was stated that there are two basic ways of gathering information from respondents: observation and survey, i.e. you can watch them or you can ask them questions.

But when describing the way in which questions could be asked, or should be asked, it soon became apparent that not every research topic is best served by the interrogative style of questioning. Knowledge of facts and the reporting of past and present behaviour patterns are all "grist" to a questioner's "mill". But there were other topics which were not so well treated in this manner; embarrassing or anxiety-inducing questions, those concerned with prestige, with motivation, with privacy and with those topics to which people cannot reply through an inability to put their answer into words.

For such topics, marketing research has invented, or more properly, appropriated, a range of methods from other disciplines, notably sociology, psychology and anthropology.

The techniques so annexed include group discussions, individual depth interviews, projective/enabling methods and observation. They are referred to, as a group, as qualitative research methods.

Qualitative research is principally used for answering the "how", the "why" and the "what" types of question. It is not used for the "how many" questions; that is the provenance of the survey and quantitative research schools of thought.

Gordon and Langmaid (1988), in their fascinating book *Qualitative Market Research*, provide a comparison between qualitative and quantitative research.

Qualitative	Quantitave
Open-ended, dynamic flexible	Statistical and numerical measurement
Depth of understanding	Sub-group sampling or comparisons
Taps consumer creativity	Survey can be repeated in the future and results compared
Database—broader and deeper	Taps individual responses
Penetrates rationalised or superficial responses	Less dependent on research executive skills or orientation
Richer source of ideas for marketing and creative teams	

Gordon and Langmead state that qualitative research is used optimally for situations which will increase understanding, expand knowledge, clarify the real issues, generate hypotheses, identify a range of behaviours, explain and explore consumer motivations, attitudes and behaviour, identify distinct behavioural groups and provide an input to a future stage of research/ development.

Qualitative research, they add, is most often used for:

basic exploratory studies,
new product development,
creative development,
diagnostic studies,
tactical research projects.

Group discussions and individual depth interviews have both advantages and disadvantages. In certain circumstances each may be more appropriate than the other; in other situations both may be used, their individual strengths and weaknesses acting as a complement to each other.

Projective techniques involve presenting a stimulus or stimuli so that their interpretation or meaning comes out of the experience of the respondent. The reasoning is that this "meaning" will reveal personality, interests, opinions and attitudes of the respondent; by using projective and enabling techniques, such barriers as "repression and the unconscious, self-awareness, rationality and social influences" (Braithwaite and Lunn, 1985) may be overcome, allowing researchers to explore individuals at a deeper level than respondents are conscious of or are capable of putting into words.

Group discussions

All people, at some points in their lives, gain experience of being a member of a group; in their education, in their profession and in their leisure activities. The latter experience is of only peripheral interest in the context of this work, but the work experience and, particularly the experience gained in education, is of some pertinence.

We learn in several ways, by being taught in formal, highly structured classes and lectures, by practising a piano or by trying to plane a length of wood, and also from the experience of others; the "experience of others" is the basis on which group discussions partially rest.

But merely gathering a number of people together in a room and asking them a set of questions and then recording their answers is not, in marketing research terms, what is understood as a group discussion—there does not seem to be much "discussion" in a process organised in such a manner.

Group discussion, in modern marketing research terms, means not only the involvement of a question and answer component, but also the dynamics and the process of interaction between respondents.

Group discussions usually last from one hour to two hours and the number of respondents can vary between six and ten: "with less than six the advantage of reducing numbers often begins to taper off", with larger groups it "... becomes hard for the interviewer to control. More timid people easily get squeezed out. The group tends to fragment, different sub-groups pursuing their own conversations simultaneously" (Hedges, 1981).

Bellenger, Bernhardt and Goldstucker (1976) say that group discussions may be used for the following purposes.

(1) Generating hypotheses that may be further tested quantitatively.

(2) Generating information helpful in constructing questionnaires for use with consumers.

(3) Providing background information on a product category.

(4) Gaining reactions to new product concepts in the absence of secondary data.

(5) Stimulating new ideas concerning older products.

(6) Generating ideas for new creative concepts.

(7) Helping to interpret previously obtained quantitative results.

However, as a balance to the above list, Gordon and Langmaid (1988) provide the following list to show where group discussions alone are not the most appropriate techniques.

(1) In intimate or personal situations.

(2) In situations where there are strong social norms which pressure people into conformity.

(3) In cases where a detailed life history is important.

(4) In situations where a group is likely to be too heterogeneous with respect to the characteristic of interest.

(5) In cases where an understanding of "complex psycho-sociological issues" is involved.

(6) In cases where it is difficult to recruit the required sample, e.g. specialists or those who are physically widely dispersed.

The group discussion in practice

Getting started
Respondents may be selected for inclusion in a group discussion by sampling the population of interest using either probability or non-probability techniques, the choice being primarily dependent upon the overall objectives of the research.

The respondents will arrive at the chosen location, which should be conveniently sited, in a wide range of nervous states: shy, boastful, self-conscious, nervous, worried, full of false bravado etc. In other words, they will act exactly as one would expect normal human beings to act, given that they are about to face a novel situation of which they know very little and may fear a great deal; hardly the atmosphere which will render useful, valid data.

A point to bear in mind when conducting group discussions is that of the conflict that occurs when an individual is placed in the setting of a group. On one hand there is the need to be seen as an individual with his/her own unique personality and characteristics and, on the other, the desire to be part of a group, to be "one of the gang". It is the moderator's job to accept that this conflict exists and to use, in a constructive way, the resultant tension.

It is incumbent on the person in charge, usually called the moderator, to put all the respondents at their ease, to bring out those that would like to crawl under the carpet and to calm down those who hold the potential to be overbearing and to dominate the proceedings.

This can be done in the following ways:

(1) Use a relatively formal physical setting, with comfortable chairs placed round a large conference-style table.

(2) Keep all recording instruments, such as video cameras and tape-recorders as much out of sight as possible without impairing their function.

(3) Have a ready supply of tea/coffee and soft drinks. With an especially "frosty" group, a glass of wine may help to "unfreeze" them a little.

(4) Introduce yourself individually to each respondent as he/she enters the room.

(5) Get each respondent to introduce him/herself, when everyone is present, and to tell the group a little about him/herself.

(6) Give a short introduction to the group and tell them the "rules" that will be followed when the discussion proper starts.

The discussion

Gordon and Langmaid (1988) have divided up the process of the discussion into five groups, which they call "forming, storming, norming, performing and mourning". The group, they say, will not be aware of these different steps, but the moderator should be conscious of the stage that has been reached, so that the moderator "may work with them to facilitate the completion of the task rather than against them or in spite of them". Without knowing what stage has been reached, the moderator will not know "when it is possible to introduce new material, invite disclosures, close up or finish the group in a satisfactory manner".

The following five sections are substantially based on the work of Gordon and Langmaid (1988).

Forming
As this is a group activity, everyone should be given the opportunity to speak within the first five minutes of the start of the discussion; otherwise the anxiety of those excluded will build. If individual respondents are not included they may feel rejected and the others, acting as a group, may either band together to "rescue" the neglected discussant or dissociate themselves from that individual.

Storming
This is the stage where power relationships within the group are worked out. Some may start "storming" at the first available opportunity, others will hold back until they have assessed the "competition".

"Storming" can erupt at any time during the discussion process, but it is particularly prone to happen when a new topic or a new form of stimulus is introduced.

Norming
This is the stage of "acceptance and agreement'; or when differences are accepted and where experiences begin to be shared.

Once this stage has settled, it is time to go on to the next stage, "performing", where the real task, for which the group has been assembled, is to be undertaken.

Performing
Gordon and Langmaid (1988) call this "task-orientated cooperative activity". Revelations and insights should appear, they say, and the mood of the group is constructive.

New task/stimulus may start up a bout of "storming", but this will soon settle and the group will revert to the "performing" phase.

Mourning
Warn the group, about five minutes before the end of the allotted time, that the "end is nigh" and ask them if there is anything they said that they did not mean, if there is anything that they want to say or if they have any final remarks.

Diagrammatically the entire process may be represented thus:

forming → storming → norming → performing → mourning

Group dynamics

Two important factors have a profound influence on the group dynamics—on the manner of the interactions between individual group members:

(1) The mood of the group members
If respondents arrive for the discussion in an anxious, fearful, frightened mood, they are likely to react in several ways. They might stay cowed for the remainder of the meeting, not offering any opinions, seeking to take a back seat etc. Or they might be angry at being placed in such an uncomfortable position and adopt an "angry silent" state (what was once described to the author as the ability to "radiate misery"). Or they might go another way altogether and try to bluff and fight their way out of their embarrassment.

It is the responsibility of the moderator to reduce all of these fears; they can be corrosive and destroy the conducive atmosphere which is important if a group is going to be capable of listening to each other and of learning from each other.

(2) The group itself
As far as moderators are concerned, groups fall into one of two main camps: good and bad. A sweeping generalisation, it is true, as in the course of a discussion, a single group may vary from one to the other. But it is usual, in the main, for it to remain "good" or "bad".

A good group tends to be open, friendly, humorous, vital and focused. A bad group tends to be defensive, tense, closed and hostile (Gordon and Langmaid, 1988). The former is obviously to be preferred, so how does one arrive at such an enviable state?

The responsibility falls heavily on the shoulders of the moderator. As well as keeping tabs on what stage the discussion has reached he/she is also trying to map out the areas that still have to be covered. Simultaneously, the moderator will be controlling (or trying to control) the dynamics of the group. And this means that the shy members will have to be encouraged to speak out, the "angry silent" types to abandon their self-imposed Siberia and the dominators to keep quiet for a while to give the others a chance to voice their views.

The shy ones can be encouraged to speak by directly asking them "What's your opinion on that?", but do not make them feel as if they have suddenly been brought before the inquisition. One way to soften the blow, as Hedges (1981) suggests, is to say, after an important remark, "That's an interesting point, I'd like to get everyone's view on that", and then ask around the table. The same method can be used to close down someone who has been a little too free with their comments.

However, if that is seen as too strong, then make use of eye contact. People tend to carry on speaking if they are being looked at; when their conversational partner looks away, they tend to stop talking. Use eye contact with the shy members to encourage them to speak; withdraw eye contact to quieten a dominant personality.

The use of the much mocked concept of body-language may also be of some help. Retiring, shy group members can be encouraged to speak by leaning towards them; dominant members can be discouraged from further loquacity by leaning away from them. Smile to encourage, do not smile to discourage.

If some member of the group makes a point which causes a large amount of disagreement, then in order to stop that member being shouted down the moderator can "legitimise" the remark by saying something like "That's an interesting point of view. I have heard that at other sessions in this room." It stops the sole respondent from becoming swamped but does not mean that the moderator has to put forward his/her own views as a way of defending the lone voice.

Advantages of group discussions

Cost and speed
As one moderator can interact with between six and ten respondents, it is both quicker and cheaper than interviewing them individually. It provides the opportunity to save both time and money while the actual discussion is in progress, but also in the amount of time and the costs which must be devoted to the analysis of the data which will be generated.

The social dimension
Many of the decisions made by an individual are taken against a social background; groups provide that context. The requirements and perspectives of

other members of society are considered as part of the discussion process and not as an "add-on", a situation which might occur in an individual interview.

Observation

Group discussion allows the observation of non-verbal communications, which enables the moderator and/or those analysing the results (when they have been recorded on video) to make an assessment of the validity of the respondent's statements.

Stimulation

A wide range of opinions, which will be provided by the respondent's colleagues, helps to stimulate individual respondents to analyse their own beliefs, attitudes, opinions and feelings. Respondents can find it difficult to articulate their inner beliefs etc., and this is a major drawback to many of the research methods in survey research. In a group setting, people are both helped and stimulated by other group members and by the interaction with them to articulate such beliefs and attitudes.

Creative

Stimulation not only helps respondents to articulate buried beliefs, it has also been found useful in generating ideas.

Less threatening

Respondents in a group may feel "comforted" and less exposed than they would in an individual interview. Their anxiety is reduced, which may allow them to produce more honest, valid and accurate responses.

Probing

The unstructured or semi-structured nature of group discussions allows the moderator to probe behind those respondent answers that are vague, incomplete and ambiguous.

Disadvantages of group discussions

Unrepresentativeness

Because of the small numbers of respondents used in group discussions, the problem of unrepresentativeness is raised. The ability to generalise about a population may thus be constrained. But this does not totally invalidate the method as a viable research tool, if it is used in those situations where statistical projections onto a population are not required, e.g. in exploratory research.

Embarrassment
This is the converse of the case "less threatening", as mentioned above. Some members of a group may feel overawed and inhibited by the other members of the group, thus, maybe, encouraging them to respond in a way which presents themselves in a good light, or to "trade-up" their reported behaviour.

Reactions to other respondents
Shy respondents may get "shouted down" by those with louder voices and/or more dominant personalities.

Reactions to the moderator
In group discussions the moderator occupies a pivotal position; much depends upon him/her. If the group reacts against the moderator, then the chances of obtaining valid and useful data are much reduced.

Case study: qualitative research for consumer products

In 1977, the Milk Marketing Board decided to investigate consumer attitudes and behaviour towards fresh cream cakes. The research was commissioned to answer a need for up-to-date information, which might have changed since the last study, on which to found strategies for future marketing and advertising exercises.

Stage One. A preliminary qualitative study to "provide a qualitative understanding of consumer attitudes and behaviour in this market..."

Stage Two. A quantitative study designed to produce data concerned with purchasing and eating behaviour, product image and related consumer attitudes.

Stage Three. A qualitative creative study to guide the formulation of a new advertising campaign for the product.

Stage One

This consisted of using 14 group discussions, comprising six groups of "heavy" buyers of cream cakes—housewives from BC1C2D social classes in the South, the Midlands and the North, six groups of "high" and of "non-buyers" of cream cakes from the same mix of social classes and geographical locations; and two groups of freezer owners who bought cream cakes at least once a month. Analysis of the results from the group discussions revealed, amongst other factors, that the cakes' appearance was "highly motivating", that the cakes were thought of as a "treat" and that they were seen as more of an "adult" confection.

Stage Two

This part of the research consisted of a survey of 1250 housewives from five categories of cake buyers: very heavy, heavy, medium, light and non-buyers. The results of this survey suggested that any future advertising campaign should seek to maintain the allegiance of current and future purchasers of cream cakes and that the advertising should try to enhance the appeal and eating pleasures to be gained from fresh cream cakes, "concentrating upon personal self-indulgence versus family treat motives".

Stage Three

Taking the results of the first two stages, a range of creative ideas was developed, the best three of which were made into "rough" TV advertisements. Stage Three's function was to investigate the potential strengths and weaknesses of these three "routes" and to guide directions as to which might be the most effective in meeting marketing strategies and to suggest possible improvements.

Concentrating upon the "heavy" user stratum of buyers, six group discussions were conducted.

The results of these discussions were that the "naughty cakes route" held the potential to be able to fulfil the strategic objectives.

The subsequent advertising campaign was based upon the "naughty... but nice" theme: a campaign which ran successfully for eight years. (From Dickens, 1987.)

Individual depth interviews

In some sectors of the social sciences, individual depth interviews have become very important. Indeed, Benney and Hughes (1956) talked of modern sociology in terms of it becoming the "science of the interview". In marketing research the situation has not reached that stage, but in certain circumstances it is a most valuable and widely used instrument. The two extremes of the interview spectrum could be said to be the structured–direct and the unstructured–indirect. The former would appear to be our old friend the administered questionnaire where an interviewer reads out a series of set questions, with fixed wording in a predetermined order; not much "interviewing" there! The latter method, unstructured–indirect, as has been noted before, is better suited to a psychiatrist's consulting room. The current zone of interest is somewhat towards the centre of the range, what Kinnear and Taylor (1991) have defined as "an unstructured personal interview which uses extensive probing to get a single respondent to talk freely and to express detailed beliefs and feelings on a topic". Thus although the "conversation with a purpose" has to have a purpose—it must be going somewhere—the lack of rigid structure is important.

In a work which is worth quoting at length, Jones (1981) has said

> "Interviews in which interviewers have prepared a long list of questions which they are determined to ask, come what may, over a period, say, of an hour and a half, are not depth interviews. This is so even if the researchers are contingent enough to alter the exact wording and order of their questions and even if the questions all centre around the same broad topic. For in this way the interviewers have already predicted, in detail, what is relevant and meaningful to their respondents about the research topic; and in doing this they have significantly pre-structured the direction of the enquiry within their own frame of reference in ways that give little time and space for their respondents to elaborate their own."

Individual depth interviews and group discussions are both techniques which are trying to understand, to search out, to explore. And in so doing, one of their main requirements is a flexibility of approach which can alter and respond to the different and changing circumstances of the situation. Explorers do not explore, detailed map in hand; if they did so they would not be explorers (there would be no need for an explorer in such cases) but tourists. Structured questionnaires or research methods which rely on strict interview schedules are the "Guides Michelin" of the research world.

The interviewer will not be totally cast adrift; there is a purpose to be accomplished. There is an implicit contract between interviewer and respondent to explore a certain part of the terrain. The respondent has to provide an amount of information, the interviewer, with the research objectives in mind, has to try to uncover and "decode" this information.

In-depth individual interviews have been found to be particularly useful in the following circumstances:

(1) Where the situation under discussion holds the potential to be embarrassing, to be stressful or to be of a confidential nature.

(2) Where a detailed analysis needs to be conducted of complex situations, such as attitudes, beliefs and feelings.

(3) Where peer pressure may cause some respondents to say that they conform to societal norms which are against their true behaviour.

(4) Where the interviewer needs to gain a progressive set of images of a decision process, such as buying behaviour.

(5) In novel, complex situations where the prime intention is to explore rather than to measure.

Getting started

Just as with other research methods that take place within a social context, the nature of the interchange between the researcher and the respondent is important; perhaps more important in this case than in the others. It is a one-to-one experience; the respondent is out there in full view of the interviewer, picked out in the glare of the spot-light. They cannot run away (or if they could, it is most unlikely that they would), and there are no other respondents who can be used to draw the fire; at its worst an individual depth interview can be a very frightening and unnerving experience.

All the suggestions that have already been given concerning the early establishment of rapport are to be employed.

The reaction of the respondent to the interviewer can dominate the way that they (the respondents) view the research situation. The interviewer's accent, mode of dress, body language, facial expressions, timbre of voice etc., are all factors which the interviewer will have to be prepared to manipulate to give a first impression to the respondent which reassures, encourages, flatters. Conducting interviews can feel a bit like giving a "performance". No one will suggest that an interviewer has to like all the respondents that are examined, which is why it is being suggested that one must give the impression of liking them. In any case, interviewers have to examine such a wide range of respondent types that even if all of them are likeable, an amount of "acting" is called for to establish rapport across the board. One would not present to an interviewee, a managing director for example, the same type of "face" as one would to an eighteen-year-old reformed drug addict.

Incidentally, rapport is not something that one "establishes" and then dives into the heart of the interview and forgets about. Rapport does have to be established, but it also has to be maintained throughout the length of the interchange.

"Performing" aside, a further way of establishing rapport is to describe to the interviewee the boundaries that circumscribe the interview situation. This will give the respondent a context for the research and for their answers. Respondents should also be told as much about the purpose of the research as is possible; why the interview is to be recorded (if it is), and above all, the interviewer should stress the value that will be placed upon the respondent's answers and the fact that they will be treated *in the strictest confidence*. No one will talk freely to an interviewer if they think that they will be mocked or that by answering they expose themselves to danger. If that occurs, respondents react by not answering at all or by lying to "protect" themselves.

The interview

Very little can be prescribed, in advance, as to the way in which an interview *must* be conducted; so much is dependent upon the respondent, the subject matter and the skill of the interviewer.

As with survey research methods, it is always better to start with the rapport establishing questions (and once established, rapport will need to be maintained for the remainder of the interview) and then build to those areas which hold the potential to be embarrassing for the respondent. On top of this schema is the idea that the interviewer should try to move from the general to the specific, and from topic to topic, in a logical manner.

Interviewer skills

It must be quite clear by now that the abilities of the interviewer are of paramount importance when conducting in-depth individual interviews. It is their skills which "tame" the "difficult" interviewee and which "entice" the shy and the nervous.

What then are the skills that a competent interviewer requires?

The Market Research Society (1979) produced the following list:

intellectual ability/common sense,

imagination/logic,

conceptual ability/an eye for detail,

detachedness/involvement,

"neutral" self-projection/"instant" empathy,

non-stereotypical thinking/capacity to spot the typical,

expertise with words/good listener,

literary flair/ability to summarise concisely,

analytical thinking/tolerance of disorder.

While it would be difficult to imagine such a paragon of virtue, it does give prospective interviewers some guidelines as to those qualities that should be aimed for. It might also provide a salutary experience for those who think that interviewing, like the ability to ride a bicycle, is learnt once and never forgotten!

Advantages of individual depth interviews

(1) The great depth and richness of the data.

(2) The ability to ascribe, directly, a response to a single individual (something which may be difficult when a group discussion is in progress) (Kinnear and Taylor, 1991).

(3) The ability to develop a close rapport and a high degree of trust between interviewer and respondent; this may encourage a freer flow of conversation and more valid results.

(4) Lack of overt peer pressure to conform to societal, or other, norms. The one-to-one relationship between the partners in an interview situation

allows for the expression of non-conformity without fear of sanctions, mockery or embarrassment.

Disadvantages of individual depth interviews

(1) Costly in terms of time and money to conduct the interview and to analyse the results.

(2) The need to find and recruit highly skilled interviewers, on whose facility the whole principle of individual depth interviewing rests.

(3) Because of the time and cost constraints, it is usually possible to work only with small samples which may limit the ability to generalise about complete populations.

(4) With the necessarily high amount of subjectivity that an interviewer has to exercise, it may be difficult to compare the results obtained by one interviewer with those from second and third interviewers.

Projective techniques

Two of the most commonly imitated tests in psychoanalysis are the word association test and the Rorschach ink-blot test; both of these are examples of projective techniques. They rely on the assumption that the way a respondent goes about organising those relatively ambiguous stimuli will give some indication of the respondent's perceptions of the outside world and the way in which they react to it.

As Kidder (1981) says, projective techniques are useful in "...encouraging in respondents a state of freedom and spontaneity of expression where there is reason to believe that respondents cannot easily evaluate or describe their motivations or feelings... or where topics on which a respondent may hesitate to express their opinions directly for fear of disapproval by the investigator or when respondents are likely to consider direct questions as an unwarranted invasion of privacy or to find them threatening for some other reason".

Respondents are asked either to talk about other people, their (the other people's) feelings, attitudes and opinions or about objects or situations. By talking about third parties or objects the theory is that respondents will "project" their own feelings—feelings which would previously have remained covert—onto the third party or object. Once they are overt—out in the open—they may be discussed.

Projective techniques may be used with individuals as well as with groups. They may be classed as a structured–indirect way of investigating the "whys" of a situation. They are not usually used to measure (that is more the territory of other techniques such as the survey), but to uncover those topics such as feelings, beliefs, attitudes and motivation which many respondents have difficulty in articulating.

Projective techniques may be used to:

(1) Explore and generate hypotheses.

(2) Uncover feelings, attitudes, behaviour patterns and motivations.

(3) Gain access to respondents' answers which are denied the researcher when using other, more direct, methods of investigation.

There are a great many different types of projective technique, certainly far too many for a work of this kind to be able to describe them in anything other than rather simple terms. The techniques may be described under the following headings: completion; association; construction; choice ordering; expressive techniques.

(a) Completion

Respondents are asked to complete sentences, stories or conversations.

Sentence completion
The beginning part of a sentence is read out to the respondent who then has to complete it. For example, "I think that people who smoke in theatre bars are..."

The beginning of the sentence should be constructed so as *not* to suggest the way in which the respondent is supposed to answer; i.e. it should not lead.

Brand mapping
Brand mapping, according to Gordon and Langmaid (1988), is a completion exercise widely used in industry. A variety of competing brands are displayed to respondents who are then asked to group them according to some respondent-stipulated characteristic. It may be used to reveal gaps in the market for a product; this technique has been found useful in new product development. It may also be used as a way of gaining an understanding of how respondents view a product market.

(b) Association

Word association
A series of words is read out to the respondent who is then asked to speak or write the first word that comes to mind. In marketing research, the technique may be used to test potential product names, advertisements, packaging and personalities who are being considered as possible endorsers of a product.

Examples include:

"What is the first thing you think of when I say breakfast?

"Give me a word you associate with Buster Keaton?"

Results are commonly analysed by noting the frequency with which words or groups of words occur after each stimulus word.

Word association can be fun; it is an excellent way of breaking the ice when starting out on a qualitative research session.

Pictures and words

Respondents are given a set of pictures and a set of words printed on cards. They are asked to put together a picture and a word and then to explain their choice.

For example, respondents may be given a picture of a bottle of malt whisky to which they attach the word "slippers". In explanation, the researcher discovers that the respondent only ever drinks whisky as a night-cap, an insight which can be considered when formulating an advertising campaign.

Brand personalities

For this exercise, respondents are asked to associate a brand or a product with a person or a personality type. It can be used to evoke a strong image of the product/brand.

Thus, a Sony compact disc player might be viewed as "a white coated scientist; clean, accurate and objective". A Brand X compact disc player might evoke an image of a "rather grubby little man with an unkempt raincoat and a battered hat".

Another variant is to present respondents with a set of pictures of, say, various types of car or the interiors of houses and then to ask them with which picture they associate the object under discussion. Thus a cheap brand of a product might be seen as beer, while a luxury brand is imagined as being akin to champagne.

(c) Construction

These are more complex exercises, the most well known (and probably the most widely used out of all the projective techniques) being the Thematic Apperception Test. In this, the respondent is presented with a picture or a series of pictures to which he/she has to react. For example, the respondent might be given a picture of someone in the process of buying a washing machine. They then could be asked to explain the situation, to describe the lifestyle of the purchasers and what experiences have led up to this picture and what is the likely course of events in the near future. The process of answering, it is hoped, will reveal what the feelings of the respondent are when going through such a purchase sequence; something which would probably be difficult to get from a respondent by straight questioning.

Cartoon tests

Respondents are given a picture or set of pictures which depicts an ambiguous situation in which the research has an interest. The respondent's job is to fill in the thought "bubbles" of the characters in the cartoon. It might show a drawing of a housewife, opener in hand, about to tackle a can of soup; the woman has an empty thought "bubble" coming out of her mouth into which the respondent has to write his/her "thoughts".

(d) Choice ordering

Respondents are asked to rank or to order or to put into categories certain factors associated with a product, brand or service.

For example, respondents might be presented with a list of words from which they have to select those they think are more appropriate to describe a bank. Or they could be asked to rank, in importance, the various services that a bank provides.

(e) Expressive techniques

The most popular and widely used of these techniques is that of role playing, where a respondent enacts the role of another person or of a product/brand. The theory is that the respondent will imbue that third party/object with his/her own feelings.

Thus a respondent might be asked to play the part of a salesman trying to door-step his way round a neighbourhood with a suitcase full of domestic cleaning impedimenta or be asked to play the role of a lawnmower.

Advantages of projective techniques

(1) Useful in the exploratory stages of a research project, where ideas and hypotheses are required.

(2) The techniques enable the researcher to gain access to information which is denied them by using other methods of investigation.

(3) May be used as a way of "breaking the ice" with a group when starting a qualitative research project.

Disadvantages of projective techniques

(1) Expensive because of the cost of having to employ highly skilled research staff.

(2) Because of the cost, it is usually possible only to work with small sample sizes; this restricts the possibilities of generalising about the results in relation to the population as a whole.

(3) Very time consuming, both to run the exercises and to analyse the results.

(4) Non-response. Some respondents may not agree to take part in such exercises as role-playing.

(5) Great opportunities for measurement error, as the role of the researcher/ interpreter assumes a very high profile.

Projective techniques: summary and comment

It would be a most unusual research project indeed that used only projective techniques. The small sample sizes involved, the difficulty in interpretation and the limited ability to extrapolate from the sample to the entire population all play their part in, more or less, confining this particular technique to the earlier parts of the research project.

It is usual for projective techniques to be used to "flush out" respondents' attitudes, feelings, beliefs etc., which are normally hidden. Once they have been brought out into the open, other research techniques may then be employed; research techniques which *do* have the ability to render results that can be used to generalise about characteristics/variables possessed by a population; such techniques as have been described in other parts of this work, e.g. survey methods, attitude scales.

Projective methods of research are easy to talk and write about; they are not so easy to put into operation and the analysis of their results can be very difficult. On a personal note, the author would like to add a small word of caution. Many of the techniques that have been described in this chapter have been derived from the realms of psychology and psychoanalysis. Marketing researchers should *never* think of themselves as "amateur" psychologists or psychoanalysts. People's feelings may be covert for reasons which are not the concern of a marketing research project; therefore, great caution, skill and tact needs to be exercised when using these methods. At a party, with friends, it may be acceptable to joke about ink-blot tests, for example, but in a marketing research setting, with "innocent" respondents and with the consultant being viewed in a professional light, it is *not* acceptable.

Observation

Observation, in marketing research terms, could be said to be the institutional-isation of seeing. All members of society observe: shoppers note new retail outlets, sales staff notice when their competitors introduce new models or alter their prices, service staff become aware of a sudden increase in the number of customers returning faulty items. All these are examples of observation, but they are casual observations. And being casual, they are subjective and likely breeding grounds for high measurement error.

Therefore, by institutionalisation is meant an attempt to turn the casual into the planned with an associated change from the subjective to the objective.

Observation may be used for two main reasons:

(1) It may be the only way of gathering certain types of data.

(2) It is a way of confirming that the results obtained by other research methods are valid. So in this case, observation does not stand alone as a research technique, but exists as part of a two-pronged investigation into a situation.

Before an action can be deemed a fit subject for observation it must meet three criteria (Tull and Hawkins, 1990):

(1) The data must be accessible, i.e. it must be overt. (This, of course, will rule out the measurement of such items as feelings, beliefs, motivations and attitudes.)

(2) The action to be observed must be frequent, repetitive and predictable.

(3) The action to be observed can only occupy a reasonably short timespan.

Forming a taxonomy of observational styles is neither easy nor particularly useful.

There are five main components which may be incorporated, in varying degrees, to create a method which is appropriate for the investigation in progress.

These components are:

(1) degree of naturalness,

(2) degree of openness,

(3) degree of structure,

(4) degree of directness,

(5) ratio of human to mechanical observation.

(1) Natural versus contrived observation

Natural observation takes place in the "wild", contrived observation takes place in a "zoo".

Natural observation stands an increased chance of observing real behaviour, free from the effects of an "artificial" setting, but one might have to wait a very long time before the behaviour occurs. Contrived observation involves creating, for example, a supermarket in a laboratory setting and then watching the actions of the respondents. It loses in its naturalness but it gains in its ability to "guarantee" that there will not be too long a wait before the required behaviour occurs. It also, to a certain extent, can be used to reduce the actions of extraneous variables; variables which can affect the results which would be obtained in a natural setting.

(2) Open versus disguised observation

In an open situation the observer can clearly be seen by the respondent. If the presence of the observer is likely to affect the behaviour patterns, then the observer will have to remove him/herself from direct view. This can be done by physical disguise, by observing through a one-way mirror, or via a closed-circuit television system.

(3) Structured versus unstructured observation

With structured observation, the researcher must know what is to be observed; i.e. when the research situation and research objectives have been sufficiently formulated for the data requirements to be unambiguously stipulated. (In this case, structured observation could be used as a confirmation of previously completed research.)

In unstructured research, the situation has not allowed for the data requirements to be predetermined. The technique is mostly used in exploratory research, the investigator being able to check on those actions or behaviour patterns which seem relevant to the research situation.

(4) Direct versus indirect observation

Direct observation takes place while the action/event is actually occurring. Indirect observation involves the examination of evidence relevant to the occurrence of the action/event in the past.

Direct observation is noting a car drive up a path, indirect observation involves the examination of the tyre tracks along a path/road. Other indirect measures are dustbin/garbage audits, as described in Chapter Five; and, for example looking at the noseprints on a museum's glass cases to try to find the most popular items on display.

(5) Human versus mechanical observation

Almost all the techniques described so far have involved humans examining, interviewing and measuring other humans. However, in some situations, the use of a human as a "recording" device is inappropriate or impractical; in such cases they can be replaced by an electrical or mechanical device. Incidentally, video or closed-circuit cameras which either record images for later analysis or transmit them to a monitor screen where the observation takes place will not be covered in this section. They are electro-mechanical devices, but their use is quite straightforward. The instruments discussed here are mostly used in a laboratory setting where they measure the physiological responses of a subject to various stimuli.

Psychogalvanometer
Humans react to stimuli; that is a basic sign of life. One of the ways in which this reaction manifests itself is through perspiration, the amount of perspiration being dependent upon the level of the emotional reaction to stimuli.

Psychogalvanometers are used to measure the changes in perspiration rates of a respondent. Stimuli might include advertisements and brand names.

Eye cameras
It is possible, by the careful alignment of lighting and camera, to track the movements of a respondent's eyes in relation to their field of view. Thus, when exposed to packages, advertisements, film/television commercials etc., researchers can follow the movement of the respondent's eyes, note what they look at first, how long they spend on various portions of the image and what aspects are skipped altogether.

Observation summary

Casual observation has an important role to play in the general day-to-day running of an organisation. But it is not sufficiently rigorous a method for marketing research; for that a more scientific and structured approach is required. Because of its potential to contain large amounts of error, both in measurement and in interpretation, observation is a method best kept for those occasions when all other avenues of research have been eliminated or for the exploratory stages of a research project.

References

Bellenger D., Bernhardt K. L. and Goldstucker J. L. (1976) *Qualitative Research in Marketing*, Monograph Series No. 3, American Marketing Association, Chicago.

Benney M. and Hughes E. C. (1956) Of sociology and the interview, *American Journal of Sociology*, **62**, No. 2, 137–142.

Braithwaite A. and Lunn A. (1985) in *Applied Qualitative Research* (ed. R. Walker), Gower.

Dickens J. (1987) in *Applied Marketing and Social Research* (ed. U. Bradley), John Wiley & Sons, New York, 2nd edition.

Gordon W. and Langmaid R. (1988) *Qualitative Market Research*, Gower.

Hedges A. (1981) An Introduction to Qualitative Research. Paper presented to the Market Research Society, Winter.

Jones S. (1981) Listening to complexity—analysing qualitative marketing research today, *Journal of the Marketing Research Society*, **23**, No. 1, 26–39.

Kidder L. H. (1981) *Sellitz, Wrightsman and Cook's Research Methods in Social Relations*, Holt, Rinehart & Winston, 4th edition.

Kinnear T. C. and Taylor J. R. (1991) *Marketing Research*, McGraw-Hill, 3rd edition.

Marketing Research Society (1979) Sub-committee on Qualitative Research: "Qualitative Research—a Summary of the Concepts Involved".

Tull D. S. and Hawkins D. I. (1990) *Marketing Research; Measurement and Method*, Macmillan, New York, 5th edition.

CHAPTER EIGHT

Measurement and Scales

Introduction   134
Concepts and definitions   136
Measurement in marketing research   137
Variables in marketing research   138
The process of measurement   139
Levels of measurement and marketing research   140
Variations in measurement   142
Validity, reliability and sensitivity   144
Summary   149
References   149

Introduction

Chapter Two outlined the sequence of steps that typically takes place in a marketing research project. After having set the research objectives, defined the research problem(s) and constructed the research proposal, choices have to be made on the type of data collection methods that are to be employed and the technique(s) of measurement that are to be used; this latter question is the subject of this chapter.

Unless a research project is to be purely qualitative, some form of measurement will be necessary. This chapter will discuss the concept of measurement itself, types of measurement and where/how measurement fits in with the overall subject of marketing research.

Chapter Four drew attention to how common sampling is as a part of everyday life; this chapter will draw attention to the universality of measurement. A pound of butter, a litre of gin, a yard of ale, a ton of coal; measures all, and in everyday usage. Each of the measures so described has a physical and quantifiable base against which they can be compared. National governments keep a set of standard weights and measures against which all the other measures in the country can be assayed.

But imagine this situation: a damp, draughty attic, lit only by a single, guttering candle. Condensation shimmers on the rain-sodden tiles, a half-starved rat scratches for some scrap behind the skirting-board. In the centre of the room, hunched over a rickety table sits a totally starved lecturer in marketing research, his fingers, racked with cold and an unseasonably early bout of rheumatism, tries to grasp the well-chewed stub of his pencil. In front of him on the desk, amidst the debris of unwashed coffee cups, curled sandwiches (well past their sell-by date) and a positive Vesuvius of smouldering cigarette-ends, sits the manuscript of a book on marketing research; his last, feeble attempt to hit the publishing big-time.

What types of measurement can be taken in this room?

The gas and electricity meters could be read (both bills would remain unpaid, however); there is a half-starved rat, half a pencil, a packet of cheese and pickle sandwiches. Then there is the lecturer himself (fully starved); we could measure his weight (going down rapidly) his blood-pressure (going up rapidly) his bank account (see weight measurement), his hair (receding), his age (advancing), his eye-sight, the bags under the eyes.

These are all physical characteristics and the assignation of a number to describe them is relatively obvious and straightforward.

But there are other things in that dank attic that are not quite so easily seen (or are impossible to see) and for which measurement is a far from easy task, e.g. the lecturer's mood (frustrated) or his attitude towards his editor (unprintable).

Marketing research faces the same problems as that rather disgusting microcosm; a mixture of measurements, some easy, because the variable of interest is overt and straightforward, and some difficult, because the variable is covert.

Those that commission research might want the demographics of their customers to be detailed. This would entail measuring their ages, income levels and the style/size of their places of residence. The research might have to investigate what type(s) of car they drive, how many packs of macrobiotic vegi-burgers they bought last month or the proportion of their income that was spent on holidays in the past 12 months. In these cases, the question "what is to be measured" can be answered easily and unambiguously; for age, it is the characteristic "number of years since birth"; for income, it is the characteristic "size of of annual monetary gain"; for car type, it is the characteristic "car type".

But commissioners of marketing research are not only interested in those characteristics to which an unequivocal, concrete number can be assigned. Many research projects have to investigate a potential target market's attitude towards a product, for example. In such a case the question "what is to be measured" does not, because it cannot, receive such a glib and unambiguous statement as in the case of physical characteristics.

Torgerson (1958) said that measurement is "the assignment of numbers to objects to represent amounts or degrees of a property possessed by all of the objects". However, in attempting to measure such characteristics of respondents as attitude, intention, behaviour or effectiveness, there are many ways in which the problem could be approached.

Concepts and definitions

To talk of the "concept" of a dog or of a book or of a house may, to many, appear to be an unnecessarily complicated way to go about things. We do not really need to talk about "concepts" of such concrete, physical items. They can be seen, touched, described and fully and unambiguously defined. But what about the concept of attitude or of behaviour or of brand loyalty; has anyone seen any of these, or touched them?

The answer would have to be *no*.

They are abstract constructions whose meaning is conveyed "... in terms of still other concepts whose meaning is assumed to be more familiar to the inquirer" (Green, Tull and Albaum, 1988).

In marketing research, there are many such concepts: attitude, social class, brand loyalty. And, if the subject of marketing research is anything, then it must be classed as practical; linguistics are indeed fascinating, but they do not offer much solace to a hard-pressed market researcher when confronted by a red-faced client, noisily demanding answers.

Marketing research is, to a large extent, an attempt to understand what is happening in a particular situation. And after understanding comes a need to be able to describe and to communicate this understanding to others. Even relatively simple situations have a complex set of factors and variables at work. It is hardly possible to convey, to a third party, the way in which a situation is "working" by the use of words. The phrase "a big man" may convey one meaning to listener X, but the size of the man conveyed by the use of the word "big" may be quite small in the estimation of listener Y. A manager tells his employees that, for the amount of work they do, their salary is "huge"; their assessment of the situation may be that the decimal place is one or two places too far to the left!

Tell a managing director that the potential market for his new product is "vast" and he will, quite rightly, say "define 'vast'". Words carry emotional resonances; numbers are objective and precise. A 150 lb man is always going to be 150 lb, no matter who does the measuring. A salary of £10 per month will always be that. Where the ambiguity enters is in the evaluation, the interpretation of those figures, but that is no fault of the original measurement and is dependent, to a large extent, on the context in which the numbers are presented.

So, to come to grips with a particular circumstance, there is a need to measure factors and variables which are relevant to that situation. The difficulty in making the measurement does not remove the fact that it still needs to be accomplished. Not only is there a *requirement* to measure, there is also a need to know *what* to measure.

Thus before we can proceed with measurement, there is a requirement to define what is to be measured. The definition can be made at what will be called the conceptual and the operational levels.

At the conceptual level, attitude might be defined, as Samovar, Porter and Jain (1981) did, as "... a learned tendency to respond in a consistent manner with respect to a given object of orientation", a definition of the concept made, as was stated earlier, "in terms of still other concepts".

That is undoubtedly interesting, but it brings us no closer to a practical way of measuring attitude; the concept is still being stated in terms of other concepts.

The second level of definition, the operational, is obviously the one that is closer to the marketing research situation; one that will turn the concept into something that is precise and quantifiable, something that can be measured. An operational definition of attitude to a product could be stated thus "When asked which luxury the respondent would take on to a desert island (apart from the eight discs) our product was chosen".

Attitude, for example, can be defined in many other ways, some of which have more and some of which have less relevance to the specific situation in which the attitude is being investigated. Attitude is not a unidimensional concept; attitude to a product has a very large number of components. And in choosing our definition of attitude, we are necessarily excluding many of them. It is a condition of measurement that it is never totally able to translate reality; the representation can only ever be incomplete. And, moreover, that representation is drawn not directly from the measurements, but by making inferences from those measured values which are assumed to be relevant to the event or object concerning which the investigation is being mounted.

Measurement in marketing research

As has been stated many times already, any marketing research project must have an overall and overt objective, one that is known and agreed upon by all concerned parties. Without an objective there can be no control of the process of research or assessment of the results. With an objective—an aim—decisions concerned with the research proposals, the plan, the sampling, and the data collection methods can be coordinated. It also means that those variables that need to be measured to fulfil the research objectives will be measured. Thus before any measurement commences, the research proposal will need to know

(1) why the research is being carried out, and

(2) what is the best way of achieving that end.

Without those questions being answered satisfactorily, there can be no way of determining what needs to be measured.

Variables in marketing research

In a marketing research situation, the usual subjects of the process of measurement are variables.

A variable is a factor which has been defined as being relevant to the situation in which the research has an interest; it is a factor which varies and in the process of varying affects the state of that situation. For example, many research projects are concerned with predicting the outcome of changes in the packaging of a product; the outcome of interest usually being the consumer response. This consumer response is termed the dependent variable and it is the outcome of all the effects of the factors that are at play in that particular market situation; these factors are termed the independent variables and their effects may be assessed by research. Such factors might include the price of the product, the price and packaging of competing products, and brand loyalty.

But, a single research project cannot measure every factor that could be relevant; how is the choice of what to measure made?

The research objectives will have stated what is the outcome of interest—the dependent variable; there will also have been some implicit assessment as to what the independent variables (the factors which affect the outcome) of interest are. But an implicit assessment is something which can only be used as a basis for deciding what particular independent variables are to be measured. The implicit needs to be made explicit.

One way to carry out this decision process is to construct a model of the situation in which the research has an interest. It is possible that those involved with the project do not know what the important and significant factors are; in that case, there is a need to mount exploratory research to uncover the significant variables. It is also possible to discover the significant variables by a thorough search of published literature reporting investigations into other relevant marketing situations.

Literature or exploratory research might suggest that factors to be investigated include such variables as brand loyalty and consumer attitude. But as has already been noted, these definitions are conceptual; they are not explicit statements of what has to be measured. The researcher will then need to proceed to make an operational definition of the variables and, again, published literature may be able to help in this process of translation from the conceptual to the operational.

The process of measurement

The definition of measurement that has been used so far is that of Torgerson (1958) which says that measurement "... is the assignment of numbers to objects to represent amounts or degrees of a property possessed by all of the objects". Weiers (1988) offers something very similar but adds a further useful comment. His definition states that measurement is "... the assignment of numbers to objects or phenomena according to predetermined rules".

As Southan (1988) says, these two definitions draw attention to three important components of measurement:

(1) Measurement is a process. The assignment of numbers occurs as a result of a "controlled overt system, not an arbitrary, not an intuitive process".

(2) Measurement translates characteristics/qualities into numbers; it turns a quality into a quantity. These numbers can then be stored, compared and analysed using statistical and other methods. But it must be remembered, he notes, that the numbers must at all times represent the qualities/characteristics of the object/person as they are present. Numbers do *not* have any meaning of their own and those that manipulate the means by which they are processed must be aware that care is required if the validity of the relationship between number and the measured characteristic is to be preserved.

(3) Measurement is governed by formal rules. The rules may vary according to who is carrying out the measurement and the objectives of the research. But once the rules are set they must be followed in a consistent manner if reliability of the data is to be guaranteed.

"If a characteristic or property or behavioural act is to be represented by numbers, there must exist a one-to-one correspondence between the number system used and the relations between various quantities (degrees) of that which is being measured" (Green, Tull and Albaum, 1988).

Real number systems have three important characteristics or features:

(1) Order: numbers have an order.

(2) Distance: differences between numbers are ordered.

(3) Origin: the series of numbers will have a unique origin indicated by zero.

When we measure, we assign numbers to people or to objects such that the relationship between the numbers reflects the relationships between the people or objects with respect to the variable/characteristic in which we have an interest. This allows us to construct a scale of measurement which enables a comparison to be made of the changes and of the amounts of the characteristic/variable under measurement.

Levels of measurement and marketing research

Measurement can be made at different levels, the level of measurement being dependent upon the size of the characteristics of order, distance and origin possessed by the numbers.

There are four main levels of measurement:

nominal,
ordinal,
interval,
ratio.

Each one makes different assumptions concerning the way in which the numbers reflect the actual situation under measurement. Because they each make different assumptions, each may be used to carry a different meaning about what is being measured.

As the level of measurement increases from nominal (the lowest) to ratio (the highest), first, the conditions for entry to the level of measurement become more exacting and, second, the manner in which the numbers may be analysed becomes less exacting, i.e. more mathematical operations are allowed.

Nominal scales

This is the lowest level of measurement, with the least stringent requirements for entry and the most limited "room" for mathematical manoeuvre.

Numbers are assigned to objects, people or variables to indicate that they belong to a category, categories covering the full spectrum of objects etc., without overlapping; i.e. they are mutually exhaustive and mutually exclusive. Numbers on a nominal scale have no mathematical value. People who own a dog could be assigned to a nominal scale value of 4; people who do not own a dog could be assigned a value of 2. Because the numbers have no mathematical value, these numbers of 4 and 2 could just as well be replaced with the symbols for "Keep Left" and "Low Bridge".

The only mathematical function that can be carried out on such a scale is to count the numbers of objects, people etc., inside each category.

Age, train numbers, bank accounts, telephone numbers, football team shirts are all nominal scales; they name things/variables.

Nominal scales do not have order, distance or origin.

Ordinal scales

This is a ranking scale and possesses only the characteristic of order.

For this scale to be of use, the respondents in a research project must be able to distinguish between the items of interest in relation to a single attribute: the ability to say that this is the best tasting ice-cream, this (second one) is the next best tasting ice-cream, this (third one) etc. The respondents are saying, in effect, that each ice-cream has more or less of the attribute "good taste"; some have more of the attribute and are placed higher on the scale than those which have less of the attribute. The one with most "good taste" is placed first.

But, an ordinal scale does not allow us to say what the differences are between the ice-creams with regard to the attribute "good taste". It is not possible to know, or to infer, from such a scale if the difference between first place and second place is the same, or more or less, than the difference between the second place and the third place.

Students are ranked on an ordinal scale for examination results, first, second, third etc., as are runners in a race.

The mathematical operations allowed are the calculation of the median and the mode, but *not* of the mean (average). Median may be defined as the central/middle value of a set of factors/items which have been ranked in an ascending or descending order of magnitude. Mode may be defined as the value which occurs most often in a set of data.

For example: we ask 500 people to rate Yeti Frozen Yoghurt against four other confections for taste.

Taste position	Number of respondents giving ranking to Yeti
First place	75
Second place	150
Third place	125
Fourth place	100
Fifth place	50
	500

"Second place" is the mode and "third place" is the median.

Interval scales

Interval scales possess the characteristics of order and distance, but the zero point is arbitrary.

Having these two characteristics enables meaningful statements to be made concerning the differences between two objects.

Thus, with an interval scale it is permissible to say that the difference between scale point 2 and scale point 3 is the same as the difference between scale point 52 and scale point 53.

The most commonly quoted examples of interval scales are the Fahrenheit and Centigrade temperature scales.

But interval scales do not allow a meaningful statement to be made that one value on a scale is a multiple of another value on the same scale.

For example: it is not true to say that 50°F is twice as hot as 25°F, because when the centigrade scale is consulted, it is found that 10°C (the equivalent of 50°F) is not twice the centigrade equivalent of 25°F, this figure is − 3.88°C; the 2:1 ratio has been broken.

Almost all statistical operations can be carried out on interval scale measurements, including the calculation of the arithmetic mean.

Ratio scales

These scales possess order, distance and origin, i.e. a unique origin given by the number zero.

All operations are possible with ratio scales, so here, one can say that a reading of 3 is three times larger than a reading of 1. Equal ratios amongst the scale points is a translation of equal ratios amongst the variable being measured.

Three feet is three times larger than one foot, the ratio being 3:1, and, in inches, 36 inches is three times larger than 12 inches—the ratio remains 3:1. Height, market share, income and price are all ratio scales.

All statistical manipulations are permissible.

Variations in measurement

The objective of all styles of measurement is to provide an exact translation of the variable/characteristic of interest into a numerical value. But such an achievement is rarely, if ever, possible; the real value will always be "contaminated" by errors arising from a variety of sources.

Measured value = real value + error

With any system of measurement there is a problem in deciding whether the differences in recorded measurements are due to the real differences that are being detected in the variable of interest or to errors in the process of measurement.

Some of the error will be systematic, resulting from bias and some will be non-systematic from random sources.

Sampling error (non-systematic) can be reduced, in probability sampling, by the use of larger samples. But the effects of many other sources of non-systematic error cannot be reduced by using similar methods.

When a measurement of a respondent's attitude, for example, is taken, the researcher needs to know that the differences in what is being recorded (the measurements) are due to actual differences in the variable being investigated (the attitude) and are not due to random, short-term error having their origin in any of the following factors.

(a) The respondent

At the exact moment that an interviewer asks a respondent a question, there are an infinite number of factors which might condition their reply. Their upbringing, income level, position of their favourite football team in the league, state of the weather etc., could all contribute towards the way in which the respondent answers.

These conditioning factors may be, very crudely, divided into two main types, the stable and the capricious.

The former are likely to comprise such factors as social class, personality, nationality etc.; the latter, the capricious, are the factors that are more likely to contribute towards the creation of error. The respondent might have terrible toothache, or be in a tearing hurry or it might be raining; all of these may "contaminate" the true answer. Respondents might guess at an answer, not being in possession of the information that is sought. They might "trade up" their answer—increase the reported size of their income or say that they hold a higher position in their place of work than they actually do—in order to impress the interviewer. The interview might be long (or thought to be long) and the respondent might give a terse answer to speed the end of the interchange.

All of these factors may move the respondent's answers away from the true answer; error has been introduced into the process of measurement.

(b) The environment

An interview which takes place on a one-to-one basis in a quiet office may yield answers which are quite different from those obtained when the same questions are put in a busy street or in a room with other people present. If it is freezing cold or swelteringly hot, the respondent may not feel inclined to linger over a street interview or in completing a questionnaire, their answers may be curtailed in order to finish as quickly as possible.

Factors such as these, though not as important as such items as good questionnaire design and careful sampling, for example, should be borne in mind when the research plan is being drawn up.

(c) The measurement process

The chosen measurement instrument, questionnaire etc., may be badly worded, full of leading and/or biased questions or too long; all of these may affect the measured values.

The interviewer, an important factor when there is face-to-face contact with a respondent, may have an influence on the answers given. Their dress, voice, accent, etc., may either encourage valid responses or cause the respondent to react in an atypical manner.

Also, the chosen measuring instrument may be inappropriate in the circumstances of the research. Observation, for example, may have been chosen to record and measure some action, where a telephone interview would have been much more successful in gathering the required data.

The three factors that have just been described may contribute error to the research project. It is the consultant's function to be aware of potential sources of contamination and to reduce as much of their effects as possible. But, it must be remembered, marketing research is a practical subject. The eradication of all errors may not be a practical option; their reduction to a minimum is, unfortunately, the best that can be expected.

However, the idea that a consultant can smugly drop a research report onto his/her client's desk and say "Yes, I know the thing's full of error, there's just nothing I could do about it" is not acceptable. Consultants must make some assessment of the size and likely effects of error on the measured values; the three concepts that are used in helping to make this assessment are reliability, sensitivity and validity.

Validity, reliability and sensitivity

Validity, reliability and sensitivity in marketing research may be defined thus:

Validity. The extent to which a scale of measurement is capable of measuring what it is supposed to be measuring. Valid measurement instruments have the ability to detect real differences amongst groups/individuals at one time or in groups/individuals over time.

Valid measurement instruments are free of bias (systematic) error.

Reliability. The extent to which a scale of measurement delivers consistent results. Consistency may be applied to measurement of different groups/individuals or to measurement of the same groups/individuals at different times.

Reliable measurement instruments are free of random (non-systematic) error.

Sensitivity. The degree to which a scale of measurement can discriminate meaningful differences in the characteristic/variable of interest.

There is an asymmetrical relationship between reliability and validity; a valid measurement is always reliable, a reliable measurement may not be valid. A sensitive measurement, like validity, also needs reliability as a precondition, since if a measure is unreliable a researcher cannot be certain whether measured values are due to real differences in what is being measured or to random fluctuations.

For example, a clock measures time. A well maintained clock that keeps good time will always show the correct time; it is both valid and reliable. A clock that is always ten minutes fast will be reliable—it will always be ten minutes fast, but it will not be valid, the time shown will be wrong. A clock that has a faulty escapement, and as a result is sometimes fast and sometimes slow, is neither reliable nor valid.

Marketing research design should aim for both validity and reliability, but, in absolute terms, this is not always possible. If a project is going to be mounted over an extended time-scale then the measurement instruments should be reliable; if the project is a one-off, then it should be valid.

Validity is the more important of the two criteria.

The assessment of validity

A valid measure detects only real differences in the characteristic of interest. But when conducting research, it is not as if the consultant was marking a mathematics examination paper, where there are known right and wrong answers. When carrying out research, there is no way of knowing if the answer that is received is "right" or "wrong". If the answer was already known, there would be little point in doing the research at all.

There are seven ways to make an estimation as to the validity of measurements.

  (i) Content/face validity.

 (ii) Predictive validity.

(iii) Concurrent validity.

(iv) Construct validity.

 (v) Convergent validity.

(vi) Discriminant validity.

(vii) Nomological validity.

(i) Content/face validity
This is the extent to which the measure "appears" to be measuring what it is supposed to be measuring. When something is measured in marketing research, because of temporal and financial restrictions, it is usually not practical to include all the possible items that could have been included. The content/face validity of a measure is concerned with the degree to which the scale is capable of representing the characteristic/variable of interest. If a foot-ruler is marked only with inches and we are going to have to use it to measure

objects that are less than one inch or are objects that are greater than 12 inches, then the measuring instrument does not have the ability to measure what we want it to measure and will have little or no content/face validity. A questionnaire which seeks to investigate a population's ownership of motor cars, but in a multiple-choice answer only presents three alternatives (when it is known that there are many more makes of car than three) does not have full face validity.

Content/face validity assessment is primarily a subjective one, made using one's own judgement or the judgement of an expert. A consultant, or an expert, makes a judgement as to whether the measurement instrument is capable of measuring what it is supposed to be measuring.

Green, Tull and Albaum (1988) show how "known groups" may also be used to judge content/face validity. For example, a measurement instrument for attitude assessment is applied to a group of respondents whose attitude towards some product or other is known to be positive. The results of such a measurement could then be compared with results obtained when the measurement instrument is applied to groups who are presumed to have negative attitudes towards the product. If the measuring instrument does not discriminate between the two groups, then its ability to measure attitude would not appear to be very great. However, the authors give a warning: there may be other differences between the two sets of groups apart from that of attitude; such differences might account for the measurement variations. "Known group" content/face validity assessment is therefore to be used with caution.

(ii) Predictive validity

Predictive validity concerns the extent to which the variable that has been measured is able to predict some future state/value with which it is associated. For example, when carrying out research into the possible future actions of a sample of the population, there is a question included on a questionnaire which asks, "If the price of this good falls by 10%, do you think you would buy it?" The predictive validity of this measure would therefore rely on the ability of the measure to predict future sales figures if the price were to drop by 10%. If the measure has little predictive validity it may be due to one of two main reasons:

(1) the possible future action is not being measured;

(2) what is being measured—what the respondents say—is not closely related to their actual actions, i.e. what they do.

(iii) Concurrent validity

Predictive validity is concerned with a comparison between a predicted future value and the value that is actually measured; the validity test takes place over time. In concurrent validity the test takes place with another measurement (made at the same time or at a closely related time) of the same, or a closely associated, variable.

(iv) Construct validity
Construct validity does not stop after successfully answering the question, "Does the measurement work?", but attempts to develop/establish criteria that enable the researcher to ask "Why is the measurement successful?" It requires that the researcher has a firm grasp of the underlying variable that is measured by the scale.

There are three sub-divisions of construct validity: convergent, discriminant and nomological validity.

(v) Convergent validity
This test is concerned with the relationship between the results obtained when measuring the same construct by means of two or more different methods. If there is a close correlation between two independent measures of the same variable, they are said to converge; there is convergent validity.

(vi) Discriminant validity
This concerns the extent to which tests differ when they are supposed to differ. For a measure to have discriminant validity there should be "low correlations between the measure of interest and other measures that are supposedly not measuring the same variable or concept" (Campbell and Fiske, 1959).

(vii) Nomological validity
In nomological validity there is an attempt to correlate the measure of interest with other measures of related but different constructs. According to Peter and Churchill (1986) it involves the "... theoretical relationship between different constructs and the empirical relationship between different measures of those different constructs".

The assessment of reliability

Results which are free of random (non-systematic) error are reliable. Reliability is concerned with consistency of results over different individuals/groups at the same time, or over time when measuring an individual or a single group.

A scale may be reliable without being valid; if a scale is not reliable then it cannot be valid.

A valid scale is one free of both random error and bias (systematic) error. There are three measures of reliability.

(1) Test–retest reliability

In measuring the reliability of a scale, research is interested in the consistency of the results after repetition of application; the research wants to know how stable is the response to the measurement. The greater the difference between the results of repeated applications, the lower the reliability.

Problems with test–retest situations include the following.

(a) Some test situations cannot be repeated; e.g. a population's initial reaction to an advertising campaign.

(b) The "destructive nature of measurement" case; i.e. a measurement of a population's attitude. Once it has been measured, the population's attention has been drawn to the topic which may, in some instances, cause that attitude to change as a result.

(c) There may be a reaction to the first test which causes changes in the way the population responds to the retest. Such a reaction may be reduced by leaving a sufficient time interval between measurements.

(2) Alternative forms

The alternative forms method of reliability test attempts to overcome some of the problems outlined in the above case by administering to the same population, or to equivalent samples, alternative but equivalent forms of the measurement under investigation.

Problems with the alternative forms reliability tests include: (a) the cost in time, finance, personnel in constructing the equivalent forms of the measure, (b) the difficulty of getting two or more versions of the measure which are exactly equivalent.

(3) Internal consistency

Reliability tests measure the reliability of a measure on a single test application.

The most commonly used form of this test is the split-half reliability test; the test measures the consistency of items within a scale and may only be used on scales with multiple items. The scale items for assessment are split into equivalent groups, usually two, a correlation then being made between the responses from the different groups. Splitting the measurement instrument may be accomplished using random selection or by apportioning odd numbered questions to one group and even numbered questions to the other group.

For example, a 10-item scale that has been constructed to measure students' attitudes towards marketing research is given to a sample of students. After administration, the scale items are then split into two groups using either of the methods outlined above. If the measure has internal consistency, i.e. all 10 scale items are measuring the same construct—student attitude to marketing research—a single respondent's score for the first five items should be the same as their score for the second group of five scale items.

Sensitivity

A sensitive scale should be able to discriminate slight changes in the subject of measurement from one individual/group to another. It should also be able to detect subtle changes in a single individual or group when applied at different times.

Sensitivity may be increased by increasing the number of points on the scale, i.e. there should be sufficient scale points to capture the variations, the range, in what is being measured. However, too large an increase in scale points will reduce the reliability of the measurement. This is because measures that have few points on their scales, such as yes/no/don't know, are capable of "soaking up" a great deal of variability in the possible responses before changes would be detected when going through a test–retest process (Aaker and Day, 1990).

On the other hand, a scale measure which has too many points for the limited range of possible responses may cause unnecessarily random variations in measurement.

Summary

Measurement, the assignment of numbers to objects or phenomena according to predetermined rules, is a basic component of marketing research; without the ability to measure, the subject could hardly exist.

Facts and behaviour, being overt, are measured in a relatively straight-forward manner, though the difficulties of so doing should not be under-estimated. Covert variables/characteristics, such as feeling, attitude and motivation, are much harder to measure. To tackle their measurement, they are conceptualised. However, these concepts are but steps in the complete process of measurement; to be of practical use, the conceptualisation of a variable must be translated into an operational definition.

Once this has been done, it may be turned into a quantity by the application of a scale of measurement.

The ability of these scales of measurement, nominal, ordinal, interval and ratio, to reflect, accurately, that which they are supposed to be quantifying depends upon their validity—the degree to which they are free from bias—and reliability—the degree to which they are free from random error.

References

Aaker D. A., and Day G. S. (1990) *Marketing Research*, John Wiley and Sons, New York, 4th edition.

Campbell D. T. and Fiske, D. W. (1959) Convergent and discriminant validation by the Multi-trait-Multi-method matrix, *Psychological Bulletin*, **56**, 81–105.

Churchill G. A. and Peter J. P. (1986) Research design effects on the reliability of rating scales: a meta-analysis, *Journal of Marketing Research*, **21**, November, 360–375.

Green P. A., Tull D. S. and Albaum G. (1988) *Research for Marketing Decisions*, Prentice-Hall, Englewood Cliffs, New Jersey.

Samovar L. A., Porter R. E. and Jain N. C. (1981) *Understanding Intercultural Communication*, Wadsworth, Belmont, California.

Southan J. (1988) in *Marketing Research*, University of Strathclyde, Distance Learning Unit, MComm.

Torgerson W. S. (1958) *Theory and Methods of Scaling*, John Wiley and Sons, New York.

Weiers R. M. (1988) *Marketing Research*, Prentice-Hall, Englewood Cliffs, New Jersey, 2nd edition.

CHAPTER NINE

Attitudes and their Measurement

Introduction	151
What are attitudes?	152
Attitudes and the prediction of behaviour	157
The measurement of attitudes	159
Rating scales	160
Attitude scales	166
Comment	171
References	171

Introduction

Attitude; how many times have you heard that word recently?

"I do not like the idea of animals being hunted merely for sport, therefore my attitude to leopard skin coats is negative."

Managing Director to marketing researcher: "I'd like you to measure our customers' likely attitude to a 34% price increase."

In all our lives, whether conducting marketing research or not, the concept of attitude is omnipresent; it is another of those factors such as sampling and measurement from which there is no escape. They are constantly referred to in our everyday conversations, though the word "attitude" is sometimes used incorrectly. One often hears friends says something similar to this: "That sales assistant in the newsagent short-changed me again. He's got a rotten attitude." Here the concept of attitude has been mixed up with that of behaviour. Now, while the link between the concepts of attitude and behaviour is strong, the two are not interchangeable. It is for reasons such as this, where a word/concept/construct is used as part of everyone's daily lives without much thought being given to its true meaning, that it is necessary to explain first exactly what is meant by the concept of attitude when it is used in the context of marketing research.

Marketing research workers are constantly being asked to measure attitudes to some thing, some service or some proposal, the most sophisticated of these measures being known as attitude scales.

But before those types of scales are described, it is necessary to answer the question, "What are attitudes?" This is because, as Oppenheim (1984) says,

> "... in the past, much attention has been paid to the technical and statistical problems of scaling and not enough to the psychological problem of what is being scaled. The most advanced scaling techniques and the most error-free procedures will not produce an attitude scale worth having unless there has first been a good deal of careful thought and exploration, and unless the ingredients of the scale (the attitude statements) have been written and rewritten with the necessary care."

The chapter will go on to describe the components of attitudes, how they may be measured, attitude scaling techniques and their applications.

What are attitudes?

Many writers have attempted to define what an attitude is; here are two of the more well known and well respected definitions.

Allport (1935) says that an attitude is "... a mental and neural state of readiness to respond that is organised through experience and exerts a directive and/or dynamic influence on behaviour".

Parasuraman (1986) defines attitudes as "... underlying mental states capable of influencing a person's choice of actions and maintaining consistency across those actions".

There are almost as many definitions of attitude as there are attitudes themselves, but all seem agreed that it is a mental state of readiness, a way an individual structures his own particular world, such that when confronted with certain stimuli he acts in a certain manner. Thus, though an individual may possess an attitude to, for example, the use of animal fur as a fashion item, it only becomes manifest when the topic of fur coats is mentioned; the attitude to fur coats does not have an all pervasive influence, drenching the whole of that individual's psyche. Attitudes are not generally held to be the only cause of human behaviour. Behaviour is the end result of a very complex interchange between factors both internal and external to that person whose behaviour is under investigation; though attitudes are constituents of the internal factors, they are conditioned through external experience. And the gathering of that experience is not a random process; it is organised through a process which is known as learning.

Attitudes are hypothetical constructs; they are abstract but to those that hold them, they are real enough. Attitudes can be held on any topic, and although many people share common attitudes, a certain part of the population may have attitudes that only a few others share. It is in the interest of the research project, therefore, to ensure that the population being investigated holds the attitude that is under investigation.

There are other areas connected with the concept of attitude that need to be discussed before any further progress can be made. Oppenheim (1984) brings to our attention, the labelling of attitudes, their mapping, their intensity, their endurance and their relationships with other attitudes.

The labelling of attitudes

Attitudes may be specifically named: anti-English, pro-capital punishment etc., or they can be couched in more general terms, such as bravery, left-wing, radical. When we, or others, give an attitude a name it is very important to know exactly what is being implied by that name. Is, for example, the attitude that has been called "anti-English" only a single dimension, are there a multitude of facets to the concept, or is the attitude "anti-English" a sub-component of a much larger conglomeration of attitudes that could be called "xenophobia"? If this question is not resolved it might mean that the research measures the wrong attitude, only part of an attitude, or a whole complex of attitudes simultaneously, only a certain number of which have a direct bearing on the case in which the research has an interest.

The mapping of attitudes

In attempting to measure attitudes, many projects assign a numerical value or a rank order to an individual's attitude (to something or other) by means of a placement on a linear scale that runs from a positive value, through a neutral (zero) point to a negative value. Oppenheim (1984) says "... for all we know, attitudes may be shaped more like concentric circles or overlapping ellipses or three-dimensional cloud formations".

However, if a linear scale is to be used, then one must ask oneself if the positive and negative wings of a scale are, or are not, to be mirror images of each other. For example, to be "anti-English" may not necessarily mean that one has to be "pro-French": to be "anti-capital punishment" does not automatically mean that one is also "pro-murder". Each side of a scale may have a set of particular situation specifics. Thus the factors that give rise to a person being "anti-capital punishment" may not apply, in the negative sense, to the conditioning of the attitude of "pro-murder". In such cases, it would be unwise, therefore, to measure the concept "anti-capital punishment" versus "pro-murder" on a single continuum; two independent scales would be preferable.

Another point to consider is whether scales should be symmetrically splayed around the neutral/zero point. On a scale that measures the positive versus the negative aspects of education, there are many positive things that may be said in favour of the subject, but very few negative things. Researchers must thus consider if it is worthwhile offering the negative factors as much space on the scale as the positive ones. Exploratory research will help the project in determining the balance of the scale.

The strength of attitudes

Attitudes may be weakly held or very strongly held; what is of overriding interest to one person, may be of little more than passing concern to another. The passion/intensity with which a person holds an attitude is of interest to market researchers as it may be a useful way to predict behaviour.

Suchman (1950) found that there was a U-shaped relationship between an attitude and the intensity with which it is held. That is, the more extreme the attitude, the more likely it is that it will be strongly held. Suchman recommends that in seeking to find the neutral point on a scale, the point of minimum intensity/passion should be discovered.

The endurance of attitudes

An individual's attitude towards X may last his/her entire life, while his/her attitude towards Y may be held at only a superficial level and may change as often as do the seasons. A person's attitude towards a political party, his/her religion etc., may be held with great fortitude, whereas a person's attitude towards the height of a hem-line, the width of a tie or a brand of baked beans may alter frequently. The reason why there is such a wide difference in the endurance of attitudes would appear to be the way in which attitudes are organised and developed within an individual's mind.

As Ajzen and Fishbein (1977) say, "there appears to be general agreement among investigators that attitudes towards any object are determined by beliefs about that object. Generally speaking, we form beliefs about an object by associating it with various characteristics, qualities and attributes. Automatically and simultaneously we acquire an attitude towards that object." Ajzen and Fishbein propose that although at any one time an individual may hold many beliefs about any given object or act, he/she can only cope with a small number, between five and seven, at any given time; these they term the "salient beliefs".

Since beliefs are a major factor in the formation of attitudes it would appear logical to propose that the more strongly these salient beliefs are held, the more they are likely to endure and the more enduring will be the attitudes that they help to form.

One person may refuse to eat pork because of a belief, gained from recent news media stories, that the pigs have been badly treated in the way that they are farmed; that negative attitude may be changed, quite easily, if the person can be persuaded that new farming methods are more humane. A second person may refuse to eat pork because of a religious proscription concerning dietary laws; no amount of advertising/promotion on behalf of the farmers will persuade those consumers to consume pork. The underlying belief, or it might be termed "value" in this case, is far too strongly held.

The relationships of attitudes

The relationship between personality, beliefs/values and attitudes might be represented thus:

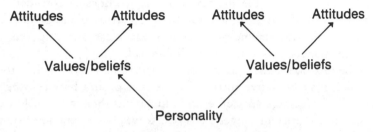

In the discussion so far, attitudes have been treated as if they were isolated entities, whereas reality would suggest that there are complex interrelationships between attitudes. An attitude may be linked with many other attitudes and with other values/beliefs. This presents the research worker with a problem. While the actual situation may suggest that there is a complex web of beliefs/values and attitudes; financial, temporal and personnel constraints deny the investigator the opportunity to investigate the situation fully. Practical research can only take place within well defined areas. Oppenheim (1984) suggests that this hurdle may be cleared in the exploratory stages of the project by using in-depth individual interviews to:

(1) investigate the "origins, complexities and ramifications" of those attitude areas which are the subject of the study, so that the research may more clearly focus on what is to be measured, and

(2) gather accurate and wide-ranging expressions of respondent attitudes in a form that might be used as a basis in making statements for use on an attitude scale.

The components of attitudes

Attitudes are generally considered to be composed of three components:

(1) the cognitive,

(2) the affective,

(3) the behavioural.

They are related in the following manner:

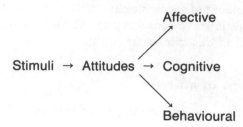

In marketing research, the measurement of attitudes is considered to be important because of the supposed link between attitude and behaviour. But researchers should not assume that this link is a clear unambiguous one; in certain circumstances there may be no link at all.

Even if the link does exist, it is prudent for the research to consider the other factors which may be active in the process that occurs between the covert attitudes, beliefs, feelings etc., of an individual and their overt behaviour.

Just because an amateur singer's attitude towards singing the title role in Verdi's "Otello" at La Scala is thoroughly positive, does not mean that audiences in Milan can look forward to a full-throated "Esultate" from him in the near future. The all too obvious truth is that his vocal chords hardly enable him to "vamp" his way through a bathroom-aria; this will tend to affect his actual behaviour!

In researching the link between attitudes and behaviour, marketing may attempt to use the information in two ways:

(a) by measuring the cognitive and affective components to predict future behaviour;

(b) by altering the cognitive and affective components to influence future behaviour.

(1) The cognitive component
This represents an individual's awareness, beliefs and knowledge about an object, person etc.

Respondents say: "I have heard of product X." "I believe that product X will carry out such-and-such a function."

In marketing research, a company may wish to estimate a market segment's knowledge of their products, its features, or price.

(2) The affective component
This represents an individual's feelings, both positive and negative, towards an object; the liking of an object, person etc., is usually expressed as a preference.

Respondents say: "I do not like product Y." "I like product X more than I like product Y."

Marketing research may be called upon to estimate an individual's feelings (both positive and negative) towards a product, or to make a comparison between a company's products and those of its competitors.

(3) The behavioural component
This represents an individual's predisposition to action prior to the actual decision being made or their expectation(s) of possible future behaviour towards an object, person, etc.

Marketing research may be employed to learn if a target market would be likely to purchase super-improved "Suddso" if the washing powder were to be reduced in price, for example, or packaged in a different range of sizes.

Activities in marketing may be intended to bring about some change in a target market, the change occurring at the cognitive, the affective or the behavioural level.

Ray (1973) has suggested that buyers pass through an ascending hierarchy of: awareness, knowledge, liking, preference, intention to purchase and then purchase. Ray, as reported in Kinnear and Taylor (1983), suggests that "... these stages can occur in different sequences depending upon the degree of buyer involvement with the purchase and the degree of differentiation among the alternatives".

Figure 9.1 shows the relationships.

Attitudes and the prediction of behaviour

Fishbein and Ajzen (1975) define an attitude as "... a learned predisposition to respond in a consistently favourable or unfavourable manner with respect to a given object".

The authors considered what attitudes would best act as predictors of behaviour towards an object. They developed a theory of attitude which is what is called the "expectancy-value" school of thought; their theory says that "attitudes be viewed as overall evaluations". For them, the "affective" component of the attitude is the most important.

When they used this model in an attempt to predict how people with a given attitude towards an object would behave towards the object, they found a low correlation between the measured attitude and their subsequent behaviour.

To improve the predictive power of the measurement, Fishbein and Azjen (1975) moved the focus of attention from the respondent's attitude about the object to the respondent's attitude concerning behaviour towards the object.

Thus those who are interested in attempting to predict, for example, future buying behaviour of banking services should not only concern themselves with the measurement of a person's attitudes towards banking services but

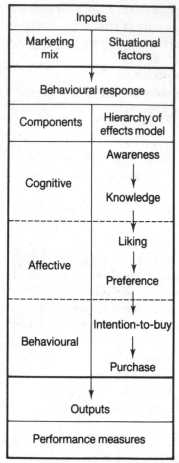

Figure 9.1. Relationship between cognitive, affective and behavioural components of attitudes. (From Kinnear and Taylor (1983) *Marketing Research: An Applied Approach*, 3rd edition, McGraw-Hill, with permission).

should, in addition, concern themselves with measuring a respondent's attitudes towards purchasing banking services. A respondent may be in favour of banking services, yet he/she does not purchase them; in such a case, what he/she is saying is, "Though I am in favour of banking services, I am *not* in favour of purchasing banking services for myself".

Another example, this time using a negative attitude.

Almost everyone has a personal "bogeyman" in the shape of their dentist, yet they continue to visit him/her. If we had measured respondents' attitudes towards dentists, the vast majority would probably be negative. And using that as a basis, we would predict that the "vast majority" of respondents would not have any contact with a dentist; yet people do. Not a very good predictor, yet, using Fishbein and Azjen's revised theory we should not have measured the respondents' attitudes towards dentists but towards visiting the dentist. This would give a much more "positive" value and would be a more valid predictor of behaviour. While people may not have a very favourable predisposition to dentists, they do have a positive attitude towards visiting a dentist—they think it will be of benefit.

Thus, if prediction of future behaviour towards an object is part of the research brief, one should use a measure of the attitude towards a specific action with the object, rather than measure attitudes towards the object itself.

The measurement of attitudes

Cook and Sellitz (1964) have offered the following list of the ways in which measurable responses may offer clues concerning an individual's attitude:

(1) by drawing inferences from observed, overt behaviour,

(2) by drawing inferences from an individual's reactions to or interpretations of structured or ambiguous stimuli,

(3) by drawing inferences from the performance of a task, where the function may be conditioned by his/her attitude towards the object/person which is the focus of the research,

(4) by drawing inferences from physiological reactions to the object/person,

(5) by drawing inferences from material which has been self-reported: beliefs, feelings, behaviour towards an object/person.

Case 1 may be recognised as observation, Case 2 are projective techniques, Case 4 are techniques which use such instruments as psychogalvanometers and eye cameras. All three of these cases have already been detailed in Chapter Seven.

Case 3 may be illustrated by the following example presented in Parasuraman (1986).

A representative sample of the target population is given an essay containing numerous facts and figures pertaining to the subject for which an assessment of the population's attitudes is required. The essay should be well balanced, containing an equal number of points both for and against the subject. After a suitable time lag, the respondents are examined on the contents of the essay. What parts of the essay are recalled and how well they are recalled will offer clues as to the respondent's attitude towards the subject. If a respondent shows a firm grasp of a disproportionately large amount of the "cons" of the argument, this would tend to indicate a negative attitude towards the subject.

Case 5 techniques, which will now be discussed in detail, are those concerned with self-reporting. They rely upon a relatively direct style of question which the respondents answer in such a way as to show the strength and direction of their attitude towards the topic under investigation, the respondent usually being required to state his/her attitude on a scale of measurement. These scales of measurement are referred to as direct response attitude scales.

Measurement scales may be divided into two main groups.

Rating scales. Where a single component of an attitude to some object, person or product etc. is measured.

Attitude scales. Where combinations of rating scales are designed to measure some/all of a respondent's attitudes towards some thing or some object.

All types of rating and attitude scales are systems of measurement, such as were discussed in Chapter Eight.

Rating scales

Rating scales typically require that the subject indicate his/her attitude towards the topic of interest by demonstrating a position somewhere along a continuum of numerical values, or a series of ordered categories. The scale operates by the respondent picking one object/category of object over others in respect of a given attribute, or by allocating a numerical value to an object or category of object depending upon the strength with which they possess a given attribute.

Rating scales can be used to assess:

(1) a respondent's overall attitude towards something,

(2) the degree to which that something possesses a certain attribute,

(3) a respondent's feelings (both positive and negative) towards a given attribute,

(4) the importance a respondent assigns to a given attribute.

There are a multitude of ways in which a respondent may be presented with a continuum or with numerically assigned categories to represent a range of possible attitudes. In this chapter they will be discussed under the following headings:

(1) Non-comparative rating scales.

(2) Comparative rating scales.

(3) Rank order rating scales.

(4) Constant sum rating scales.

(1) Non-comparative rating scales

In non-comparative, or monadic, rating scales, the respondent is asked to rate the object of interest in isolation—they are not given a standard against which to make a comparison.

(a) Graphic
In graphic rating scales, respondents have to mark their attitude position on a continuum that covers the full range of possible attitude positions. Respondents might be asked to rate their opinion of a chocolate bar on a scale thus:

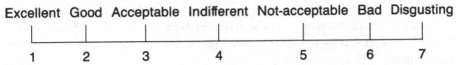

(The inclusion of such a scale-point descriptor as "indifferent" will be discussed further in the later section on forced versus unforced choice scales.)

or

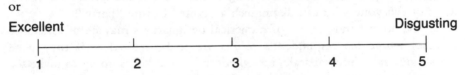

The inclusion of numerical values along the continuum is to assist the respondent, not to provide categories of response.

(b) Itemised-category scales
Respondents are directed to pick their response from a limited number of ordered categories which constitute the scale. Below are two examples.

What is your reaction to the news that the brewing industry has been taken into state ownership?

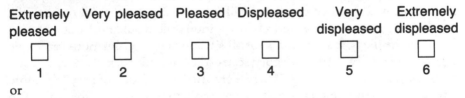

or

To what extent has your new washing-machine fulfilled your expectations?

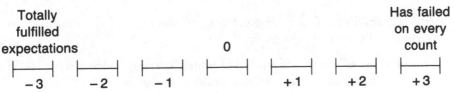

The following factors must be considered when constructing a non-comparative rating scale.

Numerical designations versus verbal descriptors. The first scale of each of the two pairs of scales presented above has each of the continua labelled with a verbal descriptor; the second scale of each of the pairs only has the extremes labelled, the categories in between being designated numerically. Because of the lack of precision when using words such as "very" and "extremely", one can never be sure that the distances that those that construct the scale place between a "very" and an "extremely" or between a "quite" and a "somewhat" are the same distances envisaged by the respondents. Also, there is the question of equality; are all the words on the scale "extremely", "very", "moderately", "quite", "somewhat"—the same psychological distance from each other on the continuum?

However, the use of verbal descriptors has been found to be a useful aid to respondents when they are completing the scale. If verbal descriptors are used, those who construct the scale should try to use clear, unambiguous adjectives; it is not everyone who can distinguish a "quite" from a "fairly"!

On the other hand the use of numerical designations may be of assistance in cases where the respondent's results are to be treated as if they were answering on an interval scale, i.e. where the researcher is going to make the assumption that the distance between the scale points $+4$ and $+5$ is the same as the distance between the scale points -1 and -2. The research will have to conduct a "benefit analysis" on these two competing factors; verbal descriptors aid the respondent by making the scales easier to use, and numerical designations are easier to use for the research workers—enabling the results to stand proxy as an interval scale.

Number of categories. In cases where a respondent's attitude is likely to be dramatically polarised between, for example, "in favour of" and "against" then a scale with just two categories will suffice to capture the full range of the respondent's attitude. However, a two-position scale would not be able to represent all the likely attitude states for all situations; many situations cannot be captured merely by a two category scale—they are not such black and white cases, there are shades of grey. Where there are these "shades of grey" the more categories of response there are, then the more precise will be the scale. The two factors which will help in deciding the number of categories are:

(a) the capabilities of the respondents in discriminating, meaningfully, between different categories, and

(b) the amount of detailed knowledge which the respondents have, or are likely to have, about the attribute under investigation.

In practice, most researchers use scales with between five and seven categories.

Balanced versus unbalanced scales. Balanced scales have an equal number of positive, favourable responses and negative, unfavourable responses; there is a mirror image of response categories on each side of the centre. In an unbalanced scale there are more of the positive or of the negative categories. Before deciding upon the type of scale to use, researchers must estimate the possible distribution of the respondents' attitudes. Exploratory research can help here.

An example of an unbalanced scale might be the following:

What is your attitude to the provision of health care in a retirement home?

Negative	Indifferent	In favour	Very much in favour	Essential
☐	☐	☐	☐	☐

Forced versus unforced choice scales. With a balanced scale with an even number of categories, respondents are forced to make a choice of response; with an odd number of categories respondents may use the central, neutral, position to avoid making such a choice.

For example:

Forced choice scale: What do you think of the idea of compulsory car seat-belts?

Very good idea	Good idea	Bad idea	Very bad idea
☐	☐	☐	☐

Unforced choice scale: What do you think of the idea of compulsory car seat-belts?

Very good idea	Good idea	Indifferent/ no opinion	Bad idea	Very bad idea
☐	☐	☐	☐	☐

Some respondents may genuinely have "no opinion" or are neutral on a subject, so a scale with an even number of categories will deny them the opportunity to express their true feelings. However, many market researchers argue that everyone will have a degree of attitude towards the object of the research and that respondents should be forced to make a decision.

Weiers (1988) suggests that an odd number of categories should be included in the scale, which will give a central neutral/indifferent position, and that an, additional "do not know" or "no opinion" box be provided, "... whenever it is likely that a significant number of respondents may not be aware of the object or have never tried it".

(Respondents should be made aware that to be "neutral" or "indifferent" about a topic is *not* the same as to be a "don't know".)

(2) Comparative rating scales

In non-comparative rating scales, respondents are not presented with any standard brand or object against which to make an assessment. The researcher thus has no idea as to the standard which the respondent is using against which they make their comparison. In order to inject some degree of unity into the rating system, comparative rating scales ask respondents to make a rating assessment against a stated standard.

There are two main types of comparative rating scales: paired-comparison and graphic/itemised comparative rating scales.

(a) Paired-comparison rating scales
In order to show the product features you look for when purchasing a new car, select one of each of these pairs. Each attribute will appear more than once.

Price or colour	Price or acceleration
Engine capacity or power-steering	Wheel size or power-steering
Wheel size or price	Colour or engine capacity
Power steering or colour	Acceleration or wheel size
Acceleration or engine capacity	Engine capacity or price
Power steering or price	Power-steering or acceleration
Colour or acceleration	Wheel size or colour
Engine-capacity or wheel size	

This scale contains six items presented in pairs; each item is compared with each of the other five items—all comparisons are therefore made. The ranking is found by counting the number of occasions on which an item is preferred over its pair.

Many researchers, however, think that this method is rather cumbersome and rarely use it.

(b) Graphic/itemised comparative rating scales
The above method may be simplified by presenting the scale as follows:

Compared with being dragged naked over broken bottle glass, marketing research is:

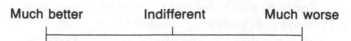

       Much better   Indifferent   Much worse

or

☐   ☐   ☐   ☐

Much better   Better   Worse   Much worse

(3) Rank order rating scales

In rank order rating scales, respondents are asked to rank a list of things, people, features etc., against some stated criterion: taste, height, weight etc.

For example:

Please place the following list of foods in an order according to their energy value; 1 = the highest energy rating, 5 = the lowest energy value.

> Brown bread
> Bananas
> Chocolate
> T-bone steak
> Cream of parsnip soup

Rank order scales are ordinal scales and have the advantages and disadvantages associated with such scales, i.e. respondents can show the order of their preferences, but from that order no inference can be made as to the "distances" between any of the objects.

(4) Constant sum rating scales

The problem of not knowing the "distances" between the points on a measure may be overcome by using a constant sum rating scale. With this method a respondent is asked to allocate a constant sum, usually a round figure such as 100, among the objects, attributes, features etc., in a way which reflects the object's attributes under investigation. This not only gives the objects a rank order but also indicates the size of the difference that the respondent perceives between the various objects.

For example: in the case of the rank order rating scale presented above, respondents were asked to rank five foods according to their energy values; supposing a respondent made the following reply:

> First: T-bone steak
> Second: Chocolate
> Third: Brown bread
> Fourth: Cream of parsnip soup
> Fifth: Bananas

This gives an order, but it does not tell us by how much T-bone steak is thought of as having more energy than brown bread.

With a constant sum scale, this drawback may be overcome.
For example:

Please allocate 100 points between the following foods according to the energy value you think they have.

T-bone steak	45
Chocolate	20
Brown bread	15
Cream of parsnip soup	15
Bananas	5
	100

This result would seem to imply that the respondent thinks that they are ranked in a certain order, but also that steak has three times the energy value of brown bread and parsnip soup.

The scale is best restricted for use with a relatively small number of objects, as respondents may have difficulties in allocating their points if the range of objects etc., is too wide.

Attitude scales

In the rating scales that have been described above, a basic assumption has been that a respondent's attitude to some object, person or feature is unidimensional; this is not a realistic proposition. People's attitudes are rarely confined to a single dimension; indeed, attitudes to such topics as education, health and government are very complex, far too complex to be assessed with only a single measure.

The weight of a chemical is assessed with a set of scales, its colour with a spectrometer, its structure by using the techniques of X-ray crystallography. Each of these systems of measurement, scales, spectrometers etc., could be thought of as the equivalent of a rating scale, each measuring a single quality of the chemical: weight, colour, structure.

An attitude scale would be the equivalent of a machine that could combine the measurement of all three characteristics at the same time.

Attitude scales are an attempt to overcome the unrepresentativeness that arises from inferring an individual's overall response towards something or other by measuring the attitude to only one characteristic of that "something or other". They do this, in various ways, by combining sets of rating scales so that more than one facet of an individual's attitude towards something or other may be measured.

The three most popular and widely used attitudes scales which will be discussed are the Likert scale, the semantic differential scale and the Stapel scale.

(a) The Likert scale

The Likert scale, sometimes referred to as a summated scale, requires that respondents indicate their degree of agreement or disagreement with a series of statements which are associated with the attitude under investigation. Their responses are given a numerical value and/or a sign which reflects the strength and the direction of the respondents' attitude to each of the statements; thus respondents who agree with a statement will be marked positively or with a high mark and those who disagree with a negative or low mark.

Thus scales can run from, say, 1 to 5, from 5 to 1, or from $+2$ through zero to -2.

For example:

An hotel chain's drinks buyer is presented with five statements about a company's product:

(1) Dean's Beer is expensive.

(2) Dean's Beer has too high an alcohol content.

(3) Dean's Beer tastes as beer should taste.

(4) Dean's Beer is good with cheese sandwiches.

(5) Dean's Beer contains too much gas.

The buyer has to respond to each of these statements using one of the points on this scale:

> strongly agree
> agree
> neither agree nor disagree
> disagree
> strongly disagree

For statements which are in favour of Dean's Beer, Cases 3 and 4, their responses are marked from, for example, five to one—five for "strongly agree" through to one for "strongly disagree".

For statements which are against Dean's beer, Cases 1, 2 and 5, their responses are marked from one to five, one for "strongly agree" through to five for "strongly disagree".

When the score is totalled it will give an indication of the buyer's attitude towards Dean's Beer; 25 being very favourable and 5 very unfavourable.

Alternatively, it could be marked using a scale that runs from $+2$ through zero to -2. But in this case, an individual's responses to unfavourable statements must be multiplied by -1 "... for the purposes of directional consistency—so that positive responses will reflect favourable attitudes and negative responses will reflect unfavourable attitudes" (Weiers, 1988). Thus, in those Cases 1, 2 and 5, which are unfavourable to the beer, a respondent's answer of "strongly agree" is, in fact, expressing an unfavourable attitude towards the product. By multiplying this figure ($+2$) by -1, only the direction of the response is altered (not its strength). This is in line with the idea that positive represents a favourable response and negative an unfavourable response.

After the identification of the object about which attitudes are to be measured Sellitz, Jahoda, Deutsch and Cook (1959) present five steps in the construction of a Likert scale.

(1) Generate a number of statements, both favourable and unfavourable, which are thought to be relevant to the object under investigation.

(2) Give the statements to a representative sample of the population to be investigated. Respondents show their agreement or disagreement with the statements marking them on a scale of, say, $+2$ for strong agreement and -2 for strong disagreement.

(3) The score for each statement is summed by aggregating the individual's scores for each statement.

(4) Analyse the statements to determine which of them discriminate between the high attitude scorers and the low attitude scorers. Those statements which do not show a robust correlation with the total score are discarded.

(5) Those statements which remain will form the Likert scale and may be administered to respondents to measure the attitude in question.

Likert scales are relatively simple to construct and easy to administer; they are thus most useful in those circumstances where there is no interviewer/moderator to explain how to use the measuring instrument—for example, mail questionnaires and self-administered questionnaires.

(b) The semantic differential scale

Semantic differential scales are probably the most widely used measures of attitude, especially for brand and corporate image investigations.

Respondents have to indicate the position of their attitude towards the object on an itemised seven-point scale. This enables the researcher to evaluate both the direction and intensity of the respondent's attitude towards the object. The extremities of the scale are secured by a pair of polarised adjectives, statements or phrases.

For example: A group of respondents might be asked to record their attitude towards the Hotel Graham

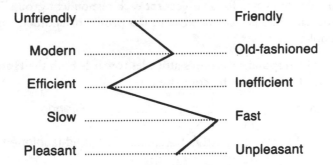

Unfriendly	....	Friendly
Modern	....	Old-fashioned
Efficient	....	Inefficient
Slow	....	Fast
Pleasant	....	Unpleasant

Osgood, Suci and Tannenbaum (1957), who originated the scale, developed approximately fifty pairs of bipolar adjectives, grouped to measure three fundamental components of an attitude towards an object:

(1) Evaluative: negative–positive, good–bad.

(2) Activity: active–passive, fast–slow.

(3) Potency: strong–weak.

Dickson and Albaum (1977) showed that by using descriptive phrases, rather than single adjectives, the scales will have more meaning to respondents which will lead to a higher degree of reliability.

The research may include any number of pairs; Weiers (1988) says that between 20 and 30 pairs may be included. In addition Luck and Rubin (1987) recommend that each side of the scale is not reserved exclusively for either the positive or the negative aspects of the adjective-pair, statement or phrase. This, they say, will avoid the "halo" effect where respondents tend to tick only down one side of the marking schedule.

The evaluative type of bipolar adjectives are the ones most often used in studies concerned with uncovering respondents' attitudes towards brand and corporate image.

There are two main ways in which the results of semantic differential scale measurements may be analysed: aggregate and profile.

Aggregate analysis
Aggregate analysis involves summing the scores for each individual respondent for all the pairs of adjectives, statements etc.; thus for each respondent there is a numerical value of his/her attitude towards the object.

Using these aggregated scores, individuals may be compared with other individuals with respect to the same object, or two or more objects may be compared with respect to the same individual or a group of individuals.

Profile analysis

Profile analysis involves calculating the arithmetic median or mean value for each pair of adjectives etc., for an object for each respondent group. The profile thus derived can then be compared with the profile of another object.

For example:

The profiles of a respondent group's attitudes towards both the Hotel Graham and the Hotel Donald may be compared.

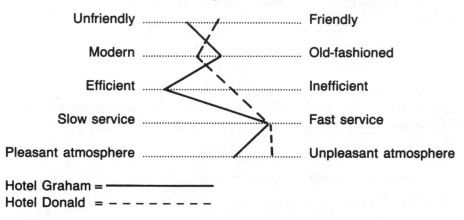

Unfriendly .... Friendly

Modern .... Old-fashioned

Efficient .... Inefficient

Slow service .... Fast service

Pleasant atmosphere .... Unpleasant atmosphere

Hotel Graham = ————————
Hotel Donald = – – – – – – – –

If an aggregate analysis had been used, it might have showed that both hotels have a similar score with an overall positive image, but it would not have revealed the quite different profiles that each hotel has in the minds of the respondents.

A profile analysis will show which are a product's individual weak and strong points. Marketing strategies may then be devised to improve the former and to capitalise on the latter.

The main disadvantage of semantic differential scales lies in their construction. To render valid results the scales need to be composed of truly bipolar pairs of adjectives; however, some of the pairs chosen may not be true opposites in the minds of some respondents.

The Stapel scale

The Stapel scale is a modified version of the semantic differential scale and uses a unipolar, 10-point non-verbal rating scale with values which range from + 5 to – 5. The scale thus measures both the direction and the intensity of an attitude simultaneously. The Stapel scale differs from the semantic differential scale in that it measures how well only one adjective, phrase etc., fits the object being evaluated.

For example: respondents are asked to evaluate how well each of the following adjectives describes the object under investigation.

Annie's mousse tastes:

+5	+5	+5
+4	+4	+4
+3	+3	+3
+2	+2	+2
+1	+1	+1
Creamy	Fruity	Expensive
−1	−1	−1
−2	−2	−2
−3	−3	−3
−4	−4	−4
−5	−5	−5

The Stapel scale is easy to administer and does not require that the adjectives be tested to ensure true polarity as is necessary in the case of the semantic differential scale.

Comment

This chapter has attempted to describe attitudes and the ways in which they may be measured as part of a marketing research project. It has purposely done so in simple terms; the subject is extremely complex and those students who wish to delve deeper into the subject are advised to consult specialist texts which offer a fuller and deeper analysis of the subject.

References

Allport G. W. (1935) in *Handbook of Social Psychology* (ed. C. Murchison), Clark University Press, Worcester, Mass.

Ajzen I. and Fishbein M. (1977) Attitude–behaviour relations: A theoretical analysis and review of empirical research, *Psychological Bulletin*, **84**.

Cook S. W. and Sellitz C. (1964) A multiple-indicator approach to attitude measurement, *Psychological Bulletin*, **62**.

Dickson J. and Albaum G, (1977) A method for developing tailormade semantic differentials for specific marketing content areas, *Journal of Marketing Research*, February.

Fishbein, M. and Azjen I. (1975) *Belief, Intention and Behaviour*, Addison-Wesley Publishing Company, Reading, Massachusetts.

Kinnear T. C. and Taylor J. R. (1983) *Marketing Research: An Applied Approach*, McGraw-Hill, New York, 2nd edition.

Luck D. J. and Rubin D. S. (1987) *Marketing Research*, Prentice-Hall, Englewood Cliffs, 7th edition.

Oppenheim A. N. (1984) *Questionnaire Design and Attitude Measurement*, Heinemann, London.

Osgood C. E., Suci G. J. and Tannenbaum P. H. (1957) *The Measurement of Marketing*, University of Illinois, Urbana.

Parasuraman A. (1986) *Marketing Research*, Addison–Wesley Publishing Company, Reading, Massachusetts.

Ray M. L. (1973) Marketing Communication and the Heirarchy-of-Effects, unpublished research paper no. 180, Stanford University.

Sellitz C., Jahoda M., Deutsch M. and Cook S. W. (1959) *Research Methods in Social Relations*, Methuen, London.

Suchman E. A. (1950) The Scalogram Board Technique, in *Measurement and Prediction* (ed. S. A. Stouffer), Princeton University Press, New Jersey.

Weiers R. M. (1988) *Marketing Research*, Prentice–Hall, Englewood Cliffs, 2nd edition.

CHAPTER TEN

Experimentation

Introduction   173
Terminology   174
The nature of causality   176
Experimentation and validity   177
Internal validity   178
External validity   181
Experimental designs   182
Laboratory and field experiments   185
Summary   191
References   191

Introduction

A theme that has run constantly throughout this work has been that of validity—truthfulness.

Unless that which is being sampled is sampled in a valid way or that which is being measured is measured in a valid way, then the results could almost be thought of as less useful than no information at all. A further example of where validity assumes an important role is that of experimentation; the subject of this chapter.

In marketing, as in many of the social sciences, there are constant attempts to experiment. For marketing in particular, managers regularly alter the constituent members of the marketing mix; for example, the products themselves are subject to development and modification, their packaging is transformed, the prices go up/go down, the promotional and advertising campaigns are rethought and refocused, distribution policies are reviewed. These "experiments" are tried and at the next meeting of the board of directors it is proudly proclaimed, that as a result of a packaging rethink, sales of Washo, in the last quarter, have increased by 38%.

Now while objective observers are not in a position to be able to question the rise in the sales figures, they are quite legitimately able to take the reason for the sales increase with a "pinch of salt". Can managers, they ask, put their hands on their hearts and state, quite categorically, that the increase in sales is solely the direct effect of a change in the packaging?

Are these managers, under the rules of experimentation, in a position to be able to make a valid causal relationship between the change in the packaging and the sales increase? Before that statement can be accepted as valid, all other potential and/or actual sources of possible influence that could have contributed to the increase in the sales of Washo must be excluded. Without considering, accepting and excluding such influences how can they say that, for example, sales revenue increases were not due to the fact that their main competitor went bankrupt last month, that adverse publicity about another rival had a severe effect upon the rival's sales, that Washo's own sales force had transferred to another and more sales-volume-orientated bonus scheme?

This chapter will explain the conditions for causal relationships, the nature and variety of experiments and the threats which can arise to their validity. The chapter will conclude with a description of one of the more common ways in which marketing concludes experimentation—test marketing.

Terminology

To remove any misunderstanding concerning the exact meaning of the following text, here are explanations of some of the more important words that will be used.

Experiment

An experiment is a process whereby one or more variables are consciously manipulated to evaluate the effects on one or more other variables.

Independent variables or treatment

The independent variable is that variable which is manipulated, the effects of which are to be evaluated. Independent variables include price and package changes, advertising and promotional changes or different modes of distribution.

Dependent variables or measurement

Dependent variables are those variables which are thought likely to be affected by changes in the independent variable. They include sales volume, brand preference, awareness and market share.

Extraneous variables

Extraneous variables are those variables that lie outside the knowledge and control of the manipulators of the experiment. If their effects become too strong, they can so confuse the situation as to substantially reduce the researcher's ability to make valid causal inferences.

Much of the process of experimentation is concerned with the control of extraneous variables.

Test units

Test units are those individuals/bodies/groups to whom the treatments (manipulations) are applied and whose responses form the basis for measurement.

Test units may be individuals, people, shops or geographical areas. Test units may take two forms: experimental and control.

(1) Experimental groups: those groups which are subjected to the experimental treatment.

(2) Control groups: those groups which are not subjected to the experimental treatment. They continue to be the focus of the normal environmental forces before, during and after the treatment is presented to the experimental group.

Experimental design

Experimental design consists of the specification of four factors:

(a) treatments that are to be used,

(b) test units that are to be used,

(c) dependent variables to be measured,

(d) process(es) to cope with extraneous variables.

Notation

The following symbols will be used during the course of the chapter.

X: the independent variable/treatment; $X_1 X_2$ indicates multiple treatments.

O: observation/measurement of the dependent variable.
$O_1 O_2$ indicates multiple observations.

R: indicates the random assignment to separate treatments or that individuals have been assigned, at random, to separate treatment groups.

Symbols should be read as the English language, i.e. from left to right. Movement from left to right indicates movement through time.

For example:

$$XO$$

indicates that observation took place after treatment.

Symbols placed vertically above each other indicate that both events took place simultaneously.

For example:

$$O_1$$
$$O_2$$

indicates that two observations took place at the same time.

The nature of causality

Deterministic causation

If there is a relationship between two events A and B so that B is a function of A, then the relationship may be written

$$B = f(A)$$

If the value of f is known, i.e. the nature of their relationship is known, then by giving A a value, the value of B may be determined.

A is a deterministic cause of B.

Probabilistic causation

In marketing and the social sciences, however, the nature of the relationship(s) is usually said to be only probable. Because of the multitude of variables that could be in operation, it is not possible, conclusively, to prove a causal relationship; the best that can be achieved is to infer a relationship.

Consider the following example from Green, Tull and Albaum (1988).

$$B = f(A_1 \cdot A_2)$$

Even if f can be given a value, then A_1 and A_2 are jointly necessary to determine the value of B.

A known change in A_1 is not sufficient to cause a change in B; it would depend on what happened to A_2. Where there are multivariable relationships it is said that a change in a variable (e.g. A_1) is a probabilistic cause of the effect on B.

There are three cases in which causal inferences may be drawn:

(a) Concomitant or associative variation.

(b) Sequential variables.

(c) Absence/elimination of all other possible causal factors.

(a) Concomitant or associative variation. A measure of the extent to which the presence of variable A is associated with the presence of variable B, or a measure of the extent to which changes in variable A cause an effect in variable B.

(b) Sequential variables. For an effect to be detected in variable B, it must be preceded by a change in variable A, or the effects in variable B are detected simultaneously with the changes in variable A. If the change in variable A occurs after the effects have been detected in variable B, then there can be no causal relationship.

(c) Absence/elimination of all other possible causal factors. If in an experimental situation it were possible to account for or eliminate all other possible causative factors apart from the one in which we have an interest, then it is possible to infer that that variable was the one that caused the changes.

Experimentation and validity

Imagine that you are in a physics laboratory and have been asked to determine the effects of temperature on the frequency of vibration of a tensed wire. Temperature would be the independent variable and frequency of vibration the dependent variable.

To be sure that changes in the detected frequency of the wire's vibration were solely due to changes in temperature all other variables would have to be excluded. So the physicist would have to control humidity, barometric pressure, light intensity etc. Only when all other possible causative factors have been stabilised could he state, with any degree of validity, what the causal relationship was between temperature and the frequency of the wire's vibration.

Even in physical terms, that is a very simple experiment; the control of the extraneous variables was accomplished with relative ease, and in such a way that the experimenter could be sure that they had been excluded or stabilised. A parallel situation in the environments in which a marketing experimenter has to operate is far more complex and the opportunities to be absolutely sure that all extraneous variables have been excluded/stabilised are far more rare.

The outcome of these environmental factors is that in marketing there are many sources of error which can affect the validity of the process of experimentation.

Validity in experimentation will now be discussed under two main headings internal validity and external validity.

Internal validity

Internal validity seeks to ensure that a change in variable A was the sole cause of the effects detected in variable B. If there are other possible reasons why a change in variable B was measured, then the experiment cannot achieve full internal validity.

The major sources of threats to internal validity, according to Campbell and Stanley (1966) are as follows.

(1) History

History, in this context, refers not to some long past event, but to events that take place during the course of the experiment. History in experimentation is concerned with those events which occur, outside the control of the research design, and which affect the dependent variable. The longer an experiment runs, the more likely it is that historical events will cause some significant changes in the measured variable.

For example: during the course of an experiment to measure the changes in sales of a blue cheese after a price increase, there is a news story that blue cheese may contain a new, and potentially dangerous, strain of bacteria. How then can experimenters establish a valid causal relationship between price and sales volume when the drop in sales volumes may be due, partially, to consumers' fears of eating contaminated food?

(2) Maturation

Maturation refers to changes that takes place inside the test units between two measurement times.

For example: suppose that we measure a sample of respondents' attitudes towards a new type of insurance policy. The policy is left with the respondents for a week, after which time we return and again measure their attitudes. Unfortunately, an hour before we knock on their doors, another marketing research agency has administered a questionnaire to them on their attitude towards the latest EC regulations pertaining to microwave ovens. By the time we arrive, they are hardly going to be in a sympathetic mood to our questionnaire. The answers they give, if they open the door at all, might be quite different from those answers they would have given if the rival agency had not intruded.

And as with the case of "history", the longer the period between the two measurements, the more likely it is that maturation effects will have arisen.

(3) Testing

Testing is concerned with the ways in which a measurement taken before the experiment commences can influence the final results, these results can be affected by:

(a) The main testing effect
Testing effects occur when, by the taking of a measurement, the results of following measurements are affected.

For example: suppose a group of respondents are asked, as part of a marketing research project, if they have heard of and/or bought Brand X instant mashed potato: only 30% of them reply in the affirmative.

As a result of this enquiry many of the respondents decide to try the product. At the next respondent meeting, two weeks after the first, the same question concerning knowledge and experience of Brand X is again asked; this time the response is very much higher—one of the main causes of this elevated figure is the initial marketing research question.

(b) The interactive testing effect
The interactive testing effect introduces error into the experiment when the pre-measurement process changes the respondent's reactions to the independent variable(s). Errors due to interactive testing effects are particularly prone to occur when the measurement of attitudes is the subject of the experiment.

For example: suppose a group of respondents were involved with a set of projective exercises concerned with a particular brand of brandy. In the next two weeks these respondents are likely to be more than usually interested in any advertisements and promotional campaigns that the drinks company might run. If a questionnaire is then administered to this group it will most likely result in a heightened knowledge of this particular brand or will record attitudes to that brand which few of the respondents had previously possessed.

(4) Instrumentation effects

Instrumentation effects occur when there are changes in the measuring instrument or process over time.

For example: on the first day of a marketing research project, the interviewers are presented with a questionnaire of brain-numbing complexity. For the first few days the interviewers are "all at sea" over how to use it. As time passes, they become more adept in its use and by the last few days of the project they can whizz through the questions with no thought as to its complexity.

(5) Selection

Selection error occurs with the way in which respondents are allocated to the test and the control groups.

Randomised assignment may overcome this problem, but if the assignment is by some purposive method—self-selection or by the experimenter—then large systematic errors may arise. What concerns those running the experiment is that the groups which result from such a selection process will differ in some significant way with respect to the dependent variable.

For example: supposing a group of respondents has to be divided into a test group and a control group; they are split by the respondents themselves volunteering for one of the groups. The test group sits at a table in the centre of the room, with a view of nothing, and the control group sits by the wall in close proximity to where the wine is dispensed. It is possible that those who volunteer for the control group could differ in some manner from those who opted for the test group.

(6) Mortality

Respondents, for many reasons, may choose not to remain as part of the experiment for its full duration.

Those who fall by the wayside from a single group may differ in some significant way from those who choose to remain.

In experiments which use several groups, those who drop out of group A may differ from those who drop out of groups B, C and D.

As the length of the experiment increases, the opportunities for respondents to leave increase. It may be that a test group, particularly if it is a "difficult"/inconvenient experiment, loses more than the control group; those that remain being keener or more concerned with the subject of the experiment. The differences between the respondents in the two groups may give rise to results which stem mainly from the make-up of the groups, not from their interaction with the subject of the experiment.

(7) Statistical regression

Statistical regression is a form of selection error and occurs when respondents are included in an experiment because of their scores on a previous test.

Where the scores are unreliable or unstable, those with higher scores will reach a relatively lower score on a further measurement and those with lower scores will reach a relatively higher score on a retest, even if there has been no change in that factor which is being measured. There is a tendency for the scores to move towards the population mean of the group (Cook and Campbell, 1979).

External validity

External validity refers to how good the experiment is as a basis on which the researcher may found generalisable comments about the population as a whole. Can the results which were gained through a process of experimentation be applied to the rest of the population?

It is of little use to make general comments about a population based on an experiment that does not even have internal validity; thus internal validity should be considered as a necessary, but not as a sufficient, condition for external validity (Parasuraman, 1986).

External validity is therefore required over and above internal validity for the results of an experiment to be applied, in a general manner, to a population.

There are three main sources of threats to external validity.

(1) Reactive bias

Reactive bias occurs when respondents act atypically because they know they are part of an experiment; it is especially likely to occur if the experiment takes place in a laboratory setting. Respondents may suddenly start to "see" differences between two objects that in a normal everyday setting they would have found indistinguishable, purely because they are being tested to determine if they can see differences between the objects. In field experiments, too, reactive bias may be present. It has previously been mentioned, though not by name, when panel research was discussed. There, a cautionary note was sounded, highlighting the problem that may occur as respondents begin to act differently when they become members of a panel.

(2) Reactive effects of experimentation

This source of error is concerned with what happens to respondents when the test takes place in a surrounding with which they are not familiar, i.e. respondents react to the surroundings and to the experimenters rather than to the variable(s) under examination.

The more unusual (to the respondents) the setting and the more they react to it (are aware of the surroundings) the more likely it is that the results cannot be "projected" on to the population.

(3) Sample bias

Sample bias occurs when those who are the subjects of the experiment are not representative of the general population. This is a problem of sampling, and a fuller discussion of the problem may be found in Chapter Four.

Even if an experiment has total internal validity (an enviable but unlikely state) but is being used on a biased sample, the external validity of the experiment is suspect and the ability to generalise about the population as a whole will be compromised.

Experimental designs

There are three major categories of experimental design: pre-experimental, quasi-experimental and true experiments.

(a) Pre-experimental. So called because they offer the researcher the minimum amount of control over the experimental situation. They are hardly any better than descriptive studies in their ability to establish causal relationships between variables; they are best described as exploratory techniques.

(b) Quasi-experimental. This technique does offer a degree of control over the experimental situation and also renders the opportunity to take more measurements and to gather more data than in a pre-experimental design. There is no opportunity, however, to assign test units randomly to the experimental and control groups.

(c) True experiments. Using this technique, a researcher has the ability to control the experimental situation thus reducing the size of the potential threat(s) to the internal and external validity. True experiments use both control groups and the random assignment of the test units to the control and experimental groups.

Experimental designs for pre- and quasi-experiments

Three types of experimental design are appropriate for use with pre-experiments and quasi-experiments: (i) time-series and trend designs, (ii) cross-sectional designs, and (iii) combinations of (i) and (ii) (Green, Tull and Albaum, 1988).

(i) Time series and trend designs

Time series designs gather their data from the same sample over a series of time intervals, as one would when carrying out panel/continuous research. Analysis of the data can be carried out at the level of the individual sample unit.

Trend designs differ from the above in that the data is gathered from statistically matched samples, and the data must thus be analysed in aggregate form.

The minimum form of these designs involves a single treatment followed by a single observation.

After-only without control group. The most simple of all experimental designs. It may be represented as:

$$XO$$

It involves the manipulation of an independent variable and a subsequent observation/measurement using a non-randomly chosen group. Since there is no measurement prior to the manipulation, there can be no valid assumptions made as to the effects of that manipulation.

Before–after without control group. The same as the design detailed above with the addition of a measurement prior to the manipulation of the variable, it may be represented as:

$$O_1XO_2$$

or as:

$$O_1O_2O_3O_4XO_5O_6O_7O_8$$

The addition of the pre-manipulation measurement gives the researcher the opportunity to calculate, assuming the intrusion of no error, the size of the effect that the manipulation has caused.

$$\text{Size of effect} = O_2 - O_1$$

or

$$\frac{(O_5 + O_6 + O_7 + O_8)}{4} - \frac{(O_1 + O_2 + O_3 + O_4)}{4}$$

However, errors such as history, maturation, pre-measurement and mortality (Tull and Hawkins, 1990) may exert their influence.

Multiple time series. A method used to allow for the effects of history, maturation etc., is that of multiple time series design. In this method a control group is included in the experiment; it may be represented as:

$$\text{Experiment:} \quad O_1O_2O_3O_4XO_5O_6O_7O_8$$

$$\text{Control:} \quad O_1O_2O_3O_4 \ O_5O_6O_7O_8$$

The control group should be as exact an equivalent of the test group as possible.

(ii) Cross-sectional designs
Cross-sectional designs involves measuring the independent variable for several groups at the same time, each group having been subjected to varying degrees of manipulation; it may be represented as:

$$X_1O_1$$

$$X_2O_2$$

$$X_3O_3$$

$$X_4O_4$$

etc.

The effects of the variations in the amounts of manipulation may be evaluated by determining the relationship between the independent and dependent variables. Although, according to Green, Tull and Albaum (1988), this type of design tends to reduce the effects of maturation and testing "to a minimal level", the effects of history may be very important, in that there may be "sizeable differential effects" of the extraneous variables between the groups under measurement.

(iii) Combined cross-sectional and time series designs
Designs which combine cross-sectional and time series experiments are thought to be well suited for use in the gathering of consumer panel information. In this method, which may be represented as in the following diagram, it is not known at the time of the administration of the treatment which is to be the experimental and which the control group.

Experiment: O_1XO_2

Control: $O_3 \; O_4$

This type of test could be used, for example, to test the effectiveness of an advertising campaign. Two sets of initial measurements are made, O_1 and O_3. The advertisements are run, X, and then two further sets of measurements are taken, O_2 and O_4. Those respondents who experienced the treatment (i.e. saw the advertisement) are assigned to the test group, those that did not are assigned to the control group. The effects of the treatment are assessed by comparing the measurements of the control and test groups.

Experimental designs for true experiments

The main difference between these types of experiments and those of the two previous varieties is that with true experiments there is a random assignment of test units to the test and the control groups. This reduces the systematic selection error and averages the effects of extraneous variables between the two groups. Also, because of the random nature of the assignment process, statistical procedures may be used for data analysis.

(i) Only-after with control group
This test is simple and requires only a treatment and a following measurement of test and control groups. It may be represented as follows:

$$\text{Experiment:} \quad RXO_1$$
$$\text{Control:} \quad R\ O_2$$

This method, by omitting a before measurement, may be of use when the effects of before measurement introduce unwanted testing and instrument error.

Although history and maturation effects are not controlled with this type of experiment, Campbell and Stanley (1966) say that the effects of history may be accounted for by repeating the experiment at different times and in various locations.

(ii) Before-after with control group
This may be represented as follows:

$$\text{Experiment:} \quad RO_1XO_2$$
$$\text{Control:} \quad RO_3\ O_4$$

This is very similar to the after-only type of experiment, but with the addition of a before measurement.

By randomly assigning test units to the test and control groups, the effects of maturation, testing and instrumentation are assumed to be spread equally between them both. The effects of history may be controlled if both the two pre-measurements and the two after-measurements are taken at the same time.

Statistical designs

There are four main types of statistically-based experimental design: completely randomised, randomised block, latin square and factorial. With these methods it is possible to use two or more levels of treatment and to assess the effects of two or more treatment variables.

These techniques, however, are beyond the brief of this book. For those who require a discussion of their properties, it is suggested that the appropriate texts are consulted.

Laboratory and field experiments

The two outer poles of the range of settings in which experiments may be conducted are the laboratory and the field.

In laboratory settings, the test units are placed in artificial surroundings; this may be done in an attempt to control the unwelcome effects of extraneous variables.

In a field setting, the test units are assessed in their natural setting: the home, the shop or the factory. This is usually done to help reduce those errors which arise because the respondent may react to the experimental setting.

Laboratory settings tend to have good internal validity because of the experimenter's ability to control confusing extraneous variables. However, the artificial setting may cause the introduction of errors which have their source in the artificial environment, resulting in a test which may have low external validity.

Field experiments, on the other hand, because of their life-like settings, may have good external validity, i.e. they are useful and truthful ways of making generalisable comments about the entire population. Their disadvantage is that the setting does not allow for the control of the extraneous variables, thus reducing their internal validity.

Those that control the project must decide, in the light of the overall objectives of the research and the given characteristics of the experimental situation, which type of experiment offers the most advantageous combination of attributes.

Laboratory tests

Under the heading "external validity", two of the potential sources of error were those called reactive bias and the reactive effects of experimentation.

Reactive bias is the error which occurs when test units, the respondents, realise that they are undergoing a test and act accordingly, i.e. they act atypically. They start to "see" differences between two objects/products that in a normal setting they would not have seen.

The reactive effects of experimentation may cause errors to intrude because the test units are reacting to the situation in which they find themselves (which, to them, is unusual) and to those organising the experiment. The latter effect is similar to the way in which respondents in surveys react to the interviewer. That is, the respondents may use the interviewer as a role model and/or they give the answers that they think the interviewers want to hear. Their effects, according to Tull and Hawkins (1990), may be reduced in the same way as interviewer effects were reduced—by using trained interviewers who have minimum contact with the respondents and who are uninformed as to the research hypotheses being tested.

Psychogalvanometers, eye cameras and tachistoscopes all find their place and their uses in laboratory experiments where they may be used to test, among other things, advertising effectiveness, package designs and product tests.

Laboratory experiments have high internal validity but also tend to have low external validity. If one of the objects of the research project is to be able to make generalisable statements concerning the entire population, then research workers should consider using field experimentation rather than laboratory-based tests.

Field experiments

Field experiments characteristically take place in life-like situations, thus increasing their external validity, but with a concomitant lowering of their internal validity.

Field experiments usually take place in a market setting where they are used for two main purposes: (a) to test market reaction to a new product or to a product concept, and (b) to test variations in the individual components of a product's marketing mix. In other words, for example, while maintaining all other marketing mix factors stable, the price of a good is increased/decreased and the resultant, if any, changes in sales are measured.

The three main types of field experiment are standard test marketing; controlled-store and mini-market test marketing; and simulated test marketing.

Standard test marketing
This experiment is one of the most widely used tests in marketing research. Typically, the project takes place in several representative cities/test areas, some being used as test areas and others as control areas.

Chisnall (1986) presents eight steps in the process of test marketing.

(1) Define the objectives. All parties should agree as to the overall objectives of the research project. This ensures that any subsequent decisions that have to be made are subservient to the aims of the project. It is usual to test only one variable per test marketing exercise.

(2) Set criteria of success. The criteria against which the success of the project is to be judged should be realistic and in proportion to the company's normal sales volumes, levels of advertising etc.

(3) Integrate the test marketing exercises. Any operations that take place as part of a test marketing exercise should be consistent with the normal operating procedures of the company. Unless this is done, the ability to generalise about the entire population will be reduced; i.e. the external validity of the project will be compromised.

Thus, neither the best not the worst sales staff should be used, and the advertising budget for the test area(s) should be in proportion to what would have been spent if this project had been conducted on a national basis.

(4) Set controls. Because the environment of a test market is a real one, there will be an almost infinite number of active variables, variables which may confuse the elicitation of causal relationships between actions and effects. One way in which the effects of these extraneous variables (they are, of course, only extraneous to the test—they are not extraneous to the environment, where they are quite legitimately present) may be evaluated is by the inclusion of control areas/cities. These areas, which are not subjected to the treatment, should be as similar as possible to the test areas with respect to those characteristics which are thought to be important in the situation under investigation. A second way in which the complexity of the research environment may be reduced is by the use of sequential measurement; i.e. measurements are taken not only during the course of the test, but before and after the test marketing exercise. Such measurements should investigate topics which include brand loyalty, levels of competition, price sensitivity and trade discounts.

(5) Select test areas. Test areas should be representative of the population; they should be populations in miniature.

Accordingly, the characteristics they should possess include the following:

(a) They should not be over tested.

(b) They should not be dependent upon a single industry, as disruptions in the normal running of that industry would have disproportionately large effects on the test area.

(c) Areas should have demographic constitutions similar to the national average, i.e. areas that include more students (e.g. Oxford) or people of retirement age (e.g. Bournemouth) than the normal should be avoided.

(d) The area should possess the full range of communications media: radio, television, the press, billboards, cinemas.

(e) The area should neither receive nor provide "media spillover" from and to other areas.

(f) The area's distribution network should be typical of the national pattern.

(6) Choose number of test areas. It is generally accepted that two or three cities/areas are the minimum requirements for testing a new product or altering a constituent of the marketing mix, to which, of course, must be added a similar number of cities/areas for the purposes of control.

Concerning this number, a practical "rule of thumb" is to consider the strategic importance of the project to the company; the more important it is, the higher the levels of risk involved—then the greater the number of test areas that should be used.

However, those involved with the research should consider undertaking a cost–benefit analysis if the number of test areas threatens to become too large;

projects should not be allowed to proceed if the value of the information generated is less than the cost of the test. How the company defines "value" will depend upon the individual company and, for example, the strategic importance of the new product.

(7) Decide on test duration. There are three factors to consider when deciding upon the length of the test.

(a) *Cost*: obviously the longer a test is allowed to run, the more data it will generate, but a time will come when the data settles to a "plateau". At that point the test could be discontinued. However, at any point in the course of the test, a cost–benefit analysis, weighing the additional costs of continuing the test against the quality of the possible future data, could be considered.

(b) *Repurchase rate*: the inclusion of one or perhaps two repurchases of the product under test will give a more valid indication as to durability and robustness of the product in the hurly-burly of the open market. The longer it takes for the product to be repurchased, the longer the test should be allowed to run, i.e. a standard toothpaste tube may be replenished every three weeks to a month, a standard pair of jogging shoes might last six to twelve months, so a test marketing exercise for the latter would have to have a greater duration than the former.

(c) *Competitor reaction*: test marketing is a real situation, however, which means that competitors will be present and active in the environment in which the test is being conducted. It is hardly realistic to expect that Company F will play by the rules of "cricket" while Company E is test marketing a product which could seriously affect their profits; it is likely that Company F will use any method(s), both fair and unfair, to disrupt the smooth running of the Company E's test marketing.

Competitors could, for example, alter the quality and quantity of their advertising campaigns, alter (by which is meant lower) the price of their own similar product to draw sales away from the product under test, buy up large quantities of the test product to give the impression that it is a more successful product than it really is, or undertake a national launch of a similar product on the "back" of the company conducting the test marketing.

(8) Evaluate the results. Straight extrapolation of the results of the test area on to the national market is a simple process, but may be flawed.

Other factors need to be borne in mind. Chisnall (1986) lists:

the demographic structure of the population;
types of available outlets;
strength of competing brands; and
particular variations in test areas in those competitor
    activities which could result in differences between the
    test area and the market for the rest of the country.

Although standard test marketing takes place in a true to life setting, which would suggest the opportunity to obtain good external validity, there are many potential sources of error which can corrupt the results. Much care needs to be expended in the design, control and administration of test marketing exercises if the results are to be reliable, valid and useful.

Controlled-store and mini-market test marketing
To many, the disadvantages of standard test marketing outweigh the advantages, and an increasing number of market researchers are turning to controlled-store and mini-market testing.

For controlled-store and mini-market tests, the product under investigation is handled, distributed, priced, stocked and placed on the shelves by a marketing research agency. In controlled store testing a number of retail outlets in a few locations are used. In mini-market testing a number of different types of retail outlet in a small area are used. The use of advertising in a controlled store test is constrained because of the limited range of outlets being used, but mini-market tests do allow some advertising.

The two main advantages that these methods hold over standard test marketing are that the test can be completed fairly rapidly and that, because of the way that the tests are organised and the results are collected, it is very difficult for competitors of the product being tested to interfere with the test and to obtain any insights into the data that is being generated.

These methods are particularly suited to take advantage of the electronic scanning methods, EPOS, that are now being used to "read" a product's unique bar code.

Simulated test marketing
Another form of test marketing, also gaining in popularity, is simulated or laboratory test marketing. There are many research organisations offering such a service; two of the best known are ASSESSOR in the USA and the "Sensor" system in the UK.

In general, these methods begin by gathering a number of respondents who fit the consumer profile of the product's/brand's intended target market and are then exposed to advertisements for the new product/brand, together with a cross-section of advertisements for its leading competitors. The respondents are then given the opportunity to buy the product in an actual supermarket or in a supermarket created in a laboratory setting; respondents may be given money for this purpose or redeemable coupons. Those who do not purchase the product under test are given a sample of it to take home and try. After sufficient time has elapsed for the respondent to have used/experienced the test product, they are contacted by telephone and asked to evaluate the product and to give their future possible purchase intentions towards the product.

From the data that is generated, the simulated test marketing may be used to forecast the market share for the new product/brand. This is done by using the preference data to predict the number of purchases of the new product/brand that respondents would make if they knew of its existence and it were available. These predictions are then paired with an assessment of the proportion of all the population who will have access to the product/brand for purchase.

Urban and Katz (1983) report that after evaluating the results of 44 simulated test markets, they found a correlation of 0.95 between ASSESSOR and test market predictions.

Summary

Experimentation, in marketing, is the main method of evaluating relationships between variables. Experimentation involves manipulating an independent variable in order to assess the effects of such a treatment on the dependent variable.

However, there are many extraneous variables, beyond the control of the experimenter, which may intrude and affect the dependent variable.

Two types of validity must be considered in experimentation: internal and external. The former is concerned with ability of the experiment to prove that the manipulation of the independent variable was responsible for the effect in the dependent variable. External validity is concerned with the ability of the experiment to generalise, from its results, to the population as a whole.

There are three main groups of experiment: pre-experiment, quasi-experiment and the true experiment. The pre-experiment has very low internal validity. The quasi-experiment, though it does not have the ability to assign, randomly, test units to experimental and control groups, does have the ability to decide to whom the test should be applied and when it should be applied. Weiers (1988) says that quasi-experimentation is "... simply doing the best we can with what we've got available". The true experiment uses randomised allocation of test units and control groups. This type of experiment has high internal validity, though because of its cost and complexity, it may not be so practical in a marketing environment.

Test marketing is the practical assessment of the value of a new product/service or of the alteration in a marketing mix variable in an experimental situation; the situation may either be real or simulated.

References

Cook T. D. and Campbell D. T. (1979) *Quasi-experimentation: Design and Analysis Issues for Field Settings*, Rand McNally College Publishing, Chicago.

Campbell D. T. and Stanley J. C. (1966) *Experimental and Quasi-experimental Designs for Research*, Rand McNally, Chicago.

Chisnall P. M. (1986) *Marketing Research*, McGraw-Hill, London, 3rd edition.

Green P. E., Tull D. A. and Albaum G. (1988) *Research for Marketing Decisions*, Prentice-Hall, Englewood Cliffs, New Jersey, 5th edition.

Parasuraman A. (1986) *Marketing Research*, Addison-Wesley Publishing Company, Reading, Massachusetts.

Tull D. S. and Hawkins D. I. (1990) *Marketing Research: Measurement and Methods*, Macmillan, New York, 5th edition.

Urban G. L. and Katz G. M. (1983) Pre-test market models, *Journal of Marketing Research*, August, 221–234.

Weiers R. M. (1988) *Marketing Research*, Prentice-Hall, Englewood Cliffs, 2nd edition.

CHAPTER ELEVEN

Writing and Reading Research Reports

Introduction to report writing   193
(1) The "target" audience   194
(2) The content of the report   195
(3) The style of the report   200
Introduction to reading research reports   203
Comment   205
References   205

Introduction to report writing

Good plays can be ruined by a badly directed cast, fine oil paintings can be rendered drab and uninteresting by ill-chosen frames and delicious food can be made to appear unappealing if it arrives at the table stone-cold and inappropriately smothered in an over-elaborate decoration.

Well thought out and executed marketing research reports can also be made to appear dreary, uninteresting, sloppy and intimidating if the presentation is not given as much thought and attention as the other components in the project.

Generally speaking, reports are not written in a manner that seeks to entertain the palates of jaded business executives, but neither should they be made to appear as "heavy" academic tomes merely to gain credibility.

The main guiding principle when writing a marketing research report is that it communicates what it is supposed to communicate, and it should do so in a manner which is appropriate to the intended reader; i.e. it must engage the interest of the reader, and address the situation which was outlined in the research objectives. If the report is too long, too short, full of grammatical and spelling errors, and/or lacking in a coherent, overall structure and logic, the data, however skilfully gained and analysed, cannot be used effectively by those who commissioned the research project.

A further point: as the report may be the only "contact" that many executives have with the research consultant, it is as well to remember that they will form their opinion of you based on your report; a report which does not fulfil expectations will reflect badly on you and on your research organisation.

Factors to be considered when writing research reports which will be discussed include the target audience, the content of the report and the style of the report.

(1) The "target" audience

When one meets a stranger for the first time, it is normal to make some type of assessment as to the character of that person; an assessment which is subsequently used as a basis for deciding on the way in which to conduct oneself in the company of that person. When authors write textbooks, before they commence the job of putting pen to paper, they decide on the type of market segment for which the book is intended, and then position the text accordingly.

Similarly, such a process should be carried out before a marketing research report is written; i.e. those that are responsible for the production of the final report should make detailed enquiries as to the intended "target" audience. Such enquiries will, of course, be facilitated by the contacts between agency/ researcher and client/executives during the course of the project.

Speaking in broad terms, marketing research reports fall into two main groups: the "technical" and the "general".

Technical reports

These types of document are intended, in the main, for those who are sufficiently well versed, or interested, in the theories of marketing research, to be able to appreciate, evaluate and derive benefit from a piece of work which goes into some technical detail concerning the research techniques and types of analysis used in the course of a project. Such personnel would include a company's marketing research specialists and those charged with the analysis of data.

The language of such a report can therefore be of considerably more technical complexity than that which would be used in a report for the "generalists" in a company; those who have no, or little, expertise and/or interest in the research's more theoretical foundations.

Technical reports should contain sufficient data and detail for the specialist to be able to assess the reliability and validity of the techniques used and for any calculations to be checked.

Technical reports are the equivalent of articles which appear in those specialist journals which encourage an academic or quasi-academic interest in a subject.

Popular reports

By the use of the word "popular", it is not the intention to imply that such a report should be down-market. It is possible to explain to a non-specialist target audience the technical aspects of a project without cheapening it, without making it seem trivial.

Non-specialist audiences are generally not sufficiently qualified to be able to appreciate, for example, a 24 page analysis of the pros and cons of probability versus non-probability sampling techniques; nor, in the majority of cases, are they interested in having to read such an exposition. They are interested in the destination, not in the route. But, they will be interested in why you preferred, for example, one particular type of sampling technique to the others, given the context of their particular research problem.

With a target audience more interested in results than techniques, it is important to avoid "talking down" or patronising them. Technical terms that are in common usage may be employed, but those of a more esoteric nature should be avoided. Marketing research reports should not be grasped by the research consultant as opportunities to "dazzle" an audience with their erudition and command of polysyllabic jargon.

Writers of popular research reports, those intended for general audiences, might consider using a slightly more colloquial style of writing and, perhaps, including more visual presentations—graphs, bar-charts etc.—than they would when writing a technical report. Graphs contain exactly the same amount of data as a table yet they are able to present the data in a more "user-friendly" way. It makes the report more digestible and it also, visually, reduces the apparent bulk of a text.

It may be possible, using appendices, to contain the majority of the report's technical aspects, to write a work which can be used for both the technical and the more general audience. However, this is not always possible; in such cases Weiers (1988) suggests that the consultant may be forced to write two reports: one technical, one general.

(2) The content of the report

Research reports are, usually, not commissioned for fun! And neither are they commissioned for inclusion in scholarly journals, or as opportunities for research consultants to pursue their own areas of interest—though some reports would seem to suggest otherwise!

Research, when commissioned by a company, is intended to help with the resolution of some area(s) of interest/concern. Those that commission marketing research reports do not do so merely to keep consultants from the unemployment statistics. They do so because they have encountered an actual situation which needs attention. Therefore, an overriding principle when deciding upon the contents of a research report is that everything included within the covers should be orientated in a direction to help focus attention on those areas of interest and/or concern. Only data that is relevant should be included and recommendations should only be included if they are requested and if they are valid, practical and firmly based on the findings of the project.

Reports which are over-wordy, contain a plethora of that which is irrelevant and impractical should be (and usually are) filed (temporarily) in the company executive's waste-paper bin.

While no two research reports are identical, Tull and Hawkins (1990) recommend, in general terms, that the following format will act as a worthwhile starting point for most types of report.

(i) The title page

The title of the report should be short and accurate and should encourage the potential reader to proceed further. Anything too academic or too sensational (the tabloid style of headline) will repel rather than attract readers.

The title page should also contain the names of those who commissioned the research, the date and the names of the company and the consultants who conducted the research.

(ii) The executive summary

Many business managers, inundated with reports, files, accounts, do not have the time (or the energy) to read every last page of every paper that lands on their desk; marketing research reports are included in this intimidating list of work.

Therefore, the executive summary may be all that an executive reads of the report, or it may be all that they are given. Its importance cannot be underestimated and it should receive the appropriate degree of care in its preparation.

It will need to contain all the major points of the report, such that a busy executive can grasp, quickly, the essence of the project. It should include the context of the research project, the facts, the findings, the conclusions and, if demanded, the recommendations.

At this point in the report, a detailed description of the methodology would not normally be considered appropriate.

The executive summary is certainly not the place for the use of highly complex technical language or jargon.

It is probably the most difficult single section of the report to construct and can only be written when the remainder of the report has been completed: i.e. it should be the final section of the report to be written.

(iii) Table(s) of contents

If the report is anything longer than between five and ten pages, then it is appropriate to include a table of contents to make the report easier to use. It is normal to give the chapters headings against which the appropriate page numbers are printed. Large, important sections/sub-divisions should also be detailed. Also, if the report contains a number of tables and figures, it is advisable to include separate tables listing both types of data. Appendices, which are presented at the end of the report, should also be detailed in the table of contents.

(iv) Introduction

Not every member of the organisation which has commissioned the research will be as well informed (1) as to the reasons for the research, and (2) on the project's topics of interest, as those who have been working alongside the marketing research consultants during the course of the project. Therefore, in order to render a wider company understanding of the report, and of the context in which the research took place, it is important to make the most of the introductory part of the report as a way of orientating the general reader.

Topics to be included in the introduction should include:

(1) The background to the research—the context is very important—and the marketing opportunity, threat or area of interest that acted as a catalyst for the commission of the report.

(2) A precise description of the research that was undertaken and the manner in which it was derived from the marketing opportunity, threat or area of interest.

(3) The way in which the report is to be presented.

(4) A precise, compact description of the procedures and processes that were used to fulfil the overall objectives of the research.

It is in the process of writing this introductory section, particularly, that report writers are faced with the problem of deciding the type of work to produce; is it intended for a technical audience or a popular one? If the argument is too difficult to resolve with the production of a single piece of work, then two reports, one technical, one popular, will have to be produced. However, as most business administrators are, in general, not so technically qualified (or, indeed, interested) in the detailed aspects of the research process, it is usual to produce a report aimed at the popular audience, with the technical aspects of the research being kept to a minimum. If the writer of the report concludes that a certain number of company members might have some interest in the research's technical aspects, then the report should include those details in the appropriate appendices.

However, while only a minority of the target audience might have an interest in the technical side of the work, almost all readers will need to know, in detail, why the research made a preferential choice of one research method over others.

The introductory section of the report should also include an exposition as to the type of research design(s) that has/have been used: descriptive, exploratory, causal etc., the sources of data, the system(s) of sampling employed, and the types of survey method utilised. Questionnaires, instructions for field workers, letters of introduction etc., should not be presented at this juncture as they would only impede the flow of the introduction without adding anything directly useful to the knowledge of the reader; better that such items be kept until the end of the report and be presented in the appropriate appendices.

(v) Results

The results section of a report is, usually, the prime reason why a marketing executive is going to read a report.

Therefore, apart from the fact that great care must be taken with this section it is vital that what is presented here is congruent with the objectives of the research; those objectives that were decided upon and mutually agreed upon at the commencement of the research process. Only that which is relevant should be included. Data of only peripheral interest, or data which the research consultant thinks might only be of interest to the company's research executives, should be restricted to the appendices.

Even if the research project was of only moderate dimensions, it is likely that there will be a mass of data to be considered. This should be organised into a coherent and logically ordered whole so that the writer's interpretation is clear to the reader.

If any analysis of the data has been undertaken, then care should be exercised in the way in which the results are presented. Nothing is more guaranteed to frustrate and anger a reader than having to plough through endless, arid tables of statistics and figures. Better by far to describe, in an accessible manner, what the research uncovered and to include only the most pertinent figures as evidence for your findings.

How far the technical aspects of the data analysis are discussed will best be determined by an assessment of the type of audience for which the report is primarily aimed. As a "rule of thumb", from experience, the author recommends that the level of technical detail, in the main body of the text, is kept fairly low, with the appendices being used for the presentation of the more complicated technical points.

Graphs, diagrams, pie-charts etc., and even cartoons, are all useful in "breaking up" solid blocks of text (blocks which can appear so intimidating when the report is first seen) and letting a little "light" into the body of the report.

(vi) Limitations

To pretend to the commissioners of the report that during the progress of the research everything proceeded absolutely "according to plan" would, rightly, open the research consultant to the criticism of being either an ostrich or entertaining a level of optimism that even Voltaire's Dr Pangloss in "Candide", might have found naive! There will be problems in the execution of the project and their incidence should be brought to the attention of the reader. Without stating them, one of the essential elements of the context in which the research took place will be missing.

Luck and Rubin (1987) bring to attention such problems as:

(1) the constraints of time,

(2) the degree to which the research results can be applied to a larger population,

(3) the potential effects of non-response,

(4) the potential effects of substituting a sample unit, in the field, because of "not at home" elements.

(vii) Conclusions and recommendations

To conclude the report, one must draw from the results, for each of the research objectives, the implications that these findings have for the organisation with respect to their marketing decision making process; implications should be drawn logically from the results of the data analysis.

It may be, because of the strategic importance of the decisions that have to be made, that the report will not be asked to make any recommendations; the research results being only one input to the process of making policy decisions.

However, the researcher may be asked to make recommendations. If this is so, care should be exercised; the researcher must remember that he/she only has knowledge of the findings from this one particular study, and that this study must be the sole basis on which his/her recommendations are to be made. Caution is recommended because of the researcher's possibly limited knowledge and view of the company's total situation.

One final point: it is within the brief of the researcher to suggest areas of interest/concern where additional investigation(s) should be directed.

(viii) Appendices

This section of the report should not be used as the "attic" of the study; as the place where all the marketing research's equivalent of household cast-offs are to be stored.

Items included in the appendices should be those which are of supplementary, but still pertinent, interest to the main body of the text. Appendices might include sampling plans, questionnaires, letters and statistical tables. They may also be used as a way of including the technical aspects of the work, which may only be of interest to a limited audience and which, if included in the main body of the report, might cause frustration and interrupt the progress of the less technically minded.

(3) The style of the report

While it is not the intention, here, to give an English lesson, some readers may benefit from the following, short section which offers a few guidelines for writing research reports.

(i) Report length

Keep it short!

Do not feel tempted to think that length necessarily equals quality. Make your points briefly, clearly and repeat them only as often as is absolutely necessary.

(ii) Formality

The use of personal pronouns such as "I", "me", "you" etc., tends to suggest a level of informality which many readers might think of as too "forward". Better to stick closely to the format which is used in scientific reports—the third person passive. Here instead of saying, for example, "I took a test-tube and filled it with sulphuric acid" it is usual to say "A test test tube was taken and filled with sulphuric acid". The use of such a style will tend to reinforce the impression that the report is an objective piece of work—one that could be repeated and reach similar conclusions, whoever carried out the research. The "scientific" style will tend to remove the "taint" that many think comes from too personalised a manner of presentation.

(iii) Sentence construction

Keep sentences short and keep them to a single point. If there are too many points in one sentence, too many subsidiary clauses, consider breaking it up into several smaller sentences. Remember, complex subjects are not explained to a reader, with their maximum clarity, by the use of complex sentence structures.

Do not become depressed when several rewrites are required. Very few people can get everything right at a first attempt.

If there are any doubts as to the clarity of a sentence, then the author has found the following two checks to be of assistance:

(1) Read the doubtful passage out aloud.

(2) Get someone, totally unconnected with the research report, to read those portions of the report which are troubling you.

Use commas, colons, semi-colons and brackets to make the meaning of a sentence clear, unambiguous and easy to read.

(iv) Technical language/jargon

Though there are times when a researcher might feel the impulse to club a particularly difficult client over the head with technical words in an attempt to beat him/her into acquiescence, it is an impulse which should be resisted.

If the report is to be aimed at a popular, non-technically literate audience, the use of technical language and jargon should be reduced to the absolute minimum. Readers do not want to have to sit with the report in one hand and a dictionary in the other. If technical words/phrases are to be used, they should be simply explained without patronising the reader. Writers can, of course, consign small explanations to footnotes and more detailed explanations to the appendices.

(v) Non-technical language

Unfortunately, it is not only technical language that can cause a problem; there are many, seemingly, ordinary words which can act as a minefield for the unwary.

Timm (1980) has shown how positive, neutral and negative emotions may be aroused when using words that, in absolute terms, have more or less the same meaning.

For example:

Positive	Neutral	Negative
scholarly	well-educated	bookworm
meticulous	exact	nit-picker
fragrance	smell	odour
converse	talk	prattle
dignified	proud	arrogant

It is prudent to consider the emotional "overtones" of certain words and to ensure, that wherever possible, a neutral version, with the same meaning, is employed.

(vi) Organisation

Use chapters, headings and sub-headings (all of which should appear in the table of contents) (a) to break up long blocks of text, and (b) to make the report easier to read.

(vii) Visual aids

Graphs, charts, diagrams, cartoons, pictures can all be used to reduce the perceived bulk of long sections of text. But they should be used to supplement the text, not to replace it.

One picture may be worth a thousand words, but it is in the words that the worth of a marketing research report is to be found.

(viii) The use of statistics

When well used, statistics can be an invaluable aid in the presentation of research reports. However, Weiers (1988) counsels that when they are used, the writer should:

(1) avoid those statistical terms with which the report's target audience may not be familiar;

(2) try to simplify the statistical terms which cannot be avoided by using, plain, understandable language when the terms are introduced. For example, use "average" instead of "mean" and "maximum error" instead of "confidence interval".

Timm (1980) adds the following:

(a) round large numbers up/down, e.g. 101,358 becomes 101,000 or 101,500;

(b) use numbers in a way which has some meaning to the report's prospective audience, e.g. percentages;

(c) if possible, try to avoid using the word "probability" as this is a statistical term which might "frighten off" some potential readers;

(d) only compare like with like: percentages with other percentages and means with means.

Introduction to reading research reports

While the main thrust of this book has been aimed at those who carry out marketing research projects, there will be others who will only read them. Of course, those that enter the profession of marketing research will also have to read reports. When coming face to face with a research report for the first time, it is unlikely that everyone will grant blanket acceptance to all that they find between the covers; a healthy degree of scepticism is a useful "tool" in business administration.

In order to guide the readers of reports and the listeners of presentations in a logical manner when making an assessment of what they have read/heard, the American Research Foundation (1981), as reported in Tull and Hawkins (1990) have produced the following guidelines.

(1) Origin—what is behind the research?

The report should contain a clear statement as to why the research was conducted, who sponsored it and who conducted it.

- Does the report identify the organisation(s), divisions or departments which initiated the research?
- Does the report contain a statement of purpose that states, clearly, what the research was to achieve?
- Are the organisations etc., that defined and conducted the research identified?

(2) Design—the concept and the plan

The research approach, the sampling plan and the analysis should be clearly stated and should be appropriate for the purpose of the research.

- Is there a complete, non-technical description of the research design?
- Are the research design and the purpose(s) of the study congruent?
- Does anything about the research design, including the measuring instrument(s), induce any bias—particularly bias in favour of the report's sponsor?
- Does the research design control for patterns of sequence or timing or other external factors which might prejudice the results?
- Are the respondents capable of answering the questions?
- Is there an exact statement of the population(s) the research is to represent?
- Is the sampling frame capable of adequately representing the population?

- Does the report specify the type of sample used and the sampling selection process?
- Does the report detail the data analysis processes?
- Are the questionnaire(s), field and sampling instructions included in the report or are they on file?

(3) Execution—collecting and handling the information

Data should be collected by appropriately qualified, competent personnel using forms and methods suitable for the task.

- Does the report describe the methods of data collection, including the "quality control" procedures?
- Does the report detail the proportion of the selected sample from which data was collected?
- Were those who collected the information treated in a way that would minimise any bias they might introduce?

(4) Stability—sample size and reliability

Sample sizes should be stated and they should be adequate to give stable results.

- Is the size of the sample large enough to render stable findings?
- Are the sampling error limits shown—if applicable?
- Is the calculation of the sampling error explained, or is its absence explained?
- Does the treatment of sampling error make it clear that it does not include the non-sampling error?
- For the major findings, are the reported error tolerances based on direct analysis of the variability of the data that has been collected?

(5) Applicability—generalising the findings

The report should indicate, unambiguously, the constraints which limit the findings.

- Does the research report detail when the data was collected?
- Does the report state, clearly, whether its results apply beyond the direct source(s) of the data?
- Is it clear which groups, if any, are under-represented in the data?

- If the research has limited applications, is it explained who or what it represents and the times/conditions under which it applied?

(6) Meaning—interpretations and conclusions

All the judgements/assumptions involved in reaching the findings, conclusions and recommendations should be clearly stated.

- Are measurements described in simple, clear, direct language?
- Does the use of the measurements make sense?
- Are the actual findings and any interpretations based on those findings clearly differentiated?
- Has rigorous objectivity and candid reporting been used in interpreting research findings as evidence of causation or as predictive of future behaviour?

(7) Candour—open reporting and disclosure

The report should be an honest and complete description of the process of research and of the findings.

- Is there a full and forthright disclosure of how the research was carried out?
- Have all the potentially relevant findings been presented?

Comment

Reports should be written in a way that communicates, to the reader, clearly and unambiguously how the research was planned, organised and carried out and what was found. Do not try to make claims that cannot be substantiated. It should be an honest and true reflection of what was done and what was found—if there were problems, state them.

In the report you should be aiming for that rather unsettling image one sees in the bathroom mirror in the clear, uncompromising light of dawn. Without great care, reports can resemble the reflection that one sees in a fairground—entertaining, amusing, but so distorted as to be of little practical use.

References

Luck D. J. and Rubin D. S. (1987) *Marketing Research*, Prentice-Hall, Englewood Cliffs, New Jersey, 7th edition.

Timm P. R. (1980) *Managerial Communications*, Prentice-Hall, Englewood Cliffs, New Jersey.

Tull D. A. and Hawkins D. I. (1990) *Marketing Research: Measurement and Method*, Macmillan, New York, 5th edition.

Weiers R. M. (1988) *Marketing Research*, Prentice-Hall, Englewood Cliffs, New Jersey, 2nd edition.

CHAPTER TWELVE

Commissioning Marketing Research

Introduction   207
(1) Specifying the research requirements   208
(2) Preparation of the research brief   209
(3) In-house research versus an external research agency   210
(4) Preparation of a list of agencies   211
(5) Evaluation of the research proposals   213
(6) Selecting the agency   213
Summary   214
Reference.   214

Introduction

When people go shopping for a long list of items, or when they are in the process of purchasing some expensive product for the house, it is usually the case that some type of advanced preparation takes place, even for fairly mundane tasks.

Shoppers do not just buy any old product they see on the shelves of their local supermarket or the first washing machine/motor car they see when they walk into a showroom. When many items are required, shoppers usually make a list; with an expensive purchase, where the repercussions of making an incorrect choice could be serious, prospective buyers gather brochures and, maybe, ask the opinion of those they think of as having some expertise/experience in that product area (in other words, they carry out a little secondary marketing research) before making their own evaluation as to the most appropriate choice given their own circumstances.

And so it should be when an organisation sets out to commission marketing research. Companies should prepare their own "shopping list" of items that they want to be investigated, before seeking out the most appropriate consultancy to carry out that investigation.

This, final, chapter seeks to offer to those who are in the process of commissioning marketing research a check-list of the areas that should be given some consideration.

(1) Specifying the research requirements

Crouch (1988) recommends that companies seeking to embark upon a marketing research project should ask the following questions:

(a) Is the research really necessary?

Almost any additional information is going to prove of some interest to someone in the company. But, there are practical limitations as to what marketing research can do. What a company should do, therefore, is to ask the question, "Is marketing research absolutely necessary?" If it is not, then the project should not proceed. The reasons for a negative answer to the above question might include the following:

- The risks/repercussions of making a wrong decision are small.
- The space in which a company has to manoeuvre is so narrow that no amount of additional information will be of help.
- The research can only be completed after the time when the decision will have had to have been made.

If the answer is "Yes, the research is necessary", then it should be allowed to proceed.

(b) What type of research is required?

Crouch (1988) makes a particularly useful comment on this point: "As with a lamp-post to a drunken man, research can be used in two ways: for illumination or for support."

The type of research that is to be carried out will depend, largely, upon the use to which the data is put.

If it is to illuminate, then it will probably be used to provide a "torch" to light up those areas of interest in which the company has little direct experience. Such areas could include idea generation and topics where a greater understanding of the situation is required, areas where qualitative research is particularly well suited to help.

Information of the "support" variety is likely to include data which will be used to confirm/deny the company's assessment of a situation. Information used as a support, can be of the exploratory, descriptive or causal variety.

(c) For what purpose will the research be used?

This question is a continuation of the one that was asked in (b) above. If a company is in, for example, the early stages of a new product development programme, then it is likely that qualitative data will be required. When the area of interest is better known, for example when deciding between two advertising/promotional campaigns, then quantitive data would be more fitting.

(d) When is the research needed?

In an ideal world, the data from the research should be immediately available to help with making those decisions which prompted the project in the first place. However, ideal worlds are in rather short supply; research, of even the simplest variety, will take some finite time to complete. Even if the data is the answer to a manager's dream, but it arrives after the decision has to be made, it will be less than useful.

Estimates will thus need to be made as to the type(s) of research which can be completed given the time-scale of the decision-making process. A short, well thought-out research project that renders practical assistance and is completed on time, is of more use than a much larger and more comprehensive investigation whose results will only arrive after the point at which the necessary steps will have had to be taken.

(e) What is the value of the research

Managements should try to ensure that they do not become like those people whom Oscar Wilde categorised as knowing the price of everything and the value of nothing!

Marketing research could be said to be a way of reducing the risks associated with a certain proposed course of action—a kind of corporate "insurance policy". But just as it would be rather strange if the cost of an insurance policy premium on an antique painting was greater than the value of the picture, so it would be if the costs of a marketing research project were to be higher than the value of the information which it generated.

Those involved in the instigation of research projects should conduct a cost–benefit analysis before starting the research. They should ask the question, "What would be the likely cost if such-and-such a course of action went wrong?" If that cost is greater than the price of marketing research that would substantially reduce the risk of making a wrong decision, then the investigation should be allowed to proceed.

(2) Preparation of the research brief

This section is covered in great detail in Chapter Two, especially sections 1, 2, 3 and 4.

However, it must be emphasised, yet again, that whatever is included in the research brief, there must be a close mutual agreement between those that commission the research and those who are charged with its discharge.

The main thrust of this chapter, so far, has been to imply that the research will be conducted by personnel outside the organisation. But it may be the case that the project could be undertaken by the company's own marketing research department, if such a body exists.

The choice as to whether the project is run in-house or "farmed out" to an external agency is the subject of the next section.

(3) In-house research versus an external research agency

Having fixed, at least as far as the commissioning company is concerned, the research brief (it will, of course, still have to be finally agreed with those charged with the discharge of the research), the next decision to be made is whether the company should carry out the research in-house or contract it to a specialist marketing research agency.

The advantages and disadvantages of contracting out the research are given below.

Advantages of using "outside" specialists

(a) The company will only have to pay for research when it is necessary, i.e. they will not have to bear the annual costs of a full-time in-house marketing research department.

(b) Contracting out offers the opportunity to gain access to a wider range of specialist skills, many of which may not be available when using the in-house research department.

(c) The research should be conducted with a greater sense of objectivity, with an associated absence of opportunity for the project to become "contaminated" by the influence of company politics.

(d) It may offer the opportunity to conduct the research anonymously.

(e) The wider range of facilities and resources, both in terms of equipment and specialised personnel, that will be available in a marketing research agency.

(f) There are research agencies which specialise in certain types of research methods/product areas. Such an agency could save the company considerable time because of their expertise and knowledge.

Disadvantages of using "outside" specialists

(a) The external research body may suffer from a lack of direct familiarity with the topic under investigation; certainly in comparison with an in-house team.

(b) As the external agency will be operating "at arm's length", there is, compared with an internal research department, the possibility that quality control may not be all that the commissioning body would wish it to be.

(c) If the external company is a specialist in a certain type of research or, more pertinently, in working in a particular product area, there is a possibility of "leaks" of confidential data to the commissioning company's competitors.

(d) And, finally, there is the additional cost of having to commission the research.

The company must balance out the competing advantages and disadvantages of carrying out the research in-house or of going to an external agency. Such a decision will need, also, to build into the equation the overall objectives of the research.

(4) Preparation of a list of agencies

If it is decided that the preferred course of action is to go outside the company and make use of the services of an external research agency, then the next step is to draw up a list of prospective organisations. There are many ways in which this can be done; they include:

(a) Using the personal experience of the commissioning company's management.

(b) The recommendation of colleagues in other companies.

(c) The recommendation of trade associations, such as the Institute of Management and, particularly, the Market Research Society. In the United Kingdom, the Market Research Society issues a booklet entitled "Organisations providing Market Research Services in Great Britain and Northern Ireland". The booklet lists all the appropriate agencies together with their sizes and specialist services. Using such data it is possible to construct a broad-list which matches the company's requirements with possible agencies.

Using such sources of information it is possible to draw up a list of agencies that might be suitable to carry out the required research. To reduce this to a short-list of, say, two or three possible agencies, each agency should be contacted and asked to make a short presentation to the commissioning company.

Presentations should be evaluated against a set of criteria; including:

(a) The technical capabilities of the research agency's key individuals.

(b) The degree of "fit" between the market, technical and/or product specialisation that the commissioning company requires/needs for its particular research project(s) and what can be provided by the agency.

(c) The orientation which the agency exhibits towards marketing management, i.e. does the agency have an understanding of the decision-making processes that have to be undertaken in the company's marketing department.

(d) The experience and the educational qualifications of the agency's staff.

(e) The research facilities of the agency; i.e. the type/range of fieldwork they can mount, the equipment they own/have access to, to process and analyse data.

(f) The level of creativity exhibited by the agency in its presentation.

(g) The communication skills employed by the agency in its presentation.

(h) Their ability to maintain rigid time-scales.

(i) The stability of the agency, i.e. are the key personnel likely to remain with the agency for the duration of your research project.

After these presentations, those agencies which would appear to meet the requirements of the company are then briefed as to the research project under consideration and invited to prepare a research proposal.

Crouch (1988) recommends that the brief to the prospective agencies should cover such areas as:

(a) The background/objectives of the research. Why the research is thought to be necessary and the context of the research.

(b) Information on the relevant population group(s).

(c) What type of research is thought to be appropriate. The commissioning company will obviously have given some thought as to the type of research they think appropriate for this project, i.e. qualitative or quantitative. However, "good" research agencies should inform the company if they think that the type of research that, to date, has been envisaged is inappropriate.

(d) The question areas to be covered. The more specific the commissioning company is concerning the detailed question areas to be covered, the better equipped will be the agency in its preparation of the research proposal (which should lead to the chosen agency being better able to carry out the project).

(e) The date when the project is to be completed.

(5) Evaluation of the research proposals

When the company has received all the research proposals, they will need to be evaluated in order that the final choice of agency can be made.

Points to look out for when making such an evaluation include:

(a) Have the agency understood the problem or area of interest/concern and have they, consequently, produced a proposal which fully covers all the areas that need to be investigated?

(b) Is there a detailed analysis of how the population of interest is to be sampled, and is there an estimation as to the likely size of the required sample?

(c) Have the agency presented what appears to be a sound methodology for this particular project, i.e. is the population going to be approached using mail/telephone/face-to-face interviews, group discussions, projective techniques etc.?

(d) If a questionnaire is proposed, is there a discussion as to the general type of questions that should be included?

(e) Is there a description of how the data editing, coding and analysis is to be accomplished?

(f) Is there a detailed breakdown of how the project is to be time-tabled and does this time-table suggest that the project is capable of being finished by the stipulated date?

(g) Is there a detailed breakdown of the proposed costs of the project?

(h) Does the proposal reveal any evidence that the agency has consulted the relevant sources of secondary data or that the agency already possesses useful background knowledge?

(i) From the proposal (and from the presentation) does the company think that they can work with the agency, i.e. is the project going to be free (or relatively free) from personality clashes?

(j) Does the proposal exhibit a "freshness" of thought, i.e. does it look as if the company has thought through this particular problem from first principles, or does it appear as if it is a "standard" proposal that has been dusted down and repackaged with the commissioning company's name on the cover?

(6) Selecting the agency

When a research agency has been chosen, the chosen company should be contracted to carry out the project.

The contract should give permission for the research to commence and set out those areas of interest which have been agreed upon. In detail, it should stipulate the budget and the date for the delivery of the final report.

Summary

Marketing research, in general, is not an inexpensive item and much may rest upon the quality of the information which is generated. Therefore, just as much thought needs to be devoted to the selection of an appropriately qualified research agency as a company would give to the purchase, say, of a costly piece of equipment.

This short chapter has shown how a company intent on commissioning marketing research should proceed; just as one would act when designing a questionnaire, i.e. move from the general to the specific—from the question of whether to carry out the research using an in-house team, through to the final selection of an agency.

Companies should not feel pressurised into making an inappropriate and unnecessarily hasty decision. If in doubt, pretend that the costs of the project are going to be deducted from the salaries of those company members who will make the final decision—that should inject the necessary degree of caution into the selection process!

Reference

Crouch S. (1988) *Marketing Research for Managers*, Heinemann, London.

eviation

…udents' height was measured and found to be the same (an unlikely …then there would be no normal distribution curve, merely a vertical …h would have the same value as the mean, the median and the mode. …mon sense tells us that this is unlikely. Some students have large grants …as grow tall on the nutritious, high-fibre diets that they are able to … Some students are poorly funded or they spend all their time in the …bar; thus they are under-nourished and so do not grow as tall as the …s. But the majority of students drink only moderately and are able to get …tion jobs to supplement their meagre grants. So the average student tends …ave an average height; this results in the fact that their heights do not …iate radically from the mean. Those that are either very tall or very short …stature do not have average heights and so their measurements will exhibit …ger deviations from the mean.

The standard deviation (SD) of a distribution of measurements is a way of …ndicating the typical amount by which all of the measured values deviate from …he mean of those values. If the measurements that are taken to construct a normal distribution curve are widely dispersed, then the deviations from the average (the mean) will be widely dispersed and, correspondingly, the SD—the amount by which the measured values deviate—will be large.

If the measurements are confined within a narrow spread, i.e. the measurements are not widely dispersed, then the deviations from the mean will be low and the SD will be small.

SD (σ) can be calculated using the following formula:

$$\sigma = \sqrt{\frac{\Sigma(x - \mu)^2}{N}}$$

x = the value of each measurement
μ = the mean of the set of measurements
N = the total number of measurements

The shape of the normal distribution curve can vary widely. They can be tall and thin, like a dunce's cap, or they can be short and flat, like a French beret. The shape of the curve depends upon the size of the standard deviation.

Small standard deviations, where measurements do not vary greatly from the mean, and where there is a small spread of results, give tall, thin curves (Figure 5).

Large standard deviations, where measurements do vary greatly from the mean, and where there is a wide spread of results, give short, flattened curves (Figure 6).

Statistics and Sampling

Introduction 215
Normal distribution curves 216
Standard deviation 218
Samples, their dispersion and marketing research 221

Introduction

In probability sampling techniques, each sample unit is selected, from the sampling frame, by chance and each unit has a known chance of selection. The major problem with a sample is that, as it is made up of only a very small part of the entire population, it is unlikely that it can be an exact representation, in miniature, of that population. The laws of probability, on which these sampling techniques are based, allows, however, for an estimation to be made of how close the sample statistic that has been measured is to the true value of the parameter in the population. The following section shows, in simple form, how the laws of probability may be used to make estimates of the representativeness of samples.

As was stated in the introduction to this work, it is not the intention, here, to include an in-depth discussion of statistical techniques; there are many excellent books on the topic which may be consulted by those interested in a more detailed study of the subject. However, in marketing research, it is rare that a consultant has the opportunity (or the finances) to conduct a census of a population to measure the characteristics in which he/she has an interest—except where the population of interest is relatively small. Time, together with financial and personnel constraints, all have their influence in propelling the consultant in the direction of sampling techniques. As a result, it is thought useful that the reader should have some basic grounding in the way in which statistics are used in marketing research sampling techniques. Even for those wary of statistics, this discussion will be "user-friendly" and will provide comfort to those who have previously doubted the way in which marketing research has projected the results of a sample onto an entire population.

Appendix

Normal distribution curves

If the height of a first year university student is measured and then plotted on to a graph of height against frequency (of that height occurring) then the graph would appear as in Figure 1.

If the measured heights of a further 25 students are then added, the graph might appear as in Figure 2.

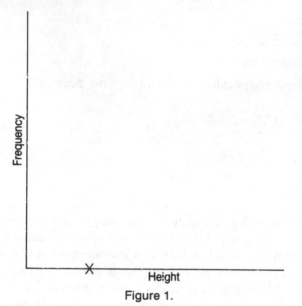

Figure 1.

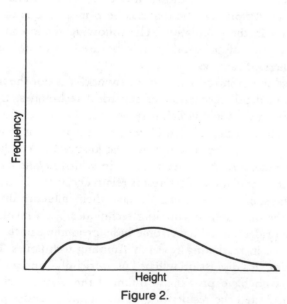

Figure 2.

A further 100 students' measurem
If 200 measurements are added, th
This graph is called a normal distrib
is that the mean, the median and the m
lie at the centre of that curve.

A further property is that the curve is sy

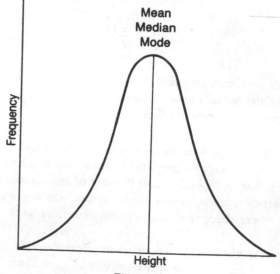

Figure 3.

Mean
Median
Mode

Figure 4.

218
Standard d

If every s
situation
line whi
But con
and th
afford
unin
oth
y

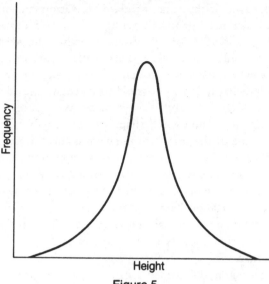

Figure 5.

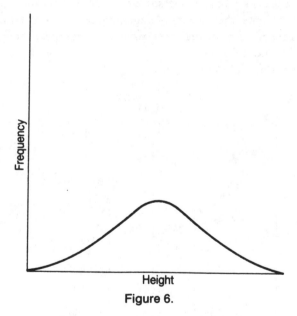

Figure 6.

Whatever their shape, though, it is very important to remember that normally distributed curves are symmetrical around their means and the areas under the curve on either side of the mean are equal.

The concept of standard deviation is useful in that it is known (the proof of which need not concern us here) that for a normal distribution curve, 68% of all measured values lie within one standard deviation on either side of the mean, 95% of all measured values lie within 2 standard deviations on either side of the mean, and 99% of all observed values lie within 3 standard deviations on either side of the mean. This is illustrated in Figure 7.

If we measure the heights of 100 students, it is possible to calculate the mean height of these students; it is also possible to calculate the standard deviation for the dispersion of their heights. Given these two figures, it is possible to make a good guess as to the overall shape of the distribution curve.

However, the shape of the distribution curve is not the market researcher's main concern. What is of interest is the extent to which we can make general-isations about the entire student population based only on the results of one sample. To return to our much researched students; if we discover, when we measure the heights of 100 of them, that the average height is 1.65 metres, the question that must be answered is: "How closely does this figure lie to the average height of all the students in the population?"

Imagine this situation:

We have already taken 100 students from the university or college (or the union bar) and have measured their heights, the average was 1.65 metres. We put these students back into their classes (or the union bar) and extract a further sample of 100 students; their mean/average height is 1.74 metres. This process of sampling is repeated a further three times and the mean heights are found to be 1.68, 1.79 and 1.59 metres.

We have seen this situation before!

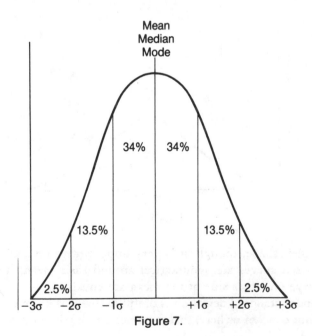

Figure 7.

Remember when we measured the heights of the first 100 students? On that occasion there was a variation in their heights. Now we are seeing a variation in the means/averages of their heights; this is called sample variation. If the number of students in each sample was increased to, say, 250, then the size of the sample variations would tend to decrease, but it would never totally go away.

How is it possible to cope with the situation of sample variation?

Return, for a moment, to the first sets of samples of students which were measured, as in Figure 4. The results of those experiments, when plotted out on a graph with axes of "height" and "frequency", resulted in a curve with a normal distribution—the classic "bell" shape. Now we can plot a second type of graph; again it will have "frequency" as the vertical axis, but the horizontal axis will be of the mean heights of the samples: this will give a distribution curve for the sample means.

This distribution curve will also have a mean value, and if a large enough number of samples of 100 students are extracted from the population, the mean of the sample means will be equal to the population mean. And just as in the case of a single sample, where the height of an individual student was more, rather than less, likely to be close to the population mean, so it is in the current case. A sample mean is more likely to be close to the population mean than it is to be placed far away from it.

It is important to note that whatever the shape of the distribution curve for the population, the sample means will be normally distributed, i.e. they will lie within a "bell"-shaped curve.

Samples, their dispersion and marketing research

One of the main drawbacks to marketing research is that it is rarely possible to plot a distribution of sample means in order to calculate a population mean. A lack of time, funds and of qualified personnel usually means that it is possible only to take one sample. Thus we have to "make do" with having to work from the results of a single sample.

So, how do we, with confidence, generalise about a population based on the results of a single sample?

When the students, in the first sample of 100, were measured, their heights varied and it was possible to work out a figure for the amount of their dispersion—the standard deviation.

A similar process can be undertaken in the case of sample means. We have seen that they too are variable in value; so an average amount for the degree of dispersion can be calculated—the standard deviation of the sample.

To avoid confusion, this is called the standard error.

Just as sample measurements are distributed normally and 68% lie within one standard deviation on either side of the mean, so sample means are normally distributed and, again, 68% of sample means will lie within one standard error on either side of the mean.

But we do not have *all* sample means, only one.

Is this of any use?

Yes! And this is how it can be used.

The standard error (SE) is calculated by the formula:

$$SE = \frac{\sigma}{\sqrt{N}}$$

σ = standard deviation
N = sample size

How can the concept of standard error be used in marketing research?

From Figure 8, it can be seen that the range, population mean + or − one standard error will contain 68% of all sample means.

Look at the area covered by the boundaries of the population mean + or − one standard error in Figure 8, this would contain a variety of sample means. And from each one of these samples we can estimate a standard error. Thus the span of any sample mean + or − one standard error will hold within it the population mean.

Point X is a sample mean, it has a standard error drawn on each side of it. You can see that the population mean lies within its boundaries. If the sample

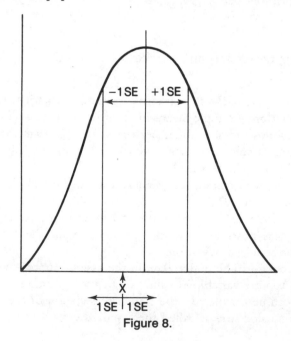

Figure 8.

mean is closer than one standard error to the population mean, the boundaries of the sample mean + or − one standard error will hold the population mean. And as we know that 68% of all possible sample means lie within one standard error of the population mean, we can say that whatever the size of the sample mean, the range sample mean + or − one standard error has a 68% probability of holding the population mean.

If the standard error of the mean heights of our sample of 100 students is 3 cm (0.03 m) and the mean sample height itself is 1.65 m we can now generalise about the mean height of the population of all students.

There is a 68% probability that the population mean lies within the boundaries of the sample mean + or − one standard error.

These figures translate thus:

sample mean = 1.65
standard error = 0.03
sample mean plus one standard error = 1.65 + 0.03 = 1.68
sample mean minus one standard error = 1.65 − 0.03 = 1.62

We can now say there is a 68% probability that the population mean lies within the range 1.68 m to 1.62 m. This range is termed the 68% confidence interval.

To increase the size of our confidence, we would have to increase the range of the students' heights and this is done by recalculating the range using + or − two standard errors or + or − three standard errors depending upon the size of the confidence interval that is required.

For example: sample mean + or − two standard errors:

$$1.65 + 0.06 = 1.71$$
$$1.65 − 0.06 = 1.59$$

Thus we can now say that we are 95% confident that the population mean lies within the range 1.59 m to 1.71 m.

Author Index

Aaker, D.A. 59, 69, 72, 83, 85, 108, 149
Ajzen, I. 154, 157, 159
Albaum, G. 35, 136, 139, 146, 169, 176, 182, 184
Allport, G.W. 152
Ansoff, H.I. 3, 4, 5
Armstrong, J.S. 82

Baker, M.J. 3, 34, 35, 42
Barban, A. 37
Bellenger, D. 114
Belson, W.A. 110
Benney, M. 121
Bernhardt, K.L. 114
Braithwaite, A. 113
Brownlie, D. 5
Buck, S. 84

Campbell, D.T. 147, 178, 180, 185
Chambers, J.D. 2
Chisnall, P.M. 89, 187, 189
Churchill, G.A. 147
Cook, S.W. 159, 168
Cook, T.D. 180
Crouch, S. 208, 212

Day, G.S. 59, 69, 72, 83, 85, 108, 149
Deutsch, M. 168
Dickens, J. 121
Dickson, J. 169
Drucker, P. 4
Duncan, R.B. 4
Dunn, S.W. 37

Emery, F.E. 4

Fishbein, M. 154, 157, 159
Fiske, D.W. 147

Glueck, W.F. 4
Goldstucker, J.L. 114
Gordon, W. 112–13, 114, 116, 117, 126
Green, P.A. 136, 139, 146
Green, P.E. 35, 176, 182, 184

Hall, R.D. 4
Hawkins, D.I. 40, 53, 61, 92, 130, 183, 186, 196, 203
Hedges, A. 113, 118
Hughes, E.C. 121
Hunt, J.G. 4

Jahoda, M. 168
Jain, N.C. 137
Jauch, L.R. 4
Jones, S. 122

Kast, F.E. 4
Kidder, L.H. 125
Kinnear, T.C. 69, 78, 84, 96, 121, 124, 157, 158

Langmaid, R. 112–13, 114, 116, 117, 126
Luck, D.J. 20, 38, 61, 103, 169, 199
Lunn, A. 113

Newson-Smith, N. 32

Oppenheim, A.N. 97, 98, 99, 111, 152, 153, 155
Osborn, R.N. 4
Osgood, C.E. 169
Overton, T.S. 82

Parasuraman, A. 152, 159, 181
Payne, S.L. 99
Peter, J.P. 147

Porter, R.E. 137

Ray, M.L. 157
Rosenweig, J.E. 4
Rubin, D.S. 20, 38, 61, 103, 169, 199

Samovar, L.A. 137
Sellitz, C. 159, 168
Sloan, A.P. 3
Southan, J. 139
Stanford, M.J. 4
Stanley, J.C. 178, 185
Stewart, D.W. 39
Stoll, M. 39
Suchman, E.A. 154
Suci, G.J. 169

Tannenbaum, P.H. 169
Taylor, J.R. 69, 78, 84, 96, 121, 124,
    157, 158
Timm, P.R. 201, 202
Torgerson, W.S. 26, 135, 139
Trist, E.L. 4
Tull, D.A. 40, 176, 182, 183, 184, 196,
    203
Tull, D.S. 35, 53, 61, 92, 130, 136,
    139, 146, 186

Urban, G.L. 191

Weiers, R.M. 36, 57, 76, 89, 139, 163,
    167, 169, 191, 195, 202

Subject Index

accounts and internal sources 39
accuracy and census versus sample 47–8
acquisition studies 34–5
advertising evaluation data 85
affective components 156–7, 158
after-only testing 183
agencies
  government 42
  list preparation 211–12
  selection 213–14
aggregate analysis 169
alternative forms reliability 148
alternative responses 105
ambiguous wording 98–9
appendices and research reports 200
applicability and research reports
    204–5
ASSESSOR 190, 191
associations 41–2
  projective techniques 126–7
associative variation 177
attitude scales 166–71
  Likert scale 167–8
  semantic differential scale 168–70
  Stapel scale 170–1
attitudes 136, 151–71
  attitude scales 166–71
  in behaviour research 70
  components 155–7
  consumer 138
  definition 152–7
  endurance 154–5
  labelling 153
  mapping 153–4
  measurement 159–60
  rating scales 160–6
  relationships 155
  strength 154
  to prediction of behaviour 157–9
audit 25

balanced alternative responses 105
balanced scales 163
before-after testing 183, 185
behaviour
  behavioural components 157, 158
  patterns 97
  in survey research 70–1
bias 53, 142
  biased wording 99–100
  counter-biasing 96
  data 36
  estimation 82–3
  negative and positive 105
  reactive 186
  samples 181–2
  body-language 118
branching instructions 108
brand
  loyalty 136, 138
  mapping 126
  personalities 127
business
  environments, turbulent 4–8
  management evolution 1–4

cameras see eye cameras; pupilometric
    cameras
candour in research reports 205
cartoon tests 128
category number and rating scales
    162–3
CATI see computer assisted telephone
    interviewing
causal
  factors 177
  research 20, 22
causality, nature of 176–7
causation
  deterministic 176
  probabilistic 176–7

census versus sample 46–8
cheating 79
check-lists 105
choice ordering in projective
    techniques 128
closed-ended questions 103–6
    balanced versus unbalanced
        alternative responses 105
    check-lists 105
    dichotomous questions 103–4
    multiple choice questions 104
    ranking 106
    responses 104–5
    scales 106
cluster sampling 57
cognitive components 156, 158
colour, questionnaire 108
comfort of group discussion 119
commissioning research reports 207–14
    agencies list preparation 211–12
    agency selection 213–14
    in-house research versus external
        research agency 210–11
    research brief preparation 209–10
    research proposals evaluation 213
    research requirements specification
        208–9
company description and acquisition
    studies 34
comparative rating scales 164
competitor reaction 189
completion in projective techniques 126
components 155–7, 158
computer
    assisted telephone interviewing
        (CATI) 77
    computerised databases 41
    interviews 24
conclusions in research reports 199
concomitant/associative variation 177
concurrent validity 146–7
confidence 123
consistency reliability, internal 148
constant sum rating scales 165–6
construct validity 147
construction in projective techniques
    127–8

consumer
    attitude 138
    panels 84–9
        diaries 86
        home audit 86
content validity 145–6
contrived observation 131
controlled-store and mini-market test
        marketing 190
convenience sampling 59
convergent validity 147
cost
    census versus sample 46
    of group discussion 118
    sample size 62
    test duration 189
cost-benefit analysis 18, 34, 36, 162,
        209
counter-biasing statements 96
courtesy 73
creativeness of group discussion 119
cross-sectional designs 184

data 36–7
    collection
        marketing research and problem-
            solving 22–5, 28
        primary data 23–5
    databases, computerised 41
    disclosure 96
    see also secondary data
debriefing method 109
dependent variables or measurement 174
depth interviews 24, 121–5
descriptive research 20, 21–2
design
    experimental 175, 182–5
    research reports 203–4
deterministic causation 176
deviation, standard 218–21, 222
dialling, random digit 76–7
diaries and consumer panels 86
dichotomous questions 103–4
direct observation 25, 131–2
directness in personal interview 75
directories 41
Directory of British Associations 42
discriminant validity 147

discussion see group discussion
disguised observation 131
dispersion of samples 221–3
disproportionate stratified random
    sampling 55–6
distribution curves 216–17, 218, 219,
    221
double-barrelled questions 93–4, 100
dustbin audit see home audit

electronic point of sale scanning (EPOS)
    87–8, 190
element and population definition 50
embarrassment and group discussion
    120
environment 143
  business 4–8
EPOS see electronic point of sale
    scanning
error 142
  frame 51, 53
  interviewer 78–9
  non-response 73–4
  non-sampling 47–8, 53
  non-systematic 142
  sampling 47, 71–2, 142
  survey 71–4
  uninformed 73
execution in research reports 204
executive summary in research reports
    196
expectancy-value 157
experiment 174
experimental designs 175, 182–5
  pre- and quasi-experiments 182–4
  statistical 185
  true experiments 184–5
experimental research 124
experimentation 173–91
  causality, nature of 176–7
  experimental designs 175, 182–5
  external validity 181–2
  internal validity 178–80
  laboratory and field experiments
      185–91
  reactive effects 181, 186
  terminology 174–6
  and validity 177–8

experts, external 43
exploratory research 17, 18, 20, 21, 138
expressive techniques 128
extent and population definition 50
external
  agency 210, 211
  experts 43
  research agency 210–11
  sources 40–3
  validity 181–2, 186, 187, 190, 191
extraneous variables 175
eye cameras 25, 132, 186
eye contact 118

face validity 145–6
feed-back loops 6
field experiments 24, 186, 187–91
  controlled-store and mini-market
      test marketing 190
  simulated test marketing 190–1
  standard test marketing 187–90
field research 33–4
final report presentation 28–9
final version in questionnaire design
    108–9
follow-up questions 102
forced scales 163–4
Ford, Henry 3
forgetfulness in surveys 72
formality and research reports 200
frame
  error 51, 53
  sampling 51, 52
free responses 102–3

garbage audit see home audit
geographical location 57
government agencies 42
graphic rating scales 161, 164–5
group 117–18
  discussions 114–21
    advantages 118–19
    disadvantages 119–20
    the discussion 116–17
    group dynamics 117–18
    in practice 115–16
  focus discussions 24
  member's mood 117

halo effect 169
home audit 86
human observation 132
hypothetical questions 101

ignorance in surveys 72
implicit assumptions 101–2
in-house research 210–11
inarticulateness 72
independent variable or treatment 174
indirect observation 131–2
individual depth interviews 121–5
  advantages 124–5
  disadvantages 125
  getting started 122–3
  the interview 123–4
  interviewer skills 124
industrial data 85
information needs 19–20
initial considerations and
  questionnaire design 92–3
inside *see* internal
Institute of Management 211
instrumentation effects 179
'insurance policy' questions 104, 105
intensity *see* passion
interactive survey 69
interactive testing effect 179
internal
  consistency reliability 148
  sources 39–40
  validity 178–80, 187, 191
interval scales 27, 141–2
interviews
  computer 24
  depth 24
  individual depth 121–5
  interviewer error 78–9
  interviewer skills 124
  mail 23
  personal 23, 69, 74–6
  telephone 23, 76–8
introduction and research reports 197–8
itemised comparative rating scales
  164–5
itemised-category rating scales 161–2

jargon and research reports 201

judgement and sample size 62
judgement sampling 59

knowledge in behaviour research 70–1

labelled response categories 97
laboratory
  experiments 24, 185–91
  settings 25
  tests 186–7
layout and questionnaire design 107–8
leading questions 99–100
Likert scale 167–8
limitations in research reports 199
location 57
longitudinal studies 34

mail
  interviews 23
  questionnaire 52, 69, 79–80
  surveys and non-response reduction
    81–2
main testing effect 179
Management Information Systems (MIS)
  39, 40
Market Research Society 211
markets and products 35
maturation and internal validity 178–9
meaning and research reports 205
measurement
  dependent 174
  destructive nature 48
  process 139, 143–4
    and scales 134–49
    concepts and definitions 136–7
    levels 137–8, 140–2
    variables 138
    variations 142–4
  techniques 26–7
mechanical observation 132
media audience data 85
mini-market test marketing 190
MIS *see* Management Information
    Systems
mortality 180
multi-stage sampling 57–8
multiple choice questions 104
multiple time series 183

natural observation 131
natural settings 25
negative bias 105
negative questions 100–1
nominal scales 26, 140
nomological validity 147
non-comparative rating scales 161–4
non-probability
    sampling 58–61
    techniques 27, 28, 115
non-respondent and projected response
        83
non-response error 73–4
non-sampling error 47–8, 53
non-systematic error 142
non-technical language and research
        reports 201–2
normal distribution curves 216–17
notation 175–6
numerical designations and rating scales
        162

objectives in marketing research and
        problem-solving 15–16
observation 131–2
    direct 25, 131–2
    of group discussion 119
    observational survey 69
    primary data 24–5
    summary 132
omnibus surveys 89
only-after testing 185
open observation 131
open-ended questions 102–3, 108
opinions in behaviour research 70
ordinal scales 26, 140–1
organisation and research reports 202
origin and research reports 203
outside see external

paired-comparison rating scales 164
panel marketing research 84–9
    advantages 88
    advertising evaluation data 85
    consumer data 84
    consumer panels 85–7
    disadvantages 88–9
    industrial data 85

media audience data 85
    retail data 84–5
    retail shop audit 87–8
    wholesale data 85
personal
    interviews 23, 69, 74–6
    surveys 81
phrasing probes 102
pictures and words 127
plus-one dialling 76
popular reports 195
population
    definition 50–1
    frame definition 51–2
positive bias 105
Post-Industrial Era 4
PPS see probability proportionate to size
pre-experimental design 182–4
predictive validity 146
prestige in surveys 73, 97
pretest and questionnaire design 108–9
primary data 23–5
primary research backdrop 33
privacy 72
    see also confidence
probabilistic causation 176–7
probability
    proportionate to size (PPS) 57
    sampling techniques 27, 51, 53–8,
        60–1, 115
    cluster sampling 57
    multi-stage sampling 57–8
    selection 28
    simple random sampling 53–5
    stratified random sampling 55–6
probing and group discussion 119
problem definition 16–18
problem-solving 14–29
    data collection 22–5, 28
    definition 16–18
    final report presentation 28–9
    involvement 13–14
    measurement techniques 26–7
    objectives 15–16
    proposal construction 19–22
    results analysis 28
    sample selection 27–8
    value assessment 18–19

products and markets 35
profile analysis 170
project design 52
projected response 83
projective techniques 24, 103, 125–9
  advantages 128
  association 126–7
  choice ordering 128
  completion 126
  construction 127–8
  disadvantages 129
  expressive techniques 128
proportionate stratified random
    sampling 55–6
proposal construction
  information needs 19–20
  marketing research and problem-
      solving 19–22
  research categories 20–2
protocol method 109
psychogalvanometers 25, 132, 186
published sources 43
pupilometric cameras 25
purposive sampling 59–60

Qualitative Market Research 112
qualitative research 112–32
  group discussions 114–21
  individual depth interviews 121–5
  observation 130–2
  primary data 24
  projective techniques 125–9
quantitative market research 113
quasi-experimental design 182–4
questionnaire 26
  design 91–111
    content 93–7
    initial considerations 92–3
    layout 107–8
    phrasing 97–102
    pretest/revision/final version 108–9
    reliability and validity 109–11
    response format types 102–6
    sequence 106–7
    size 107
  mail 52, 69, 79–80
questions
  closed-ended 103–6

comprehension 93
content in questionnaire design 93–7
dichotomous 103–4
follow-up 102
importance 96
'insurance policy' 104, 105
and interviewer error 78–9
leading 99–100
length 98
multiple choice 104
necessity 93, 96
open-ended 102–3, 108
phrasing
  ambiguous/vague words 98–9
  biased words and leading questions
      99–100
  clear and simple words 98
  containing estimates 101
  double-barrelled 93–4, 100
  hypothetical 101
  implicit assumptions 101–2
  length 98
  negative 100–1
  probes/follow-up 102
  questionnaire design 97–102
and required data 93–4
sequence in questionnaire design
    106–7
quota sampling 60

random
  digit dialling 76–7
  sampling 53–6, 85
  sources 142
rank order rating scales 165
ranking scales 106
rapport 78, 123
rating scales 160–6
  category number 162–3
  comparative 164–5
  constant sum 165–6
  graphic 161, 164–5
  itemised category 161–2
  non-comparative 161–4
  rank order 165
ratio scales 27, 142
reactive bias 186
  external validity 181

reactive effects of experimentation 181, 186
reading research reports 203–5
real number systems 139
recommendations and research reports 199
recording devices 25
reliability 144, 147–8
  questionnaire design 109–11
reports 200
  see also research reports
repurchase rate 189
research 10–30
  agency, external 210–11
  brief preparation 209–10
  categories
    causal 20, 22
    descriptive 20, 21–2
    exploratory 17, 18, 20, 21, 138
    proposal construction 20–2
  and marketing 1–8
  necessity 208–9
  and problem solving involvement 13–14
  proposals evaluation 213
  reports 193–205
    content 195–200
      appendices 200
      conclusions and recommendations 199
      executive summary 196
      introduction 197–8
      limitations 199
      results 198–9
      table(s) of contents 197
      title page 196
    reading 203–5
      applicability 204–5
      candour 205
      design 203–4
      execution 204
      meaning 205
      origin 203
      stability 204
    style 200–3
      formality 200
      length 200
      non-technical language 201–2

      organisation 202
      statistics, use of 202
      technical language/jargon 201
      visual aids 202
      'target' audience 194–5
  requirements specification 208–9
  time-scale 209
  type 208
  value 209
respondents
  articulateness 95
  and interviewer rapport 78, 120
  knowledge, degree of 94–5
  measurement and scales variations 143
  memory state 95
  necessary data 94
  question comprehension 93
  reaction to other respondents 120
  variables in behaviour research 70
  willingness to answer questions 95–7
response 108
  alternative 105
  error 72–3
  format types
    closed-ended questions 103–6
    open-ended question 102–3
    questionnaire design 102–6
  free 102–3
  inability to answer 72
  number 104–5
  position 105
  recording 79
  style 73
  unwillingness 72–3
results
  analysis 28
  and research reports 198–9
retail
  data 84–5
  shop audit 87–8
  revision and questionnaire design 108–9
  role playing 128
Rorschach ink-blot test 125
routing instructions 108

sales records 39–40

samples 221–3
  bias 181–2
  dispersion 221–3
  error 53
  selection 27–8, 65–6
  versus census 46–8
sampling 215–23
  cluster 57
  convenience 59
  error 47, 71–2, 142
  frame 51, 52
  Judgment 59
  multi-stage 57–8
  non-probability 58–61
  plan definition 65
  probability 53–8, 60–1
  process 45–67
    census versus sample 46–8
    method choice 53–61
      non-probability techniques 58–61
      probability techniques 53–8
    plan definition 65
    population definition 50–2
    selection 65–6
    size 61–4
    terminology 49
    unit selection 52
  purposive 59–60
  quota 60
  simple random 53–5
  stratified random 55–6
scales 106
  balanced 163
  forced 163–4
  interval 27, 141–2
  nominal 26, 140
  ordinal 26, 140–1
  ratio 27, 242
  see also attitude scales; measurement
    and scales; rating scales
SD *see* standard deviation
SE *see* standard error
seasonal effects 21
secondary data 23, 31–44
  advantages 35
  disadvantages 35–7
  external sources 40–3
    associations 41–2

    computerised databases 41
    directories 41
    external experts 43
    government agencies 42
    published sources 43
    syndicated services 43
  internal sources 39–40
  position and research sequence 38
  use 32–5
    acquisition studies 34–5
    field research substitute 33–4
    primary research backdrop 33
    sequence 37–9
    technique in itself 34
selection, internal validity 180
semantic differential scale 168–70
  aggregate analysis 169
  profile analysis 170
sensitivity 144, 149
'Sensor' system 190
sentence completion 126
sequential variables 177
simple random sampling 53–5, 85
simulated test marketing 190–1
size per cell requirement 62–3
Smith, Adam 1, 2
social change and government agencies
    42
social class 136
social dimension of group discussion
    118–19
societal environment 4
spacing 107
speed of group discussion 118
stability, research reports 204
standard deviation 218–21, 222
standard error 221, 222, 223
standard test marketing 187–90
  areas number/selection 188–9
  controls setting 188
  criteria of success 187
  duration 189
  exercises integration 187
  objectives defining 187
  results evaluation 189–90
Stapel scale 170–1
statistics/statistical 215–23
  designs 185

statistics/statistical (*continued*)
   methods, sample size 63–4
   regression 180
   research reports 202
stimulation of group discussion 119
stratified random sampling 55–6, 85
structure, personal interview 74
structured observation 131
style, research reports 200–3
sub-sampling 82
survey
   interactive 69
   methods 83
   'not at home' situation 73, 74
   omnibus 89
   refusal to take part 73, 74
   research 68–90
      data collection methods 74–80
         interviewer error 78–9
         mail questionnaire 79–80, 81–2
         personal interview 74–6, 81
         telephone interview 76–8, 81
      error 71–4
         interviewer 78–9
         non-response 73–4
         response 72–3
         sampling 71–2
      methods and applications 69–71
      non-response 81–3
      primary data 23–4
syndicated marketing research see
   panel marketing research
syndicated services 43
systematic error 142

table(s) of contents, research reports 197
tachistoscopes 186
'target' audience 194–5
task environment 4
task-orientated cooperative activity 117
technical language, research reports 201
technical reports 194
telephone
   directories 52
   interview 23, 52, 76–8
      advantages 77
      computer assisted telephone
         interviewing (CATI) 77
         disadvantages 77–8
      random digit dialling 76–7
   questionnaire 69
   surveys and non-response reduction
      81
temporal effects 21
terminology, sampling process 49
testing
   internal validity 179
   test marketing 190–1
      see also standard test marketing test
         units 175
   test-retest reliability 148
Thematic Apperception Test 127
third-party questions 96
time
   census versus sample 46
   population definition 50
   pressure 72–3
   series 182–3, 184
title page, research reports 196
treatment, independent 174
trend analysis 82–3
trend designs 182–3
true experimental design 182
turbulent business environments 4–8

unbalanced alternative responses 105
unbalanced scales 163
unforced scales 163–4
uninformed error 73
unit, population definition 50
unrepresentativeness of group
   discussion 119
unstructured observation 131

vague wording 98–9
validity 144, 145–7
   and experimentation 177–8
   external 181–2
   internal 178–80
   questionnaire design 109–11
value assessment 18–19
variables
   dependent 174
   extraneous 175
   independent 174
   sequential 177

variation, concomitant/associative 177
verbal descriptors and rating scales 162
visual aids, research reports 202

Watt, James 2
Wealth of Nations 1
wholesale data, panel marketing research
    85

words
  ambiguous 98–9
  biased 99–100
  clear and simple 98
  describing frequency 94
  word association 126–7
  see also pictures and words